FOLLOWING GOD
THROUGH THE BIBLE
STUDY SERIES

An informative **8 WEEK BIBLE STUDY** of life principles for today, to guide the church and the Christian's walk.

Judges

Who Will Lead Us?

IN THOSE DAYS

THERE WAS NO KING IN ISRAEL.

EVERYONE DID WHAT WAS RIGHT

IN HIS OWN EYES.

RICK SHEPHERD

AMG
PUBLISHERS

Following God

THE BOOK OF JUDGES: WHO WILL LEAD US?

© 2020 by Richard L. Shepherd

ISBN 13: 978-1-61715-532-1

Manuscript editing, text design, and layout by Rick Steele Editorial Services
http://steeleeditorialservices.myportfolio.com

Cover illustration by Daryle Beam/Bright Boy Design

Printed in the United States of America
2020 First Edition

This Scripture adventure through the times of the Judges is dedicated to several of the leaders in my life throughout the years. Someone has defined leadership as "influence," and many, many have certainly had significant influence in my life. Some are close; some afar; some are friends over the years; some have been fellow laborers; many have prayed for me; some have given wise counsel; some are now in heaven; some still around…

Thinking over the list of those who have influenced me, counseled me, prayed for me in some way, or prayed for our family became a journey through memory lane—so many have given leadership to us! Instead of naming each, lest I leave someone out, I simply say thank you. I say this with full confidence: "God knows" and will reward. These pages and principles are dedicated to the many who influenced me to be who I am today.

Rick Shepherd
Rossville, Tennessee (2019)

ACKNOWLEDGMENTS

The *Book of Judges* and the times surrounding it present the never-ending need for leadership; that's why this Scripture adventure is entitled "Who Will Lead Us?" The principles and precepts of leadership (or lack of leadership or wrong leadership) are woven throughout the people and places of the times of the judges. Practical applications for following our Leader and Lord Jesus abound in this journey.

The times of the judges, including the *Book of Judges* covers the period after the conquests of Joshua's day, around 1406–1390 BC, to the death of Samuel and the end of Saul's reign, around 1014–1011 BC. This period is marked by tragedies and feats of faith; we see people going widely astray from God and His Word and some following God closely. It is certainly filled with lessons for today, for though times and cultures, diets and manners, and inventions and conveniences, have changed many times in many ways, two things have not changed—God has not changed. People have not changed. We still need the leadership only God can provide. He made us. He knows us. He always knows what is best. In the times of the judges, most failed to grasp that reality. We need to grasp that today. We need to be like many of the Thessalonians of years ago who *"turned to God from idols to serve a living and true God"* (1 Thessalonians 1:9).

Three factors need to be kept in mind as we travel through this period. First, each of the judges served in a particular region of Israel, none served the whole nation like King David or Solomon. Second, some of the judges overlap in times. For example, when Samson judged for twenty years around Zorah and dealt with the Philistines in Philistia, south and southwest of Jerusalem, Samuel was serving as a prophet and judge around Ramah in central Israel, north of Jerusalem. Third, the *Book of Judges* is not in exact chronological order; for example, chapters 17-21 occurred before the times of the judges in chapters 3–16.

I owe special thanks to many. First, to my Lord Himself, for leading me, teaching me, burdening me to dig in to this Scripture adventure. Any good that comes from this study should bring praise and thanks to Him. There is no good in me but Jesus. By His Spirit, He is our Teacher and Leader, our Lord and Savior. He knows what each of us needs and readily guides us in that path.

Second, I am indebted to and grateful for my wife Linda Gail for her encouragement to write these lessons. Her praying for me means much. Third, many others in the Body of Christ have encouraged me to pen these adventures through the Scripture.

Fourth, I am greatly indebted to the people at AMG Publishers for their encouragement and guidance. Thank you, Steve Turner and Amanda Jenkins. In addition, I am most appreciative for the excellent editing done by Rick Steele, a continual encouragement and goad to clearer writing and helpful content. Thanks so much!

Fifth, I am greatly indebted to several whose resources proved very insightful, including:

Wayne Barber, Eddie Rasnake, Richard Shepherd, *Following God: Prophets of the Old Testament* (Chattanooga: AMG Publishers, 1999),

Barry J. Beitzel, *The Moody Atlas of Bible Lands* (Chicago: Moody Press, 1985),

Charles Bridges, *An Exposition of Psalm 119* (Carlisle: The Banner of Truth Trust, 1827, 1974),

Francis Brown, et al, *The New Brown-Driver-Briggs-Gesenius Hebrew and English Lexicon* (Peabody: Hendricksen Publishers, 1979),

Robert Chisholm, Jr., *Judges* in *The Bible Knowledge Word Study, Joshua-2 Chronicles*, ed., Eugene Merrill (Colorado Springs: Cook Communications Ministries, 2004),

Dictionary of the Holy Bible, rev. and enlarged ed. (New York: American Tract society, 1886, 1914),

The ESV Study Bible (Wheaton: Crossway Bibles, 2008),

Timothy J. Keller, *Living in a Pluralistic Society* (Study Notes on the Book of Judges, et al.) (New York: Redeemer Presbyterian Church, 2006),

John MacArthur, ed., *The MacArthur Study Bible* (Nashville: Word Publishing, 1997).

Charles Caldwell Ryrie, *The Ryrie Study Bible* (Chicago: Moody Press, 1976, 1978).

Sam Shaw, *Study Notes on the Book of Judges* (Collierville, TN: Unpublished material, n.d.).

William Smith, *A Dictionary of the Bible* (Philadelphia: The John C. Winston Company, 1884).

Robert L. Thomas, gen. ed., *New American Standard Exhaustive Concordance of the Bible* (Numbering Classifications from James H. Strong's Exhaustive Concordance of the Bible) (Nashville: Holman Bible Publisher and The Lockman Foundation, 1981).

Merrill F. Unger, ed., *Unger's Bible Dictionary* (Chicago: Moody Press, 1957, revised 1966).

Herbert Wolf, *Judges*, in *The Expositor's Bible Commentary*, vol. 3. Frank Gaebelein, gen. ed. (Grand Rapids: Zondervan Publishing House, 1992).

Spiros Zodhiates, exec. ed., *The Hebrew-Greek Key Word Study Bible* (NASB), rev. ed. (Chattanooga: AMG Publishers, 1984, 2008) and *The Complete Word Study Dictionary—New Testament*, (1992).

RICK SHEPHERD

Rick Shepherd

RICK SHEPHERD has served in churches in Florida, Texas, and Tennessee, and ministered over fifteen years as Team Strategist for the Prayer and Spiritual Awakening Team of the Florida Baptist Convention. He holds M.Div and Ph.D degrees from Southwestern Baptist Theological Seminary. Rick is one of the founding authors of the Following God® series. He has been married to his wife Linda Gail since 1977. They have four children and seven grandchildren. They are always glad to encourage believers and witness to listening hearts wherever they go. They make their home in the Memphis, Tennessee area.

PREFACE

Markets today are flooded with ideas about leadership—books, blogs, articles, seminars, webinars, websites—all proclaiming what it takes to be a good leader. Every field has its proposed solutions for the best leadership—for investments, financial management, retirement options, church ministries and non-profits, the food industry (from fast food to gourmet creations), the military, education and educational pursuits, government, world trade . . . the list could go on.

Many remain dissatisfied with the proposals and ideas, still looking for ways to be a better leader. What does it take to lead or to be a good leader? At least five key components come to mind.

1. **Following**—Someone or something worth following. Who is that? What is that?

2. **Fighting**—What is worth fighting for or against? What is worth my time and effort?

3. **Freedom**—What gives space, room to create and grow and be fruitful?

4. **Friends and Foes**—Who is with me, for me? Who is against me? Why? How? Where?

5. **The Forever Factor**—What matters forever? Is it last month's T-Ball winner, the Best Apple Pie at the County Fair, the latest "National" or "World" Champion in something?

It boils down to this: Whom or What can I follow? We know the answer is simple: someone or something that is good and real and true. Scripture is clear: God is good and real and true. He knows how to lead and how to guide others in leading.

Where does that thought lead us? There is one more crucial component that stands alone in discussing leadership: the absolute necessity of the heart, one's attitude and motivation in leading and influencing others. That factor can be seen from two angles. First, the impact of the Spirit of God in and with a person, then the receptivity of a person, the willingness to take in deeply what He says, what is true and right. It is a matter of one's "spirit" or heart.

We sometimes find people speaking of a company or business or establishment with "heart," referring to the good atmosphere or "vibe" in that place or with that group. When it comes to an individual, what kind of "heart" do we see? What is his or her attitude, demeanor, or even work ethic? Is it positive rather than negative, loyal rather than self-seeking, servant-hearted rather than overbearing? One's spirit must be the priority before the mental, emotional, or physical factors enter the equation. Character from the heart must always come before "confidence" in one's capabilities or the application of one's abilities.

This is where we find ourselves in looking at the "judges" of long ago. In reality, what they faced, the issues that arose, the attitude and demeanor with which they faced them are not much different today in the twenty-first century AD than in the fourteenth through the eleventh centuries BC. Why? Because, although times and cultures have certainly changed, people and "issues" of the heart have not. These factors are part of the times of the judges and therefore part of *"Who Will Lead Us?"* Another fitting subtitle for this study, *"Whom Will I Follow?"* calls us to consider "What does this mean to me, to my heart, to my life?" *"The Book of Judges: Who Will Lead Us?"* is a journey of learning from the leaders of the times of the judges. What can they show us? What do we need to know from them? What did they learn (or fail to learn) during those tumultuous times? That is the heart of this journey, what this Scripture adventure is about. Come join in, take it in, then live it out.

RICK SHEPHERD

CONTENTS

LESSON 1

THE TIMES OF THE JUDGES
COMING BACK TO FOLLOWING GOD

The *Book of Judges*—what does that have to do with today or with me? Some have noted Judges 21:25, the last verse in the *Book of Judges*, as the theme verse: "*In those days there was no king in Israel. Everyone did what was right in his own eyes*" (ESV, NASB, NKJV). All or part of that statement is also found three other times in the *Book of Judges*: Judges 17:6; 18:1; 19:1. That is a very accurate picture of those times and those people, including the lives of Eli and Samuel, who judged Israel in the transition time to the kings of Israel. Over and over the people needed to be called back to following God as their king. Could that also be true of us today? Who do we follow? Is it "me"? Or should I be following God? If so, how well am I doing? Do I, do we, need to come back to following God as He wants and as He has written in His Word?

Let's explore. What were the "judges" of these times like (Judges 2:16)? What did they do as leaders? Why were they needed, or were they needed? What did the people think of these "judges" during that time? How well did people follow those "judges"? What difference did these leaders make in their lives? What do we see in the people's lives during this period, and how do their lives relate to our lives today? In this journey through the times of the judges, we will explore these and other questions and thoughts. Hopefully we will discover some insights that apply to life today and what it means to walk with the Lord (not against Him).

 WORD STUDY
Judges

The Hebrew word translated "judges" is *shaphat* (Strong's #8199) which means "to judge," with the idea of passing sentence for or against someone. It thus carries the idea of "to govern," including the executive, legislative, and judicial elements of governing.

DAY ONE

WHO IS GOING TO LEAD?

First, a little review of history. The books of *Genesis* through *Joshua* give us history from Creation to Joshua's conquering of Canaan. In those centuries, God called people to listen, trust, and follow Him. From the start, God's desire for Adam focused on worship and obedience, based on two Hebrew words, *abad* and *shamar*.[1]

To worship is to recognize the worth or value of the Lord Himself. The word *abad* in Deuteronomy 6:13 is translated "worship"—*"You shall fear only the LORD your God; and you shall worship [serve] Him . . ."* When tested about worshiping Satan, Jesus quoted from Deuteronomy 6:13, stating in Matthew 4:10, *"You shall worship the Lord your God and serve Him only."* Recognize His true worth and do His will.

The Hebrew word *shamar* translated "guard" or "take care of" is most often translated "keep." One can see the idea of keeping something valuable or keeping a command, holding it valuable so that one obeys for the good of all involved.

WORD STUDY
"The LORD"

When the Scripture speaks of the Lord, many times it refers to Yahweh or Jehovah, found in the Hebrew text over six thousand times as YHWH (Strong's #3068), the Eternal, Self-existent God (always being). The word is rooted in the Hebrew word *hayah*, "to be" (Strong's #1961). In English translations, it is often printed in small capitals as "The LORD," which refers not only to the eternal God (who is always being), but to the covenant-making, covenant-keeping God of Israel. He revealed Himself to Moses and the children of Israel as *"the LORD God of your fathers,"* also declaring Himself as *"I AM WHO I AM."* (see Exodus 3:13–15, NKJV). Jesus made this claim numerous times (e.g., John 4:26; 6:35; 8:12, 58; 10:7, 11; 11:25; 14:6; 15:1; 18:5–8). In Moses' day, when He made the statement *"I am the LORD"* (Exodus 6:2, 6–8; 7:5, 17; 12:12; 20:2; 29:46), this matched a royal formula that most likely would have been familiar to Moses and to those who came after him. Kings in the Near East used this formula to begin a royal decree or edict. As an example, John Currid cites the Legend of Sargon in Assyria: 'I am Sargon, the mighty king.' In Exodus 20:2, The God introduces His royal decree revealing His purposes and plans for His covenant people. [For further insights see John D. Currid, *A Study Commentary on Exodus*, vol. 1 (Auburn, MA: Evangelical Press, 2000), pp. 136-137.]

If only Adam would worship and obey, he would always experience God's good will. In Genesis 2:16–17, God gave clear commands about eating from any tree except the *"tree of the knowledge of good and evil."* John Sailhammer insightfully states, "The inference of God's commands in vv. 16–17 is that God alone knows what is good . . . for man and that God alone knows what is not good . . . for him. To enjoy the 'good,' man must trust God and obey him. If man disobeys, he will have to decide for himself what is good . . . and what is not good. . ." [Genesis, p. 45].

---

1. Most translations of Genesis 2:15 state God's purpose for placing people in the Garden of Eden as to "cultivate" or "work" and to "keep" or "take care of" the Garden. The Hebrew word *abad* translated "cultivate" or "work" is translated "serve" some 200 times, with the idea being to honor a master or recognize the value of a request or task. One serves what is worthwhile. The Hebrew word *shamar*, often translated "guard" focuses on the idea of "keep," as in keeping a command or obeying. John Sailhammer has shown that the better translation is "to worship and to obey." [Genesis, vol. 2 of *The Expositor's Bible Commentary*, Frank E. Gaebelein, gen. ed., (Grand Rapids: Zondervan Publishing House), pp. 44-48].

God's desire and design have never changed. In the Garden, Adam and his wife rebelled against God and His Word, thinking they could know and choose better what was good than the Lord. They were sadly mistaken. Their rebellion is not so far from every human heart. We think we know what's best—at least we show that side of ourselves from our earliest days. Isn't that part of why we speak of the "Terrible Twos"? We do not have to teach a child to be selfish or stubborn or lie. It comes in the package.

So, what should we do? Don't we need some kind of leadership to get out of this mess? The debate has gone on for centuries: "Who is going to lead?" That is a good question. The *Book of Judges* has some good answers. Let's explore this territory.

Tradition says that Samuel wrote the *Book of Judges*. He certainly had a tremendous vantage point from which to view the people of Israel. In his days the people clamored for a king, no longer wanting a "judge" like Samuel or any of the others. In many ways, Samuel served as the last of the judges and the first of the prophets (though the Scriptures speak of Abraham and Moses as prophets in Genesis 20:7 and Deuteronomy 18:15; 34:10). The people gladly followed Samuel most of his life, but things changed. What did the people think in Samuel's latter days? What did they think of Samuel's sons? Look at 1 Samuel 8:1-5 and record what you find.

_____

_____

_____

_____

📖 The people also looked at the nations surrounding them. Read 1 Samuel 8:5, 20. What did the people see and what did they want?

_____

_____

_____

_____

The people saw Samuel advancing in age. He had turned over some of his responsibilities to his sons Joel and Abijah, but they did not do so well in following God, His Word, or their father Samuel. In 1 Samuel 8:3, we read that they *"did not walk in his ways but turned aside after gain. They took bribes and perverted justice."* The people also looked at the nations surrounding them and cried out for a *"king to judge us like all the nations"* (1 Samuel 8:5).

DID YOU KNOW?
History's First King

While Adam could be seen as the first king over the earth, the first ruler recorded in Scripture is Nimrod. Genesis 10:10 speaks of *"his kingdom."* Apparently, he first ruled in the rebellious city of Babel along with the cities of *"Erech and Accad and Calneh, in the land of Shinar."* From there he traveled to build and rule Nineveh along with Rehoboth-Ir, Calah, and Resen (Genesis 10:11–12). Throughout Scripture various leaders of villages, towns, cities, or city-states were called "kings," from the Hebrew word *melek* (Strong's #4428), rooted in *malak* (Strong's #4427) which means "to reign."

According to 1 Samuel 8:6, what did Samuel think of the people's desires and words?

As Samuel prayed and brought this matter to the Lord, what did the Lord say? Read 1 Samuel 8:6–9 and record the details along with your insights.

Samuel grieved over the people's attitude and request. He brought the matter to the Lord who told him to proceed with their request. God recognized that they were rejecting Him as their True King, just as Adam and the rest of humankind had done over and over. God told Samuel to let them have what they wanted but also to warn them of what would come with the answer to their request. Someone has wisely stated, "Sometimes we get what we want, but we find we do not like what we got." Often God will give us what we seek, knowing it will wake us up to what He wants us to seek.

> *"Sometimes we get what we want, but we find we do not like what we got." Often God will give us what we seek, knowing it will wake us up to what He wants us to seek.*

STOP AND APPLY—What Do You Seek?—What we seek says something about what we want and what we think is of value. What we spend our time and money on tells something about what we see as most valuable. Jesus tells us, *"Seek first the Kingdom of God and His Righteousness"* (Matthew 6:33). He does not say that out of egomania, but out of knowing what is best, and He and His will are always best, never second best. So, the question comes again: "What Do You Seek?" Or perhaps we should adjust it to ask, "Who do you seek?" It matters now and it matters forever. Stop and talk to the Lord. Do what He says.

Who is going to lead us? Who is going to lead you? That is an age-old question and the *Book of Judges* explores the ups and downs of people's responses. Who is your King? Who calls the shots in your life? Let's explore more through the people of Israel and hopefully discover some practical answers.

DAY TWO

JOSHUA AND HIS LEADERSHIP

When we turn to the history of the people of Israel, we discover some very practical truths. We find them sometimes following, often complaining, and wanting to get on with their lives. First, they had to get settled, and the Lord had plans for that. Joshua would lead them into the Promised Land of Canaan to settle in to what God had planned. To help know which way we should go, we need to first look at Joshua and how he led the people of God. It is important to ask, "Who is Joshua, and why does he matter?" Today we will discover how the Scriptures answer.

IN THEIR SHOES
General Joshua

In Exodus 17:8, Joshua was tasked by Moses to raise an army and fight the under-handed Amalekites while Moses stood on the mountain with the Rod of God raised. The Israelites proved victorious and acknowledged it was by the Lord's working. They acknowledged the Lord and His work by building an altar and naming it "*The LORD is My Banner*" (Exodus 17:15).

📖 What kind of leadership did Joshua exemplify? What do you find out about Joshua in Exodus 17:8–16 and 33:7–11 (especially verse 11)?

📖 What two main factors are evident in walking with God, according to Joshua 1:6–9? Hint: This was a failure in the people of Judges 2:10.

Joshua came on the scene as a victorious warrior, the leader of the people of God against the underhanded Amalekites. In that incident, it became evident that the Lord and depending on Him proved to be the key factor in victory. As Joshua grew in his manhood, he also spent time with the Lord. He listened carefully to Moses and knew God's Word. Joshua knew the Lord, and he continued to grow in knowing His Word. When the time came to lead, God focused him on knowing Him, being strong and courageous as he had been, but even more so now. Joshua would need to follow God and His Word—every day, every step.

 DID YOU KNOW?

The "Captain of the Host of the LORD"

The "Captain of the Host of the LORD" is the "Angel of the LORD." That name is found in one form or another about 35 times in the Old Testament. He is far more than an "angel." Each appearance (or sometimes simply hearing His Voice) is a "Christophany"—an appearance of the pre-incarnate Christ. When He appears or speaks, He reveals Himself as a Warrior fighting for His people and His purposes. He never loses!

How did Joshua respond to the "Captain of the Host of the LORD" in Joshua 5:13–15 and 6:1–6, (especially 6:6)?

_____

_____

_____

_____

What do these incidents in Joshua's life tell you about him? What kind of leader was Joshua? What can we learn from him?

_____

_____

_____

_____

Joshua responded to the "Captain of the Host of the LORD" in worship. When He told Joshua to take his sandals off, Joshua obeyed, just as Moses had done at the Burning Bush in Exodus 3:1–6 (another appearance of the Angel of the LORD). Joshua listened very carefully to what this "Captain" said. To Joshua, He was evidently a great leader, and anything He said about conquering this first obstacle would be very important. Joshua repeated to his men the exact instructions he had been given about marching around the city of Jericho. Joshua followed the Lord, so people could follow Joshua. That is genuine leadership. The Lord knows where He is going, and He can lead each of His children.

📖 What happened to Joshua and the people of Israel according to Judges 2:6–10?

_____

_____

_____

📖 What about Joshua's replacement? Who would the people follow? When all is said and done, what do you discover in Judges 21:25?

_____

_____

_____

_____

At the age of 110, the national leader Joshua died. Those around him in his generation also died, and most of the next generation forgot about the Lord and the great work that He had done for Joshua and for the people. They did not know the Lord, did not interact with Him, did not focus on His Word, and that, in turn, led them to follow whatever each thought was "right" in his or her own sight. Moses had Joshua as his successor; he had taught him much about the Lord and His ways. Joshua did not have a successor, so the people followed whoever was willing to lead. In most cases that meant local tribal leaders; some good and some not so good. What happened next? We will discover in Day Three.

DID YOU KNOW?
Ancient Covenants

During this period in history (around 1450–1000 BC), kings and rulers used a form of treaty or covenant containing five elements, all of which are found in Exodus 19:3–8 in the covenant instituted at Mount Sinai—a Preamble introducing the call of the sovereign or king to enter into an agreement ("...the LORD called to [Moses] from the mountain, saying, 'Thus you shall say to the house of Jacob.' . . ."), an historical Prologue recounting the nature of the relationship ("You yourselves have seen what I did to the Egyptians . . . I bore you on eagles' wings, and brought you to Myself"), Stipulations in the relationship (". . . obey My voice and keep My covenant"), Blessings promised ("then you shall be My own possession among all the peoples . . . and you shall be to Me a kingdom of priests and a holy nation"), Agreement and Acceptance in the assembly of witnesses ("Moses called the elders of the people . . . and all the people answered together. . . . All that the LORD has spoken we will do!' And Moses brought back the words of the people to the LORD."). The Lord based His words and actions during the period of the Judges on this covenant agreement.

STOP AND APPLY—How well do you know the Lord? Do you know Him as Lord and Savior? If not, now's the time, the best day of your life. What about His Word? Is it your 'daily bread' as Jesus spoke of His Father's word in Matthew 4:4? Are there any changes God is directing in your life after looking at His Word about Joshua?

God wanted the best for His people. He wanted them to follow Him and His Word. How well did they do? Did they err and, if so, where? We will look at some of their successes and failures in Day Three.

DAY THREE

SUCCESSES AND FAILURES

God's way is always the right way. He knows what is best, so it is always best to follow Him. How did the people of Israel follow Him? The Lord told Joshua to pay close attention to His Word every day, all day. That would lead to success God's way, regardless of what others thought or said. Today, we will look at their successes and failures.

What did the sons of Israel first do after Joshua died, according to Judges 1:1–3? What did God do?

IN THEIR SHOES
How Important Is Praying?

Throughout Scripture, we find people "calling on the LORD" and Him responding with love, wisdom, correction, mercy, grace, or whatever is needed (Genesis 4:26b; Luke 18:13–14). Someone has wryly stated, "coincidences happen to people who pray." It's not a coincidence to see God answering prayer. Scripture shows us that those who "*diligently seek*" the Lord, find Him becoming an answerer and rewarder (Hebrews 11:5–6). Prayer is part of our communication with the Lord, the voice of our dependence on Him. Prayer is the oxygen of our being. How important is prayer? How important is oxygen? Israel (and others in Scripture) discovered that God hears and answers prayer; He listens to the cry of His people. Psalm 145:18–19 gives great comfort and assurance, "*The LORD is near to all who call upon Him, to all who call upon Him in truth. He will fulfill the desire of those who fear Him; He will also hear their cry and will save them.*" Let's apply that—pray every day!

📖 What occurred in the life of the tribe of Judah, according to Judges 1:4–10?

The right place to start is in prayer. The children of Israel did that after the death of Joshua; they "*inquired of the LORD*," seeking His leadership in dealing with the Canaanites. In so doing, they received from the Lord the needed guidance for the battles that faced them. The people of the tribe of Judah asked the tribe of Simeon to join them, and the two tribes conquered many Canaanites and Perizzites, including the cities of Bezek and Hebron, plus a portion of Jerusalem.

IN THEIR SHOES
Why Conquer Canaanites?

Some have criticized the Lord seen in the books of *Joshua* and *Judges* as a "moral monster" or a "genocidal God" because of His command to the Israelites to conquer Canaan and rid the land of them. Is this a valid accusation? One must see this for what it is. Over four hundred years before, in Genesis 15:16, the Lord states, *"the iniquity of the Amorite is not yet complete,"* referring to the level of sin, rebellion, and moral decay that comes with sin. He proved Himself very patient and merciful (see Acts 17:30). When Israel marched into the land of Canaan, the moral decay had festered to the point of 'moral gangrene' that required national amputation (see Leviticus 18:1–30 for examples of their moral degradation). It was a moral malignancy, a social cancer of such depth that it required intense surgery; these peoples had gone beyond the limits, and execution was the only answer (Deuteronomy 20:16–18). In the midst of this, the Lord continued to show mercy to those willing to repent and trust in the Lord, the God of Israel. People like Rahab and her family became part of the people of God (see Joshua 2; 6:25; Matthew 1:5; James 2:25–26).

📖 What did Caleb and Othniel do, according to Judges 1:11–15?

📖 Read Judges 1:16–20. What do you discover about others who joined with Judah?

More successes and failures. What did other tribes do, according to Judges 1:21–36? List the tribe in the "Tribe" section in the chart given below.

Tribe	Canaanite Peoples / Cities	Scripture
	Jebusites in Jerusalem	Judges 1:21
	Beth-shean, Taaanach, Dor, Ibleam, Megiddo	Judges 1:27
	Gezer	Judges 1:29
	Kitron, Nahalol	Judges 1:30

	Acco, Sidon, Ahlab, Achzib, Helbah, Aphik, Rehob	Judges 1:31
	Bet-shemesh, Beth-anath	Judges 1:33
	Amorites in the valley, Mount Heres, Aijalon, Shaalbim	Judges 1:34

Some of the successes: Caleb led in the attack of Debir along with his future son-in-law, Othniel. Othniel proved a valiant and victorious warrior capturing the city of Debir. He won his bride, Caleb's daughter Achsah. Caleb gave them added land with springs of water since their land was in an arid region. Others joined with the tribe of Judah, including the Kenites, descendants of Jethro, Moses' father-in-law. The tribes of Judah and Simeon together conquered the towns of Zephath, the areas of Gaza, along with nearby Ashkelon and Ekron. Judah conquered much of the hill country but could not drive out the Canaanites who had iron chariots. In today's terms, these chariots would be the battle equivalent of tanks or armored vehicles, difficult to deal with. Caleb conquered Hebron, dealing a blow to the giants (sons of Anak) of that area. The people *"of Joseph"* (likely a portion of the tribe of Ephraim) conquered Bethel, formerly named Luz, in central Israel. Some of the tribes put various Canaanite peoples into forced labor. This would prove to be a bad influence on the Israelites; like drinking polluted water from a local stream, eventually sickness shows up.

STOP AND APPLY—What battles are in front of you? Are there some "unconquered" areas in your life that need attention? What is God saying to you about your "Canaanite" infections? Any infestations? Gangrene? Spiritual cancers? Ask the Lord for His viewpoint. Ask Him to show you sin like He sees sin . . . in your life. Then, look to Him for His victory. Take one step, even if it's a "baby step." Then, one step at a time. One step, then the next step. He will faithfully lead you. Simply follow with worship and obedience, trusting Jesus' righteous life in you along with His love and power for you (1 John 3:8; 4:4).

What kind of influence could remaining Canaanites bring? Could it really be all that bad? Is it really necessary to deal with sin God's way? We will explore these questions in Day Four.

Day Four

The Downward Spiral of Self-Will and Sin

Many years ago, as Jacob heard about some of the circumstances his family faced, he stated, *"all these things are against me"* (Genesis 42:36). Actually, everything that was going on was for him, not against him. He could not see it yet. Romans 8:31 reminds us that God is for us. Like a good physician who tells the truth about a physical diagnosis leading to surgery or medicine or some other regimen, the Lord knows what is best or worst for each of us. Israel was about to find out about this. Today, we will see what happens when we do what is right in our own sight, rather than seeking the Lord, His Word, and what He says is right.

📖 What should we do when God convicts us of some sin, some disobedience? What did the Lord say in Judges 2:1–5? How did the people respond?

ⓘ DID YOU KNOW?
God's Warning about Canaanite Covenants

God made it very clear that His people were to make no covenants with the people living in the land of Canaan. Moses recorded the Lord's clear commands concerning this: Exodus 23:32–33; 34:12; Deuteronomy 7:2. For the good of His people, the Lord spoke this prohibition against making a covenant agreement with any Canaanites. He spoke like a loving father or mother instructing children about what to eat or drink or what not to eat or drink; wrong choices could have serious consequences. Covenant agreements were binding. As the Lord was faithful even to disobedient people, so person-to-person or nation-to-nation covenants had to be honored. God wanted none of the infectious idolatry or immorality of the Canaanites influencing or infiltrating His people. He told them at least three times to not make a covenant with the Canaanites, but they did anyway—to God's grief and their detriment.

The Angel of the LORD appeared and spoke directly to His people concerning His faithfulness in delivering them from slavery in Egypt and their disobedience. He remained in a covenant relationship with them. Therefore, He would remain faithful to them. That also meant He would chasten them—correct, discipline, guide—when needed as any father or mother would do. He knew that often the pushback a child gives is a sign of the need for clearer, better boundaries. This proved true with the Canaanites in the land. He would allow them to be as *"thorns,"* a reminder of the curse that came with sin in Genesis 3:18. These Canaanite peoples and relationships would ever remain as a *"snare"* to watch out for. The people wept over these words, but their weeping did not lead them to repentance or permanent life change.

📖 What pattern did the people of Israel begin to follow in the days after Joshua's death? What do you discover in Judges 2:11–13?

📖 How did the Lord respond to the disobedience and rebellion of His people, according to Judges 2:14–15?

_____

_____

_____

📖 What did the people do according to Judges 2:18b? How did the Lord respond to the people?

_____

_____

_____

_____

📖 How did people act after each judge died? Read Judges 2:19 and record your insights.

_____

_____

_____

📖 According to Judges 2:20–23, what did the Lord do as the people continually strayed from Him and His Word?

_____

_____

_____

_____

"There is a way which seems right to a man, but its end is the way of death" (Proverbs 14:12)

The people did what was right in their own eyes; that proved to be "_evil in the sight of the LORD._" They believed lies, worshiped false gods, all based in demon delusions (see Deuteronomy 32:17; 1 Corinthians 8:4–6; 10:20; 1 Timothy 4:1). This was a personal relationship matter as they forsook the Lord Himself, being unfaithful to Him, and worshiping the "_Baals,_" all false gods of Canaan. It was a betrayal, a form of spiritual adultery. In loving and jealous anger, the Lord allowed foreign invaders and plunderers so that the people were "_severely distressed._" They groaned, crying out to the Lord. He had compassion on them and sent judges or deliverers to rescue them from their enemies.

They had rest and peace during the days of the various judges, but when a judge died, the people strayed even further in their faulty thinking and fatal living. They proved to be very stubborn. Because they would not listen to the Lord and His Word, He allowed several different pagan people groups to harass His people, all in order for them to see themselves and their sin for what it is. In His providence, He allowed this so that ultimately, they would turn to Him, the true God. He and His Word bring light in darkness, peace in distress, and comfort in hard times. [For an overview of the Seven Cycles of Sin and Salvation in the *Book of Judges*, see the chart at the end of this lesson.]

📖 What had the Lord warned about just a few years before, according to Deuteronomy 31:14–18?

📖 Who is the Lord? In what ways did Israel need to know Him? What do we need to know? Look at Deuteronomy 33:26–29 and record your thoughts.

EXTRA MILE
The Song of Moses

Read Deuteronomy 31:30; 32:1–43 and note what God says about Himself and His people.

The Lord knows people. He knew the people of Israel would believe lies, be deceived, and worship false gods. He also gave clear warnings about revealing His anger against covenant breaking. When His people followed fake gods and participated in false worship, He responded. He instructed Moses to write a song so the people could remember what He said and apply it to their lives and their worship. The Lord revealed Himself through Moses' testimony; *"there is none like the God of Jeshurun* [Israel]." He is *"the eternal God,"* not bound by time or earthly circumstances. He is the faithful God who cares for His people. He watches over them but will not cower under His people's rebellion; He deals with it. He will also deal with His people's enemies, so that His people will rise victorious.

DAY FIVE

WHOM WILL I FOLLOW?

There is no God like the God of Israel, the God of the Bible. He is the only God. As the apostle Paul testifies in 1 Corinthians 8:4-6, "... *we know ... that there is no God but one. For even if there are so-called gods whether in heaven or on earth, as indeed there are many gods and many lords, yet for us there is but one God, the Father, from whom are all things, and we exist for Him; and one Lord, Jesus Christ, by whom are all things, and we exist through Him.*" Today we will explore what it means to follow the one true God.

 IN THEIR SHOES
Remembering

The Lord told Moses to write a song so that the people would remember the Lord and what He said (Deuteronomy 31:19–22, 30). The Lord wants us to remember Him, what He has said, what He has done, and what He commands us to do. We find in Scripture that we need reminding; for example, in Psalm 105:5; Isaiah 46:8–11; Luke 17:32; John 2:22; 12:16; 14:26; 15:20; 16:4; 1 Corinthians 11:23–26; 2 Thessalonians 2:5; 2 Peter 1:12–15; Jude 5–7, 17–19.

Recall what the Lord told Joshua about following Him in Joshua 1:6–9. The two overarching essentials are **1)** knowing the Lord, and **2)** knowing and obeying His Word. The two things mentioned in Judges 2:10 closely match those essentials: First, they "*did not know the LORD,*" and second, they did not know "*the work which He had done for Israel.*" God works according to His perfect mind and heart. His Word reveals much of what He does and how He wants people to follow Him.

📖 Look at One who perfectly followed His Father and lives as the perfect leader. What was true of His life, according to Isaiah 50:4?

_____

_____

_____

📖 What did Jesus speak about as early as His boyhood, age 12? Read Luke 2:46–52 and note your insights about the boyhood of Jesus.

_____

_____

_____

📖 Jesus began His ministry when He was about thirty years of age (Luke 3:23). At this age, He faced a time of intense testing. What did Jesus testify about in that moment of testing, according to Matthew 4:4?

📖 What did He say during His days of ministry? Read what Jesus said in John 8:28–29. Note your insights.

Isaiah 50:4–11, one of the Servant Songs of Isaiah that prophesies about the coming Messiah, pictures the Messiah first as one who was awakened "morning by morning" to "listen as a disciple" to what His Father said. That could have begun very early in Jesus' life. Also, He would have heard and been taught the scriptures in His home with Joseph and Mary. In the weekly synagogue readings in Nazareth, He heard the scriptures read, taught, and discussed. At age 12, Jesus confounded the teachers in the temple in Jerusalem with His insights and questions. For Him, this was being "in the things of My Father" (Luke 2:49, margin). It is no surprise to find Him testifying at age thirty about living based on "every word that proceeds out of the mouth of God" (Matthew 4:4). In His ministry, He told His opponents, "when you lift up the Son of Man, then you will know that I am He, and I do nothing on My own initiative, but I speak these things as the Father taught Me" (John 8:28).

> "The Lord God has given Me the tongue of disciples, that I may know how to sustain the weary one with a word. He awakens Me morning by morning, He awakens My ear to listen as a disciple." (Isaiah 50:4)

📖 How can we follow the Lord today? Record your thoughts and applications from Psalm 1:2–3 and 119:9–11, 97–105.

📖 What did Jesus say about a relationship with Him in John 14:21, 23–24 and 16:13?

What did Jesus tell His disciples then (and His disciples today) in Matthew 28:20? How important is His Word? What does He say in John 15:7?

_____

_____

_____

God wants us to treasure and love His Word. As we read and obey what He has said, we will experience Him giving light to our understanding. This is the way to walk in purity, to live holy. Jesus treasured the Word His Father taught Him "*morning by morning*," and He promised to teach His disciples through the ongoing ministry of the Holy Spirit. We, too, are tasked with teaching believers what He said, knowing that the Holy Spirit will take that Word and work it into each disciple's life. More than simply knowing about His Word, Jesus wants us to receive His Word as authoritative, from Him personally; this is a matter of the heart. He wants us to take Him seriously, to obey what He has said in order to fully experience Him and His Word. That means valuing what He says, meditating on it, applying it day by day, and sharing that Word as God opens doors and hearts.

STOP AND APPLY—How's Your Heart?—Do you have a personal relationship with Jesus Christ as your Lord and Savior? Have you looked to Him, asked Him to forgive and cleanse you? Has He given you a new heart? Are you born from "above" or "born again"? Are you walking in fellowship with Him from the heart, or is there some issue interfering with your heart fellowship? Stop and pray. Talk to Him and deal with anything He brings up in your season of prayer or during your time in His Word. Remember, 1 John 1:7–9 promises His forgiveness and fellowship with Him.

TAKEAWAYS
The Judges

There are four takeaways from the times of the judges: **1)** God is The Leader forever, **2)** God always knows what is right, **3)** When God says "no" or "don't," "yes" or "do," then trust Him and obey, **4)** Jesus shows us perfect leadership.

Lord, You are The Leader, the Lord and Creator of all, Who knows how life is to be lived. You came as the Son of Man and Son of God and walked on this earth. You know what it means to face difficulties, temptations, hunger, thirst, and weariness. You faced all these things and continually obeyed Your Father every day, in every way, whatever You faced. Your Word is forever and true as You are true. Lead me today by Your Word and by Your Spirit. Help me lead others to You, to follow You faithfully and fully. Thank You for all You have done to provide us with Your Word, Your indwelling Spirit, and placing us in a Body of Believers who can encourage, challenge, and help us grow. In Jesus' Name, I pray. Amen.

A Chronological Overview of the Times of the Judges

The *Book of Judges* is written in a thematic form, not in chronological order. The last two judges, Eli and Samuel, are not examined in this book. Two major factors interweave in the Times of the Judges—**1)** Events occurred over different regions (not over the entire nation) and **2)** Events sometimes overlap times (not sequential). Each account is about a certain region of the country, not the entire nation, with a judge serving only a portion of Israel and the people in that region. The seasons of oppression and deliverance often overlap in time. Therefore, this chronology of *Judges* is presented with approximate dates. The intent of the *Book of Judges* is to show the self-will and idolatry of the people when no king reigned; they refused to follow the Lord as king. Each did what each considered *"right"* in his or her own sight. Throughout the nation, many were asking and seeking for "who will lead us?" This overview seeks to show the conditions and events of over 350 years, from the entrance of Israel into Canaan around 1406 BC to the end of Samuel's life around 1014 BC.

All dates are estimates and approximate. Each judge is highlighted.

Date	Events	Scripture
1446-1406 BC	The children of Israel left the land of Egypt around 1446 BC, led by Moses following the Lord in the Pillar of Fire and Cloud of Glory. This occurred 480 years before Solomon began building the Temple in Jerusalem (966 BC).	Exodus 12:40
1406-1398 BC?	Joshua led the people of Israel in conquering the major portions of the land of Canaan, but certainly not all the land. Several Canaanite settlements remained which the Israelites had to deal with.	Joshua 1
1390 BC?	Joshua led the priests and people in moving the Tabernacle from Gilgal to Shiloh. There the priests set up the Tabernacle, making Shiloh the central worship location for the people of Israel.	Joshua 18:1; 22:9, 12
ca. 1380 BC	Joshua, the strong, faithful conqueror and leader of Israel, was born in Egypt around 1490 BC and died in Canaan at the age of 110, around 1380 BC.	Joshua 24:29; Judges 2:8–9
1380 BC	After Joshua's death, the children of Israel *"inquired of the LORD"* about who should go up to battle against the Canaanites. The Lord instructed the tribe of Judah to continue the war with the Canaanites. The warriors of the tribe of Judah and the neighboring tribe of Simeon captured several cities, including Bezek, Jebus/Jerusalem (partial), Hebron, and Debir along with some of the area between the foothills and coastal plains south of Jerusalem and near the Negev. The tribe of "Joseph" also captured Bethel (Luz) (in the tribal allotment of Ephraim).	Judges 1:1

ca. 1380 BC	The tribes of Manasseh, Ephraim, Zebulun, Asher, Naphtali, and Dan failed to drive out many groups of Canaanites, placing them instead into forced labor.	Judges 1:27
ca. 1380-1370 BC	The Angel of the LORD, a manifestation of the pre-incarnate Christ, rebuked Israel for idolatry and warned of the chastening of God they would face. In Judges 2, the author presents the recurring Cycle of Sin and Salvation of the Period of the Judges.	Judges 2:1–23; 3:1–6
1381-1362 BC	Phinehas, the son of Eleazer and grandson of Aaron, served as High Priest for 19 years, possibly from around 1381 to 1362 BC. His father Eleazer served as High Priest before him and died around 1381 BC.	Exodus 6:25; Josh. 24:33; Judges 20:27–28
ca. 1375-1372 BC	Judges 17-21 present two appendices to the Book of Judges. These likely occurred early in the Period of the Judges. Most scholars see the events of chapters 19-21 occurring first, followed by the events of chapters 17-18.	Judges 17–21
ca. 1375 BC	Doing what he considered *"right in his own eyes,"* a Levite in the hill country of Ephraim added a concubine from Bethlehem to his home. She acted unfaithfully toward him, left him, and returned to her father's house in Bethlehem.	Judges 19:1
ca. 1375 BC	After four months, the Levite traveled to Bethlehem, seeking to bring his concubine back to his home in the hills of Ephraim. He stayed four and a half days at her home with her father and then they left, returning to the hills of Ephraim.	Judges 19:3
ca. 1375 BC	The Levite, his concubine, and at least one servant traveled north, bypassing Jebus (Jerusalem) and going to Gibeah, part of the territory of Benjamin.	Judges 19:10
ca. 1375 BC	Hospitably, an old man invited them into his home for food and a night's lodging.	Judges 19:16
ca. 1375 BC	The Levite gave his concubine to the men of the city of Gibeah. They repeatedly raped and abused her, leading to her death near morning.	Judges 19:23
ca. 1375 BC	The Levite took his concubine's body to his home in the hills of Ephraim. He cut her body into twelve pieces and sent one piece to each of the twelve tribes. The people of Israel became incensed at the horrendous actions by the men of Gibeah.	Judges 19:28b

ca. 1375 BC	From throughout the nation, from north to south, *"including Gilead"* east of the Jordan, men of Israel gathered at Mizpah, about two miles from Gibeah.	Judges 20:1
ca. 1375 BC	Meeting at Mizpah, the men of Israel heard the story from the Levite and, filled with shock and rage, decided to take action for the atrocities done in Gibeah. They went to the people of the Tribe of Benjamin seeking to deal with the men of Gibeah. The men of Benjamin chose to defend the men of Gibeah rather than give them up for their crimes against the concubine.	Judges 20:2
ca. 1375 BC	Apparently, the Ark of the Covenant and the High Priest Phinehas served at Bethel briefly during this time. The civil war with Benjamin occurred ca. 1375 BC.	Judges 20:27
ca. 1375 BC	After inquiring of the Lord (through Phinehas) at nearby Bethel, the men of Israel, led by the tribe of Judah, fought against the tribe of Benjamin—400,000 men of Israel versus the 26,700 men of Benjamin. 22,000 Israelites died on the first day of battle against Benjamin.	Judges 20:14
ca. 1375 BC	After their defeat the first day, the tribes of Israel gathered at Bethel to fast and pray over going into further battle against the tribe of Benjamin. At Bethel, they consulted Phinehas and worshiped. The Lord directed them to fight Benjamin again.	Judges 20:22
ca. 1375 BC	The Israelites faced defeat via the Benjaminites on the second day. 18,000 men of Israel died in the battle. That brought the number to 40,000 Israelites.	Judges 20:24
ca. 1375 BC	After their defeat on the second day, the tribes of Israel gathered again at Bethel to fast and pray over going into further battle against the tribe of Benjamin. Through Phinehas, the Lord directed them to battle Benjamin on the third day. He promised victory which they saw the third day. 25,100 men of Benjamin died that day.	Judges 20:26
ca. 1375 BC	Six hundred men of Benjamin fled to the Rock of Rimmon where they lived in the cave-filled hills for four months.	Judges 20:47
ca. 1375 BC	Several of the tribes of Israel gathered at Bethel to determine how to avoid the total annihilation of the Tribe of Benjamin. They wept before the Lord, offered burnt offerings, and sought His will in this matter.	Judges 21:1

ca. 1375 BC	They determined that none had come from Jabesh-gilead to fight against Benjamin. Therefore, they sent a fighting force of 12,000 who executed the people, except for 400 unmarried virgin women. They brought these back to be wives for 400 of the remaining 600 men of Benjamin, to whom they offered terms of peace.	Judges 21:5
ca. 1375 BC	For the remaining 200 men of Benjamin, they devised a plan for them to steal 200 young women from the Feast (likely the Fall Feast of Tabernacles) at Shiloh.	Judges 21:16-23
ca. 1375 BC	After the events of the civil war with Benjamin and its aftermath, all the men of the various tribes returned to their families in the allotted territories.	Judges 21:24
ca. 1372 BC	Living in the tribal allotment of Ephraim, Micah crafted idols for his family. He also "consecrated" one of his sons as his priest. After this, Micah hired a Levite from Bethlehem to be his family priest. Still holding to his idols, Micah superstitiously thought "the LORD will be good to me, since I have a Levite as priest."	Judges 17
ca. 1372 BC	The tribe of Dan followed in the idolatry of Micah. They sought the counsel of Micah's Levite priest about their search for another territory. He told them to "go in peace." They traveled to Laish in northern Israel, spied out the city, and returned to their tribal allotment in south central Israel.	Judges 18:1-7
ca. 1372 BC	Most of the tribe of Dan abandoned their allotted territory near the Negev and the Mediterranean Sea in south central and south-west Canaan, because of the difficulties associated with the Canaanite people (Amorites) and Philistines there (see Judges 1:24-26). They began looking for another place, an easier area to conquer. They moved north, captured, and destroyed the city and people of Laish (or Leshem) just south of Mount Hermon. They rebuilt the city, renamed it "Dan" and began living there. They also hired Micah's Levite priest as their tribal priest.	Judges 18:8-12
ca. 1372 BC	Having stolen Micah's silver idols and other idols, the Danites also took his hired priest to lead them in their new territory in Dan in Northern Israel. Judges 18:30-31 notes his name as Jonathan, the son of Gershom and grandson of Moses. Jonathan served as a priest ca. 1380-1365 BC. His sons continued as priests after this.	Judges 18:13-29, 30-31

ca.1372-722 BC	The tribe of Dan continued in their idolatry for many years "until the day of the captivity of the land," likely the culmination of the Assyrian campaign in 722 BC.	Judges 18:30
1370s, 1360s BC	The children of Israel "did evil in the sight of the LORD." They forgot Him and turned to worship and serve the Baals and the Asheroth.	Judges 3:7
1361-1353 BC	In His jealous anger, the Lord allowed Cushan-rishathaim of Mesopotamia to oppress the children of Israel for eight years (likely in the territory of Judah).	Judges 3:8
ca. 1353 BC	When the children of Israel "cried to the LORD," He raised up the first of the "judges," Othniel, the nephew of Caleb. Othniel defeated Cushan-rishathaim.	Judges 3:9
1353-1313 BC	The land had a period of rest for forty years as Othniel judged Israel. He led primarily in the region of Judah.	Judges 3:11
ca. 1313 BC	Again, the children of Israel "did evil in the sight of the LORD."	Judges 3:12a
1313-1295 BC	Eglon king of Moab, oppressed Israel for 18 years (likely the region of Ephraim)	Judges 3:7
1295-1215 BC	In the region of Ephraim, God raised up Ehud as a judge to defeat Eglon and bring about peace and rest from oppression for 80 years (1295-1215 BC).	Judges 3:15-30
ca. 1215 BC	Shamgar fought the Philistines and saved Israel.	Judges 3:31
ca. 1215	Once again, the people of Israel "did evil in the sight of the LORD."	Judges 4:1
1215-1195 BC	Jabin king of Canaan from Hazor in northern Israel oppressed Israel for 20 years (likely in the regions of Ephraim, Zebulun, and Naphtali).	Judges 4:1-3
1192 BC	Eli the priest was born around 1192 BC. He lived for 98 years, until 1094 BC.	1 Samuel 4:15, 18
1195-1155 BC	God raised up Deborah and Barak to deal with the oppression of Jabin of Canaan in the regions of Ephraim, Zebulun, and Naphtali. The Lord led them in defeating Jabin, his General Sisera, and his army. The Israelites had rest for 40 years.	Judges 4:4
1155-1148 BC	The Midianites, Amalekites, and "sons of the east" oppressed Israel for 7 years (likely in the regions of Manasseh and Ephraim in central Israel).	Judges 6:1–6
1148-1108 BC	God raised up Gideon to deal with the Midianites and their allies. The region of Manasseh and Ephraim had peace for 40 years.	Judges 6:7

1108 BC	The people of Israel (Manasseh and Ephraim) did not remember the Lord who delivered them from the Midianites through Gideon, nor did they remember Gideon and the 40 years of peace he brought.	Judges 8:33
1108-1105 BC	Abimelech, the son of Gideon by a concubine in Shechem (Judges 8:31), through conspiracy and treachery, arose to rule in central Israel (Shechem, Arumah, and Thebez in West Manasseh) with 3 years of tyranny. He was NOT a judge. He murdered 69 of his half-brothers to ascend to rulership. His half-brother Jotham escaped by hiding from this murderous rampage. Abimelech died in Thebez.	Judges 9:1–57
1105-1082 BC	After Abimelech's rule and death, Tola arose to judge Israel (West Manasseh) for 23 years.	Judges 10:1–2
Around 1100 BC	The events recorded in the *Book of Ruth* lasted about 11–15 years and occurred in the land of Moab and in Bethlehem *"in the days when the judges ruled/governed"* (Ruth 1:1). Boaz and Ruth became the parents of Obed, father of Jesse, grandfather of David. Boaz and Ruth were the great grandparents of David (born about 1041 BC).	Ruth 1:1; 4:17
1126-1105 BC	Jair the Gileadite arose to judge Israel for 22 years (likely in the region of Gilead in East Manasseh, east of the Jordan River).	Judges 10:3
1105-1087 BC	The children of Israel in the region of Gilead *"did evil in the sight of the LORD,"* serving various Baals and other false gods such as Chemosh, Molech, and Dagon. The Ammonites arose and oppressed them for 18 years.	Judges 10:6–9
1087-1081 BC	Jephthah arose to lead the Gileadites in dealing with the Ammonites. He judged Israel for 6 years.	Judges 11:1–40; 12:1–7
1192-1094 BC	Eli lived from 1192 to 1094 BC (98 years— 1 Samuel 4:15), serving as High Priest and Judge at the Tabernacle at Shiloh in central Israel. Some calculate the chronology of his judging Israel from 1134 to 1094 BC (40 years).	1 Samuel 1–3; 4:1–22
ca. 1130s BC	Sometime after reaching the age of 50, Eli turned over his duties as High Priest to his oldest son Phinehas. In wickedness and disobedience to the Word of God, Phinehas and his brother Hophni served as priests at the Tabernacle. For historical data, see Josephus, Antiquities of the Jews, Book 5, Chapter 11.2.	1 Samuel 2:12–17, 22–36; 3:12–18

1106 BC	Elkanah and his two wives Hannah and Peninnah traveled from their home in Ramah to the Tabernacle in Shiloh for the yearly Feast (likely the Fall Feast of Tabernacles). There, in deep oppression, Hannah prayed for a son and vowed to give him to the Lord as a Nazirite all his days.	1 Samuel 1:1–18
ca. 1105-1101 BC	Hannah gave birth to Samuel and weaned him at their home in Ramah in the territory of Ephraim. After he was weaned (about age 3 or 4), she brought Samuel to serve at the Tabernacle in Shiloh where Eli served as a priest and judge.	1 Samuel 1:19–28; 2:18–21
1094 BC	The Lord called Samuel as a prophet and he began to bring God's Word to Israel.	1 Samuel 3
1094 BC	Fighting in the areas of Ebenezer and Aphek (the region of Ephraim), the Philistines captured the Ark of the Covenant from the Israeli army and took it into Philistine territory (to the Philistine cities of Ashdod, Gath, and Ekron).	1 Samuel 4:1–11; 5:1–12
1094 BC	Eli's sons, Hophni and Phinehas died at Aphek. Eli died at Shiloh after hearing of the capture of the Ark of the Covenant. He had judged Israel for forty years.	1 Samuel 4:17–18
1093 BC	After seven months of horrendous plagues in several of their cities, the Philistines returned the Ark of the Covenant to Beth-shemesh in the territory of Judah.	1 Samuel 5:1–12; 6:1–21
1093-1073 BC	The men of Kiriath-jearim brought the Ark of the Covenant to the home of Abinadab in Kiriath-jearim in Judah where it remained for twenty years. Abinadab consecrated his son Eleazar "to keep the Ark of the LORD."	1 Samuel 6:21; 7:1–2
1081-1074 BC	Ibzan of Bethlehem judged Israel for 7 years. Likely, he dealt with Canaanite peoples in the region of Judah in central and south Israel.	Judges 12:8–10
1074-1064 BC	Elon the Zebulunite judged Israel for 10 years. Likely, he dealt with Canaanite peoples in the region of Zebulun in northern Israel.	Judges 12:11–12
1064-1058 BC	Abdon the Pirathonite (from the town of Pirathon in the hill country of Ephraim) judged Israel for 8 years. Likely, he dealt with neighboring Amalekites and other Canaanites in the region of Ephraim during this time.	Judges 12:13–15
ca. 1085-1014 BC	Samuel served as priest, prophet, and judge at the Tabernacle in Shiloh as well as in Bethel, Gilgal, Mizpah and Ramah (regions of West Manasseh, Ephraim and Benjamin) from ca. 1085 (perhaps earlier, 1090?) to his death in 1014 BC. He anointed Saul as king of Israel ca. 1052 BC and David as future king ca.1029 BC.	1 Samuel 3:1–21; 7:15–17

1090-1050 BC	The Philistines oppressed Israel for 40 years (ca. 1090-1050 BC) and continued to be a menace in the reigns of Saul (1052-1011 BC) and David (1011-971 BC).	Judges 13:1
1085-1065 BC	During the the 40-year Philistine oppression, God raised up Samson to judge Israel for 20 years.	Judges 13—16
ca. 1073-1014 BC	Samuel, now around 32 years of age, called the Israelites to "return to the LORD with all your heart." He spoke of the current oppression of the Philistines. They gathered at Mizpah where he prayed and "judged the sons of Israel." The Lord dealt severely with the Philistines. They no longer came "within the border of Israel" and "the hand of the LORD was against the Philistines all the days of Samuel."	1 Samuel 7:3–14
ca. 1050 BC	Likely, the Philistines destroyed the Tabernacle complex at Shiloh perhaps as early as 1094 BC to around 1050 BC. [See 1 Samuel 4:19-22; Psalm 78:56-64; Jeremiah 7:12, 14; 26:6, 9.]	1 Samuel 4:19–22
ca. 1380-1052 BC	The Period of the Judges shows the spiritual and moral degradation and lack of leadership in Israel at this time—"In those days there was no king in Israel; everyone did what was right in his own eyes" (Judges 21:25). This continued in the times of Eli and Samuel recorded in 1 Samuel.	Judges 21:25; 1 Samuel 1–12
1105–1014 BC	Samuel lived from around 1105 to 1014 BC. He served as a priest at the Tabernacle at Shiloh, at first assisting Eli, from around 1100 BC. He also served as a prophet and judge in Israel for about 80 years (to around 1014 BC). Around 1052 BC, He anointed Saul as Israel's first king (1052-1011 BC). Later, he anointed David (around 1029 BC) who would one day replace the disobedient Saul as king (around 1011/10 BC). Samuel died around 1014 BC, about three years before Saul was slain in battle with the Philistines and David became king (1011 BC). According to Jewish tradition, Samuel penned the record of the events of the Book of Judges.	1 Samuel 1 –24; 25:1; 28:3–19; Acts 3:24; 13:30; Hebrews 11:32

The Judges of Israel

Date	Time Frame	Name	Enemy Oppressors	Cities, Tribal Region	Scripture
ca. 1361-1313 BC	8 years of oppression, 40 years of rest	Othniel/ Judah	Cushan Rishathaim king of Mesopotamia	Debir, territory of Judah	Judges 1:11–15; 3:1–11; Joshua 15:15–19; 1 Chronicles 4:13
1313-1215 BC	18 years of oppression 80 years of rest	Ehud / Benjamin "a left-handed man"	Eglon, king of Moab; Ammonites; Amalekites	Ephraim, fords of the Jordan River	Judges 3:12–33; 4:1
ca. 1215 BC	Unknown	Shamgar / Uncertain	Philistines	[Asher, Naphtali?]	Judges 3:31; 5:6
1215-1155 BC	20 years of oppression, 40 years of rest	Deborah / Ephraim And Barak/ Naphtali	Jabin, king of Canaan, Army commander Sisera	Naphtali, Jezreel Valley, Megiddo, Kishon River valley	Judge 4:1–33; 5:1–31; Hebrews 11:32
1155-1108 BC	7 years of oppression, 40 years of quiet	Gideon / Manasseh	Midianites; Amalekites; "sons of the East"	Issachar, Ephraim	Judges 6:1–33; 7:1–33; 8:1–32; Hebrews 11:32
1108–1105 BC	3 years of wicked rule	Abimelech, Manasseh	Abimelech ruled in wickedness	Shechem, Beth Millo, Ophrah, Arumah, Thebez	Judges 8:31–35; 9:1–57; 2Samuel 11:21
1105-1082 BC	Unknown, 23 years of peace	Tola / Issachar	Unknown	Shamir, Ephraim	Judges 10:1–2
1126-1105 BC	Unknown, 22 years of peace	Jair / Gilead-Manasseh	Unknown	East Manasseh, East of the Jordan River	Judges 10:3–5
1087–1081 BC	18 years of oppression, 6 years as a judge	Jephthah / Gilead-Manasseh	Philistines; Ammonites; Ephraimites	Gilead, east of the Jordan River	Judges 10:6–18;11:1–40; 12:1–7; Hebrews 11:32
1081-1074 BC	Unknown, 7 years as a judge	Ibzan of Bethlehem / Judah or Zebulun	Unknown	Unknown	Judges 12:8–10

1074-1064 BC	Unknown, 10 years as a judge	Elon / Zebulun	Unknown	Unknown	Judges 12:11-12
1064-1058 BC	Unknown, 8 years as a judge	Abdon / Ephraim	Unknown	Unknown	Judges 12:13-15
1085-1065 BC	20 years as a judge	Samson / Dan	Philistines	Zorah, Eshtaol, Timnah, Gaza, Sorek Valley, Philistia, Israel's central highlands	Judges 13—16; Hebrews 11:32
1134-1094 BC	40 years as a judge	Eli / Levi Sons: Hophni and Phinehas	Philistines	Shiloh, Ramah, Bethel, Gilgal, Mizpah, and Central Israel	1 Samuel 1:1-28; 2:1-36; 3:1-21; 4:1-22; 14:3; 1 Kgs 2:27
1105-1014 BC	Samuel lived 91 years, first as a servant-priest at Shiloh (Taberacle), then as a judge and prophet (Tabernacle)	Samuel / Levi (1 Chronicles 6:27-28), Territory of Ephraim (1 Samuel 1:1). Sons: Joel and Abijah	Philistines	Shiloh, Ramah, Bethel, Gilgal, Mizpah, and Central Israel	1 Samuel 2—24; 25:1; 28:3-19; 1 Chronicles 11:3; 26:28; Psalm 99:6-7; Jeremiah 15:1; Acts 3:24; 13:20; Hebrews 11:32

The Seven Cycles of Sin and Salvation in Israel
The Cycle Summary

The Sin of Israel	The Chastening of the Lord	The Cry and Prayer of the People	The Work of the Lord in Raising Up a Judge/Deliverer	Scripture
"Israel did evil in the sight of the LORD and served the Baals, and they forsook the LORD, the God of their fathers, who had brought them out of the land of Egypt, and followed other gods from among the gods of the peoples who were around them, and bowed themselves down to them; thus they provoked the LORD to anger. So they forsook the LORD and served Baal and the Ashtaroth." Judges 2:11–13	"And the anger of the LORD burned against Israel, and He gave them into the hands of plunderers." Judges 2:14–15	"...for the LORD was moved to pity by their groaning because of those who oppressed and afflicted them." Judges 2:18b	"Then the LORD raised up judges who delivered them from the hand of those who plundered them... And when the LORD raised up judges for them, the LORD was with the judge and delivered them from the hand of their enemies all the days of the judge ... But it came about when the judge died, that they would turn back and act more corruptly than their fathers, in following other gods..." Judges 2:16, 18a, 19a	Judges 2:11–23; 3:1–6

The Seven Cycles

#	Israel Sinned, "did evil"	God Allowed Oppressors / Years of Oppression	Israel Prayed	God Sent a Deliverer / Years of Rest	Scripture: The Book of Judges
1	"And the sons of Israel did what was evil in the sight of the LORD."	"Then the anger of the LORD was kindled against Israel." Judges 3:8a Cushan-rishathaim oppressed them for 8 years.	"And the sons of Israel cried to the LORD..." Judges 3:9a	"... the LORD raised up a deliverer for the sons of Israel to deliver them, Othniel the son of Kenaz...And the Spirit of the LORD came upon him, and he judged Israel." Judges 3:9b–10 40 years of rest.	Judges 1:13; 3:7–11
2.	"Now the sons of Israel again did evil in the sight of the LORD." Judges 3:12a	"So the LORD strengthened Eglon king of Moab against Israel." Judges 3:12b 18 years of oppression	"But when the sons of Israel cried to the LORD, the LORD raised up a deliverer." Judges 3:15a	"the LORD raised up a deliverer for them, Ehud the son of Gera..." Judges 3:15b "And the land was undisturbed for eighty years." Judges 3:30	Judges 3:12–30
3.	"Then the sons of Israel again did evil in the sight of the LORD." Judges 4:1	"The LORD sold them into the hand of Jabin king of Canaan." Judges 4:2a 20 years of oppression	"And the sons of Israel cried to the LORD. (Judges 4:4, 6, 23)	God raised up Deborah and Barak. "So God subdued... Jabin the king of Canaan before the sons of Israel." Judges 4:4, 6, 23	Judges 4:1–24; 5:1–31 Hebrews 11:32

4.	"The sons of Israel did what was evil in the sight of the LORD." Judges 6:1a	The Lord raised up the Midianites to oppress Israel. Judges 6:1b 7 years of oppression	"The sons of Israel cried out to the LORD." Judges 6:7	The Angel of the LORD came and called Gideon to follow the Lord in conquering the Midianites. Judges 6:11-40; 7:1-25; 8:1-32— 40 years of peace	Judges 6:1–40; 7:1–25; 8:1–32 Hebrews 11:32
5.	"The sons of Israel again played the harlot with the Baals" Judges 8:33	Abimelech arose to rule as a tyrant. Judges 9 3 years of tyranny	Jotham spoke to the men of Shechem. Judges 9:7–21	Tola "arose to save Israel." He judged Israel for 23 years—years of peace. Judges 10:1-2	Judges 8: 33-35; 9:1-57; 10:1-2
6.	"The sons of Israel again did evil in the sight of the LORD." Judges 10:6a	"The anger of the LORD burned against Israel, and He sold them into the hands of the Philistines" and the Ammonites. Judges 10:7	"The sons of Israel cried out to the to the LORD." Judges 10:10a	"The Spirit of the LORD came upon Jephthah." The Lord gave the Ammonites "into his hand" and he defeated them. Judges 11:29, 32-33 Jephthah judged for 6 years.	Judges 10:6-18; 11:1-40; 12:1-7 Hebrews 11:32
7.	"The sons of Israel again did evil in the sight of the LORD." Judges 13:1a	"The LORD gave them into the hands of the Philistines forty years." Judges 13:1b	"Then Samson called to the LORD." Judges 16:28 and 15:18	"He [Samson] shall begin to deliver Israel from the hands of the Philistines." Judges 13:5b with 13:25; 14:6a, 19; 15:14 Samson judged 20 years.	Judges 13–16; Hebrews 11:32

"In those days there was no king in Israel; everyone did what was right in his own eyes."
Judges 21:25

The Angel of the LORD

Christ Revealing and Accomplishing His Will

The Angel of the LORD is considered a Christophany,

a pre-incarnate appearance of Christ in the Old Testament

Scripture	Event	Place
Genesis 16:1; note verses 7-13	The Angel of the LORD found Hagar and Ishmael in the wilderness running from Sarai's harsh treatment. He delivered them and instructed Hagar to return to Sarai.	Wilderness near Shur
Genesis 17:1–22, note verses 1, 22	*"The LORD appeared to Abram"* in some form when he was ninety-nine years old and promised him a son Isaac. After meeting with him, He *"went up from Abraham."*	By the oaks of Mamre near Hebron
Genesis 18:1–33	The Lord came to the home of Abraham in the form of a Man along with two angels also in the form of men. He spoke to Abraham and Sarah about their coming son Isaac and to Abraham about the coming judgment of Sodom.	By the oaks of Mamre near Hebron
Genesis 21:8–21, note verses 17-19	The Angel of God knew about Hagar and Ishmael and heard Ishmael crying. He spoke to her and provided water for them.	Wilderness of Beersheba
Genesis 22:1–19, note verses 11-19	As Abraham was offering up Isaac on Mount Moriah, the Angel of the LORD stopped him, spoke to him, and gave him many promises.	Mount Moriah (modern Jerusalem)
Genesis 28:10–22; 31:11, 13	The Lord appeared to Jacob in a dream at Bethel promising him the land, many descendants, and a seed through whom the earth would be blessed. This same Lord appeared as the Angel of God twenty years later.	Bethel
Genesis 31:10–13	The Angel of God spoke to Jacob in a dream instructing him to leave Haran and return to Canaan.	Haran

Genesis 32:22–32; Hosea 12:4–5	The Angel of the LORD wrestled all night with Jacob and blessed him at the Jabbok River.	Jabbok River
Genesis 48:3, 16	In Egypt, while blessing the sons of Joseph, Jacob testified before his family of *"the Angel who has redeemed me from all evil"* (NKJV). Only God can redeem. He invoked this "Angel" to *"bless the lads,"* something only God could do.	Testimony in Egypt
Exodus 3:1–6, note verse 2; Deuteronomy 33:16; Acts 7:30–36; Mark 12:26; Luke 20:37	The Angel of the LORD appeared to Moses in a flame of fire in the midst of a bush at Mount Horeb in the desert of Midian.	Mount Horeb (also known as Mount Sinai)
Exodus 4:24–26	The Lord met Moses and sought to kill him for failing to circumcise his son. This was possibly the Angel of the LORD.	On the way to Egypt
Exodus 14:19–20; Psalm 78:12–16; Isaiah 63:9	The Angel of God appeared in the Pillars of Cloud and of Fire guiding and protecting the children of Israel from Pharaoh's army.	At the Red Sea
Psalm 78:52–53	The Lord *"led forth His own people like sheep, and guided them in the wilderness like a flock"* (Psalm 78:52).	From Egypt to Canaan
Exodus 19–20; 24:12–18; Acts 7:38	The Angel of the LORD gave the Law to Moses on Mount Sinai.	At Mount Sinai
Exodus 24:1–11	The Lord invited Moses, Aaron, Nadab, Abihu, and the Seventy Elders to come up to Mount Sinai where He spoke and appeared to them. This was possibly the Angel of the LORD whose appearance mirrors that of the Lord in Ezekiel 1:26-28; Daniel 7:9-10, and of Christ in Revelation 4:2-3	At Mount Sinai
Exodus 23:20–23 Acts 7:35–36	Moses received God's promise that He would send the Angel of the LORD to guide Israel into Canaan. *"My name is in Him." "My Angel will go before you."* (NKJV).	At Mount Sinai

Exodus 32:34 33:1–6, 12–16	The Lord told Moses He would send a representative angel before them, not the Angel of the LORD. He Himself would not go with them because of their sin. Moses interceded and God promised, "*My presence shall go with you.*"	At Mount Sinai
Numbers 22—24, note 22:22–39	On Balaam's journey to meet Balak with the leaders of Moab, the Angel of the LORD met Balaam and his donkey.	The Plains of Moab
Joshua 5:13–15; 6:1–5	A Man, the Commander or "Captain of the Host of the LORD," met Joshua near Jericho and instructed him in how to conquer the city.	Near Jericho in the land of Canaan.
Judges 2:1	The Angel of the LORD rebuked Israel for disobeying Him in not dealing with the Canaanites as He had commanded.	Bochim (means "Weeping")
Judges 5:23	The Angel of the LORD cursed the people of the town of Meroz for not fighting with the people of God against the Lord's enemies in northern Israel.	Meroz
Judges 6:11–24, 25–27	The Angel of the LORD appeared to Gideon calling him to lead Israel against the Midianites.	Ophrah
Judges 13:1–24	The Angel of the LORD, also called "*the Angel of God*" (13:6, 9) appeared to Manoah and his wife promising them a son and then ascended in the flame of their burnt offering.	Zorah
Psalm 35:5-6	David prayed for the help of the Angel of the LORD against an enemy who was against him without cause.	Israel
2 Samuel 14:17, 20	A woman of Tekoa spoke to David about the Angel of God "*discerning good and evil*" and being marked by "*wisdom...to know everything that is in the earth*" (NKJV).	Jerusalem

2 Samuel 24:10–25; 1 Chronicles 21:1–30, note verses 12–20, 27, 30	The Angel of the LORD was involved in judging David's sin of numbering the people (probably to enhance his military might or perhaps out of pride in his military potential).	Israel and Jerusalem
Psalm 34:7 (with 1 Samuel 21:10–15)	David celebrated the protection of the Angel of the LORD in the danger he faced from Abimelech—King Achish of Gath.	Gath, city of the Philistines
1 Kings 19:5, 7	The Angel of the LORD touched Elijah twice, instructing him eat and drink in preparation for the journey ahead.	Wilderness south of Beersheba
2 Kings 1:2–17, note verses 3, 15, 16	The Angel of the LORD instructed Elijah to go and deliver a message to Israel's king Ahaziah.	Samaria
2 Kings 19:35–36; Isaiah 37:36	The Angel of the LORD struck 185,000 Assyrian troops bringing Sennacherib's threats to naught and delivering Hezekiah and the people of Jerusalem.	Near Jerusalem
Daniel 3:19 Daniel 3:19–30, note verse 28	God "*sent His Angel*" and delivered Shadrach, Meshach, and Abed-nego from the fiery furnace. To Nebuchadnezzar this fourth Man in the furnace appeared "*like the Son of God*" (or margin, "a son of the gods") (Note: 3:25, 28-NKJV).	The Plain of Dura in the province of Babylon
Daniel 6:1–28, note verse 22	When rescued from the lion's den, Daniel testified, "*My God sent His angel and shut the lions' mouths...*" That phrase is the same as that found in Daniel 3:28.	The city of Babylon
Zechariah 1:7–17, note verses 11, 12	The Angel of the LORD appeared in Zechariah's first vision as the Commander-in-Chief of the angelic hosts riding on a red horse of judgment seeking to bring mercy and restoration to Israel.	Israel and the Earth

Zechariah 3:1–10, note verses 1–2, 3–4, 6	The Angel of the LORD appeared in Zechariah's fourth vision rebuking Satan and declaring Jerusalem and the nation (represented by Joshua the High Priest) as the cleansed and restored people and priesthood of God. With that is the promise of the coming Messiah (Servant, Branch, Stone).	Israel
Zechariah 12:8	Zechariah prophesied about the future of Israel when the nation will be strong like David or like a nation with the Angel of the LORD leading them.	Jerusalem and the area surrounding it

LESSON 2

GOD'S RELIABILITY—OUR AVAILABILITY
DEALING WITH SIN AND EVIL GOD'S WAY

The people of God were doing what was "right" in their own eyes. There's a problem. What is "right" in many eyes is "evil" in the eyes of God. He must deal with it, especially when it's within His own covenant people. We see Him doing that soon after Joshua died. He knew what was best for His people and He had communicated that clearly through Moses and others. It was written down, but few knew what God had said or what Moses had written, and even fewer read it. So, God chose to use the instruments at hand to deal with His people. What instruments? The pagan peoples within the land and surrounding the land of Canaan.

What does that mean to me today? Too often we do not know what God wants, and we do not know what He has said—what we could easily read, if we would take the time and effort. As we walk through the accounts in Judges 3-5, we will discover life lessons and principles that come home to the heart, to each of our hearts. These writings and stories will help us follow God more really and more faithfully. The Lord can become very, very real to daily life—this very day.

Week 2's Scripture adventure takes us into the land of Israel once again, into the lives of some of God's well-beloved people and into some of their failures. Let's learn from them. One does not have to experience failure to know how to live successfully. There are many times when someone else's missteps can lead us into the right steps and avoid the potholes and pits that would hamper our journey.

DID YOU KNOW?
What Were the Baals?

"Baal" means "master, lord," and served as the name of the chief male god of the Phoenician people, one of the nations among the peoples of Canaan. Worshipers saw him as the son of El or the son of Dagon, the grain god. People thought of Baal as the agricultural god of crops and fertility as well as the storm god of rain (dew, fog), lightning, and thunder. Most Canaanites adopted Baal (or Baals) as their god. Their false worship included animal and human sacrifices, feasts, and immoral practices led by false priests and ritual prostitutes, male and female. Canaanites worshiped several Baals, since often a town or area focused on and worshiped their own local Baal idol.

DAY ONE

GOD'S RELIABILITY AND CREATIVITY

People did *"evil in the sight of the LORD."* What would He do? How would He respond, and how would the people respond or react to His actions? We find out by exploring the paragraphs and pages of the *Book of Judges*.

📖 Read Judges 3:7. Exactly what did the people do?

_____

_____

How did the Lord respond according to Judges 3:8?

_____

_____

According to Judges 3:9, what did the people do in response to their God-given circumstances? How did God respond to His people?

_____

_____

_____

Othniel, the first judge mentioned in the *Book of Judges*, went to battle with Israel's oppressor Cushan-rishathaim of Mesopotamia. What did the Lord do, according to Judges 3:10?

_____

_____

According to Judges 3:11, what happened as a result of the leadership of Othniel, God's appointed leader?

_____

_____

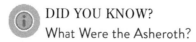 DID YOU KNOW?
What Were the Asheroth?

The Asheroth (also spelled Asherim, plural of Asherah) were the various images of Asherah, a pagan goddess, daughter of El and consort of Baal. Many Canaanites practiced false worship of this goddess along with Baal, which included immoral rites at the various shrines, groves, or "high places" dedicated to her and Baal. Often a wooden image of this goddess along with an image of Baal stood at these shrines. Names of this false goddess included Ashtoreth, Astarte, and Anath, and she is linked to the Babylonian goddess, Ishtar.

The people of Israel in the tribal regions of Judah and Simeon (south central Israel), did evil in God's sight. He knew what He saw and heard was wrong; they were sinning against Him and against themselves. The people forgot Him as their God and substituted fake gods, the various Baals (there were many) and the Asheroth (plural, with various shrines of the Canaanite goddess Asherah, Baal's "wife"). The Lord is holy and true and detests anything untrue, deceptive, and destructive. He arose in jealous anger and chastened His people by allowing oppression to come through Cushan-rishathaim, king of Mesopotamia (the area around and between the Tigris and Euphrates Rivers). The name Cushan-rishathaim can be translated as "Cushan of double evil" and his oppressive rule lasted eight years.

The oppressive years of Cushan-rishathaim caused the people of God to cry out to the Lord. God heard their prayers and raised up Othniel as "*a deliverer.*" The word "deliverer" is a translation of the Hebrew word *yasha*, meaning "wide," "open," and "free." It refers to being safe. Othniel was a "savior" or "rescuer" for the people, one who brought them out of their oppression. When he went to war against Cushan-rishathaim, "*the Spirit of the LORD came upon him,*" and he led them to victory. By the power of the Lord, Othniel served in that capacity for forty years and "*the land had rest,*" free from strife, oppression, and marked by safety and freedom. This was an answer to prayer.

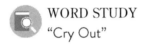

WORD STUDY
"Cry Out"

The Hebrew word *za'aq* (Strong's #2199) means "to shriek" in the face of pain, danger, or anguish of some kind. It is often translated "cry," "cried," or "cried out" and refers to the cry for help, the heart cry of need or pain, seeking deliverance and support. It is used six times in the *Book of Judges* (3:9, 15; 6:6, 7; 10:10, 14). Used twice in the *Book of Judges* is a similar Hebrew word *tsa'aq* (Strong's #6817), also meaning "to shriek." It is also translated "cried out," with the emphasis on crying out together (4:3; 10:12).

DAY TWO

WHAT DO YOU HAVE IN YOUR HAND?

When Jesus' disciples spoke to Him about the thousands of hungry people in the area of Galilee where they were ministering, He asked them a question: "*How many loaves do you have?*" (Mark 6:38). Andrew answered, "*five barley loaves and two fish, but what are these for so many people?*" (John 6:9). It seemed like an impossible situation for the disciples. They could calculate how much money it would take, but where could they get that much food? How could they get the food now? Jesus ordered them to have the people sit down in an organized manner, and then He took the loaves and the fish given to Him, prayed, and multiplied it. He did that many times in Scripture, taking what a surrendered heart gave and multiplied it beyond what a person could do. Did God do that in the Old Testament? What do we discover in the *Book of Judges*?

IN THEIR SHOES
Don't Forget the Lord

God warned His people to not *"forget the LORD,"* but to remember Him, what He had done, what He had said, and what He had promised (Deuteronomy 6:12; see also Deuteronomy 4:9; 6:10–12; 8:10–20; 32:15–18; Psalm 78:11; 106:7, 13, 21–23). In the days of the judges, they *"forgot the LORD their God, and served the Baals and the Asheroth"* (Judges 3:7).

📖 What happened after Othniel's days, after the forty years of rest? Remember Judges 3:7? It states that the children of Israel *"forgot the LORD their God,"* and He dealt with them. According to Judges 3:12, who was the next oppressor?

_____

📖 Again, we read about the children of Israel crying out to the Lord. How did He respond according to Judges 3:15? Who did He raise up?

_____

_____

_____

_____

📖 What did Ehud do? Read the account in Judges 3:15b–26 and summarize what he did.

_____

_____

_____

📖 How did Ehud lead the children of Israel to freedom from Eglon and the Moabites, according to Judges 3:27–29? Where did Ehud place his confidence, according to Judges 3:28? What results came about in this region?

_____

_____

_____

When the people forgot the Lord as their God and looked to the Baals and Asheroth, He gave them into the hands of Eglon the Moabite. The people cried out to the Lord, and He raised up Ehud as a deliverer and judge. Ehud took tribute money to Eglon, but he also hatched an assassination plot to deliver the people of Israel from their oppression. After Eglon's death, Ehud rushed back to the hills of Ephraim, where he blew the ram's horn, mustering men to fight against Moab. He focused his attention and their attention on the Lord as the key to victory over the Moabites. For the next eighty years the land remained undisturbed.

📖 What was life like after Ehud died, in the days of Shamgar? Read Judges 5:6 and note your insights.

_____

_____

_____

_____

📖 What do you discover about Shamgar in Judges 3:31? What was significant about his actions? How did his actions impact Israel?

_____

_____

_____

_____

 IN THEIR SHOES
What Is an Oxgoad?

An oxgoad is a pole about 6 to 8 feet long with a sharp blade on one end. Israelites used oxgoads to prod livestock or to clean a plow or other instrument. Shamgar used it as a weapon similar to a club or spear.

Apparently, the main roadways in Shamgar's day were dangerous, likely controlled by various Canaanite peoples. The roadways were obviously places to avoid lest harm or danger come. It appears that most Israelites avoided them, going by sideroads, byways, or "_roundabout ways_" (Judges 5:6). In that kind of climate, the Lord raised up Shamgar as a judge. Not much is said about him, but what is said is quite noteworthy. Glen Owens, quoting W. A. Criswell, summarized his life this way: "Shamgar did what he could with what he had where he was for the glory of God." What he did was for the good of Israel. Judges 3:31 says he "_saved_" or delivered Israel, a phrase using the Hebrew word _yasha_, pointing to bringing about freedom, deliverance from oppression, or salvation from enemies. Shamgar stands as a great example of looking to the Lord in difficult times and using what the Lord provides to accomplish His will.

DID YOU KNOW?
About Shamgar

Not much is said about Shamgar, only two verses mention him. Glen Owens has given a clear statement about Shamgar he heard from W. A. Criswell: "Shamgar did what he could with what he had where he was for the glory of God." What of his identity and ancestry? His name is not Hebrew. Perhaps he was not a full-blooded Israeli or could have been a Gentile who began following the God of Israel instead of a Canaanite god. "Shamgar" possibly comes from the Assyrian language similar to the name Samgar-nebu (Jeremiah 39:3). Judges 3:31 notes him as "the son of Anath," possibly pointing to the Canaanite war goddess Anath or residence in the town of Beth-Anath in the territory of Naphtali (Judges 1:33). In any case, Shamgar's activity showed his loyalty to the Lord, opposing the Philistines. Judges 3:31 notes his ministry—*"he also saved Israel."*

STOP AND APPLY—What Do You Have?—What has God given you? In 1 Corinthians 4:7, the apostle Paul tells the Corinthian believers that all they have of value each has *"received."* That should lead each of us to be grateful to God for all He has given us—salvation, spiritual gifts, daily bread, the list could be very long. Each of us can also be useful. What do you have? Like Shamgar in Judges 3:31, use what God has given you to do His will—not what you wish you had or think would be better, but what He reveals as you pray and seek Him. He has a plan. Be who He can make you and use what He gives you, where you are, for the good of people, to God's credit and glory.

DAY THREE

WHEN GOD SAYS "GO," THEN GO!

In the days of the judges in Israel, many different oppressors afflicted different areas of Israel. Today, we will see some of those oppressors in central Israel and how the Lord delivered His people, sometimes with very creative means, even using the weather to deal with one of them.

DID YOU KNOW?
Does God Use the Weather?

Judges 5:4, 20–22 reveal God using a rainstorm and flood as part of the defeat of Sisera and his nine hundred iron chariots. The people of Deborah's day thought of the stars as involved in the rains (v. 20). Job 37:1–13 speaks of God at work in the weather. Job 37:13 states that *"He causes it to happen."* That verse points to His using the winds and weather as part of His *"correction"* (literally, "the rod") or a measure of judgment, along with His maintenance on the earth, *"for His world"* (e.g., sun and rain as in Matthew 5:45), and to show His *"lovingkindness"* or mercy (e.g., Acts 14:17—*"He did good and gave you rains from heaven and fruitful seasons, satisfying your hearts with food and gladness"*).

 What oppressors did Israel face in the days of Deborah and Barak, according to Judges 4:2? How long did they have to deal with this distress? Look at Judges 4:3 and note your answers.

What did Israel face, according to Judges 4:2b–3 and 13?

📖 Read Judges 4:4–7. What did God communicate to Deborah and Barak? How did Barak respond? Find out in verses 8–10.

Because of Israel's evil, the Lord allowed Jabin, king of Canaan from Hazor (northern section of Israel) to oppress Israel. Jabin's General Sisera led his army with an impressive nine hundred iron chariots, tools of warfare that Israel could not match. The oppression lasted twenty years. When the children of Israel cried out to the Lord, He responded by speaking to Deborah who was "*judging Israel*" near Ramah and Bethel in central Israel (the hills of the Ephraim territory). The Lord directed Deborah to call for Barak to deal with this Canaanite menace. Barak was reluctant and wanted Deborah to go with him. She agreed, pointing to how the Lord would use a woman to gain a victory.

📖 Who helped fight against Jabin, Sisera, and his troops, according to Judges 4:6b, 7, 10, 14b, 23–24; 5:10–12, 14–15a?

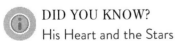

DID YOU KNOW?
His Heart and the Stars

Psalms 147:3–4 reveals the compassion and brilliance of the Lord, "*He heals the broken-hearted, and binds up their wounds. He counts the number of the stars; He gives names to all of them.*" How many stars are there? At least one billion trillion! Not only does He know where each one is (Isaiah 40:26), He calls each one by name—amazing! A lifetime of seventy years is about 2.2 billion seconds. It would take an average person five hundred billion lifetimes to only count the stars, one per second, yet the Lord calls each by name. The same God cares for "*the brokenhearted.*"

📖 According to Judges 4:14–16 and 5:4, 19–22, what happened in the battle against Sisera and his army?

_____

_____

_____

_____

📖 What happened to Sisera in the face of his retreat from battle, according to Judges 4:17–22 and 5:24–27? How does fame go to Jael? What do you read in Judges 5:24?

_____

_____

_____

_____

On the human side, we read of Barak's troops with men from the tribal regions of Naphtali (Barak's tribe) and Zebulun, along with some from Ephraim, Benjamin, and Issachar. On the Lord's side, we read of Him promising Barak to give Sisera *"into your hand,"* assuring victory, even taking several captive. In His righteousness, the Lord went with these troops. Judges 5:4, 19–21 speaks of *"clouds"* and a *"torrent,"* pointing to a God-directed deluge of rain in the Jezreel valley. Sisera's nine hundred iron chariots would not fare well in a muddy rainstorm, sinking, bogging down, while the horses sought to run away from the flooded Kishon creek bed.

Israel's men routed the Canaanite troops. Sisera abandoned his chariot and raced to his presumed allies in nearby Kadesh (4:11). There, Heber's wife Jael opened her tent to Sisera, gave him milk, then drove a tent peg in his temple as he slept. Since women set up tents in that day, she would have been very skilled with the hammer and peg. While it appears gory to most in our day, it was a desperate day in Israel, and Jael was praised for her skill, cunning, and valor.

STOP AND APPLY—Follow God's Initiative—Deborah and Barak followed the Lord as He directed them in dealing with Jabin and Sisera. The Lord worked with precision on a number of fronts, even bringing a thunderous rainstorm that flooded the Jezreel Valley, causing Sisera's iron chariots to bog down, which led to their total defeat. Jesus spoke of following His Father and of never doing anything on His own initiative. His life and ministry were received from the Father, never achieved by the flesh, by self-initiative (John 5:19; 8:28–29; 12:49–50). The same should be true for each of us. Follow God, follow His leadership in what to do and what to say.

OUR CHALLENGES—GOD'S CHOICES

God's ways are certainly not our ways. So often, we can only see what is directly in front of us. We cannot see as God sees. He sees the past, the present, the future and He sees the hearts and motives of men and women. He sees their outward words and actions. We can learn from Him and from observing people.

📖 Who stayed away from the battle, according to Judges 5:15b–17?

When Barak called for help in dealing with Jabin, Sisera, and his army, several nearby tribes ignored or refused his call. This included the men of the tribes of Reuben, Dan, and Asher, and men from the region of Gilead, east of the Jordan River. Each of these had their reasons, but it came down to not wanting to fight for what the Lord wanted to do, equivalent to taking a stand against the Lord and their fellow Israelites.

📖 What is God's evaluation of unbelieving cowardice and open rebellion against Him and His Word? Read Judges 5:23 and record your insights.

📖 What more do you find in Judges 5:28–30?

What does Judges 5:31 say about knowing and obeying the one true God?

The "*Angel of the LORD*" pronounced a curse on the city of Meroz, "*because they did not come to the help of the LORD.*" Notice that the Lord took this personally. When men would not help fellow Israelites, the Lord saw this as a stand against Him. Others, like Sisera's mother, while lamenting her son's lateness in returning, faced an even worse circumstance: her son stood against the Lord and His people. Enemies of the Lord perish in their unbelief and in the choices that spring from that unbelief. Theirs is a way of darkness, while those who love and obey the Lord are like the rising sun, bright in their walk and in their help to others.

STOP AND APPLY—Ready to Help—Who does God want you to help? Perhaps the Lord is preparing you to help someone by giving you wisdom and understanding from His Word, so that when a person or situation arises, you will be well-prepared and ready to give His Word, His counsel. Ask Him to teach you. Pray for His *"wisdom from above"* for your daily walk and for helping and praying for others (James 3:13–18).

DAY FIVE

WHOM WILL I FOLLOW?

All of us face challenges, tests, and temptations. How should we deal with those?

📖 What do you discover in John 5:19 and 8:28–29 about how Jesus faced daily life?

_____

_____

_____

_____

Jesus continually focused His attention on His Father, looking for His ways and how He was working. He listened to His teaching and meditated on His Word. Jesus knew the wisdom He had came from the Father and His Word. As the Father taught Jesus, Jesus continued to listen, not doing anything but what the Father desired. Jesus practiced the presence of His Father, never living a self-initiated life, but a Father-initiated life; never indulging in a self-pleasing life but living a Father-pleasing life. He also refused to say anything except what the Father gave Him to say, when the Father so ordered, through His Spirit (see John 12:48–50).

📖 How did Jesus face tests and temptations? Read the Scriptures for each test and for each response and record Jesus' Response in the chart given below.

The Tests and Temptations of Jesus

Scripture	Test or Temptation	Jesus' Response	Scripture
Matthew 4:3 Luke 4:3	Jesus, hungry and weary, faced the devil's temptation to shortcut God, turning some of the abundant stones of the wilderness into fresh bread. He certainly had the power to do so, if He chose to.		Matthew 4:4 Deuteronomy 8:3 Luke 4:4

Matthew 4:5–6 Psalm 91:11–12 Luke 4:9–11	The devil tempted Jesus to reveal how the Father would take care of Him, even if He jumped from the high point of the Jerusalem Temple.		Matthew 4:7 Deuteronomy 6:16 Luke 4:12
Matthew 4:8–9 Luke 4:5–7	Another shortcut. The devil promised Jesus *"all the king-doms of the world"* if He would *"fall down and worship"* the devil.		Matthew 4:10 Deuteronomy 6:13; 10:20 Luke 4:8

"Since then the children share in flesh and blood, He Himself likewise also partook of the same, that through death He might render powerless him who had the power of death, that is, the devil . . . For since He Himself was tempted in that which He has suffered, He is able to come to the aid of those who are tempted."—"For we do not have a high priest who cannot sympathize with our weaknesses, but One who has been tempted in all things as we are, yet without sin"—Hebrews 2:14, 18; 4:15

Some would say, "But I'm not Jesus, so how can I face life the way He did?" Good question.

📖 What did Paul say about his life in Galatians 2:20, 1 Corinthians 15:10, and Romans 15:15–18, especially verse 18?

The marvel of the Christian life is that God meant it to be the "Christ-in-me life." That is Paul's testimony in Galatians 2:20; he lived based on "The Great Exchange"—*"no longer I who live, but Christ lives in me."* It is a life lived *"by faith in the Son of God, who loved me and delivered Himself up for me."* Paul testified that what he was and what he did was by *"the grace of God"* working in him, with him, and through him. When he points to his extensive ministry in much of the Roman Empire, he sees it as an example of *"what Christ has accomplished through me."* Here is a good thought: Jesus gave His life for us, to give His life to us, to live His life with us, to live His life in us, to live His life through us.

Jesus gave His life for us, to give His life to us, to live His life with us, to live His life in us, to live His life through us.

📖 When we consider all the scriptures say and show us, how can we face temptations and various challenges and circumstances? What are the redeemed doing, and what do the scriptures call for us to do in Revelation 22:1–9?

God's heart from the beginning is that we worship and obey Him. That is what we see occurring in Revelation 22:1–9—everyone in a relationship of worship and obedience to the Lord forever. For today, we need to get to know Him better by knowing His Word more fully—reading, meditating, thinking through what He has said. Obey Him now. What is He saying today, to me? See His eternal worth. Follow His lead. He is called "*Faithful and True*" (Revelation 19:11), which means He will always be faithful, consistent, never deceptive or misleading, but always leading us His way.

In the period of the judges, most of the time the people of Israel did not worship and obey the Lord. They chased after and prayed to false idols, fake gods. That resulted in empty prayers, empty answers, empty hearts, filled with unrest, anxiety, and turmoil. When they did obey God and His Word, they found themselves following the right leader in the right way. They and their land had peace.

What is your situation? Consider this: It is always right to cry out to the Lord, to call on Him about whatever we are facing. He tells us in 1 Thessalonians 5:17 to "*pray without ceasing*," like a continual spring of fresh prayer bubbling up to Him. In Philippians 4:6, the Holy Spirit through the apostle Paul commands us, "*Be anxious for nothing, but in everything by prayer and supplication with thanksgiving let your requests be made known to God.*" Let every anxious thought be like an alarm clock waking you up to pray—at that moment, about that matter! What will be the result? Like the people of Israel experienced rest in their land, the Spirit promises us we can experience His peace or rest in our hearts and minds—"*And the peace of God, which surpasses all comprehension, shall guard your hearts and your minds in Christ Jesus*" (Philippians 4:7).

What do you need now? Who is God in light of your need? What do you need to ask Him? Write your prayer or a journal entry here. Spend time with the Lord. As a friend once told me, "It's time to have an honest conversation with God."

TAKEAWAYS—

Othniel, Ehud, Shamgar, Deborah, and Barak

There are three takeaways from the times of the early judges:

1) Listen carefully, Follow closely, Obey fully

2) Do what God says to do, when God says to do it,

3) Trust God for the details you do not see.

Lord, Thank You that You are the true and living God, faithful and true, not dead, not false, not deceptive. You are alive today, this moment, for what matters in my life right now. I bring before You those things and people that are weighing heavy on my heart. Lead me in Your Word to know how to pray for each person, each situation. Lead in right actions, what is right in Your sight. Show me any "blind spots," anything I am not seeing clearly. If there are any "Shamgar resources" You have given me, help me see them and use them Your way. Where I am fearful like Barak, lead me with Your fearlessness and creativity. Where I am reluctant like some of those in Israel, fill me with a ready heart, mind, and will. Thank You for caring for me this day and for leading me in prayer. In Jesus' name, I pray. Amen.

NOTES

LESSON 3

WILLING HEARTS—VICTORIOUS GOD
GOD DIRECTS WILLING HEARTS

God hates evil in any of its many manifestations, whether in an individual, a family, a town, or a nation. He grieves over sin wherever it is found. When the people of Israel faced the wicked oppression of the Midianites, they had to deal with Midianite dishonesty, the theft of their harvests, and the injustice of their oppressive ways. God heard the cries of His people, and He acted. In the events of the life of Gideon, we see Him at work in some amazing ways with a very unlikely man.

Judges 6—8 takes us on another Scripture adventure, looking at the leadership of God at a time when people found themselves in great need of leadership. The choice of Gideon as a leader seems almost comical, but God had a design and plan, and Gideon needed to follow the Lord. God uses willing hearts. How should we follow God? When we look at the life of Gideon, we learn some valuable lessons.

DID YOU KNOW?
Who Were the Midianites?

The Midianites came from east of the Red Sea, in what is today Saudi Arabia. They trace their lineage to Midian, the fourth son of Abraham and Keturah (Genesis 25:1–2). Before his death, Abraham sent Midian and others away into *"the land of the east,"* likely northern Arabia (Genesis 25:6). In the selling of Joseph by his bothers, we see Midianites closely associated with Ishmaelites (e.g., Genesis 37:25–36). The Midianites also linked themselves with the Moabites in bringing Balaam to curse Israel. Because of the immoral and corrupting practices of the Moabites and Midianites in Peor toward the people of Israel, the Lord called on Israel to fight the Midianites. This occurred not long before Moses' death and the people of Israel's entering into Canaan. They killed several Midianite leaders as well as Balaam and soundly defeated the Midianites (around 250 years before—Numbers 25:1–18; 31:1–24). With their countless desert camels, the nomadic Midianites came into Israel in the days of Gideon with Amalekites and *"the people of the east"* (east and northeast of Canaan) (Judges 6:3; 7:12), devouring the harvests. The Lord raised up Gideon to deal with them.

DAY ONE

"WHAT HAVE YOU DONE THIS TIME?"

The people of God once again did *"evil in the sight of the LORD,"* and He allowed the Midianites to oppress them. In their situation, it is like the Lord coming into the room and asking, "What Have You Done This Time?" and then dealing with what He found in their actions and words. What did the people do and what did God do as they faced their oppressors? Let's look in the *Book of Judges* and discover what occurred and what we can learn.

📖 Read Judges 6:1–2. What did the people do? How did God respond? What measures did the people take in dealing with their oppressors?

_____

_____

_____

_____

What did the people of God continually face from the Midianites, according to Judges 6:3–5?

_____

_____

Summarize what you find about the people of Israel in Judges 6:6. How did the people respond in this condition?

_____

_____

_____

 DID YOU KNOW?
What Were *"the gods of the Amorites"*?

The Amorite people descended from Canaan (Genesis 10:16). Their prominence in the land of Canaan caused some to refer to them in general as Canaanites. Before entering Canaan, the Israelites defeated Og and Sihon, leaders of two Amorite kingdoms east of the Jordan River (Deuteronomy 3:8–10). The word "Amorite" could mean "high one," perhaps referring to their settlements in the hills and mountains in and around Canaan (Numbers 13:29; Deuteronomy 1:7, 20; Joshua 10:6). The word could also mean "tall one" (Amos 2:9; Numbers 13:33; Deuteronomy 2:11). In Gideon's day, the Lord sent a prophet to the people of Israel, reminding them that He had already commanded them (numerous times) to neither fear nor worship *"the gods of the Amorites"* (Joshua 24:5–18, note verse 15; Judges 6:10). The Amorites (a word often used as a general term for Canaanites) worshiped various gods, including Baal-berith (translated "lord of the covenant") which the people of Gideon's area began to worship (Judges 8:33; 9:4). Over seven hundred years later, Jeremiah had to rebuke the people of Israel for honoring idols (Jeremiah 10:2–16).

📖 According to Judges 6:7–10, what was the first thing the Lord did as a result of the people crying out to Him?

_____

_____

_____

Because His people did evil, the Lord allowed the Midianites to ransack the land. The tribal regions of Manasseh west of the Jordan River faced hordes of Midianite and Amalekite warriors coming into the land, stealing and destroying the crops, devastating the land, and impoverishing the people. The people resorted to hiding in self-made dens and caves in the mountain areas, trying to protect themselves and their goods. All of this brought Israel *"very low"* and led them to cry out to the Lord. The Lord did not immediately raise up a deliverer, but rather sent a prophet to show them their sin and rebellion more clearly. They had been ignoring the Lord, forgetting what He had done in bringing them out of Egypt, and paying no attention to His warnings about the Amorite/Canaanite peoples and their false gods. They needed to take their sin seriously.

DAY TWO

WHEN GOD VISITS

When the people of Israel cried out to God, it appears they were crying more out of pain than repentance. God had to focus on their disobedience first. He answered their cry by sending them a prophet and reminding them of what He had told them time and again—*"I am the LORD your God; you shall not fear the gods of the Amorites in whose land you live."* It appeared that He would do nothing else, but scold. However, the next verse reveals Him coming to Gideon. What happens when God visits?

DID YOU KNOW
Where Was Ophrah?

The town Ophrah of the Abiezrites lay in the tribal region of Manasseh, west of the Jordan River, about six miles southwest of the town of Shechem. Gideon was born and buried there and led his people from there (Judges 6:11; 8:32; 9:5). Gideon placed an ephod of gold there which proved to be detrimental as many came there to worship it as an idol (Judges 8:27).

📖 The Angel of the LORD came to where Gideon was working. Where was Gideon, according to Judges 6:11?

_____

_____

_____

Read Judges 6:12. How did the Angel of the LORD greet Gideon? What does this imply?

_____

_____

_____

How did Gideon respond? Summarize what you find in Judges 6:13.

_____

_____

_____

_____

What occurs in Judges 6:14–18?

_____

_____

_____

What do you find in Judges 6:19–24?

_____

_____

_____

Gideon and apparently several others in the territory of Manasseh were trying to eke out an existence threshing wheat in hidden places. A wine press is a low point, hopefully hidden from anyone near, a place to thresh and keep a little wheat. The Angel of the LORD came to Gideon where he was; He knew the situation and the difficulties the people were facing at the hands of the Midianites, Amalekites, and others. It was not a pleasant time. He also had heard their cries, knew their pain, and was there to do something about it.

What Did Israelis Think about the Angel of the LORD?

When the Angel of the LORD came to Gideon, the people of Israel thought of Him as the One who led Israel out of Egypt and into Canaan via the Pillar of Fire and the Cloud of Glory. He is the "Captain of the Host of the LORD" that directed Joshua in how to conquer Jericho. Many longed for the day when He would come back in a Pillar of Fire or some supernatural way and bring a new day to Israel. This visit to timid Gideon certainly communicated care and confidence in those who heard or read about these events. God had not abandoned them, in spite of their sin and rebellion. He remained the covenant-keeping God.

The greeting of the Angel of the LORD to Gideon seems strange. Gideon certainly did not give the appearance of a *"valiant warrior,"* nor of one who was practicing the presence of the Lord. Gideon even responded, *"if the LORD is with us, why then has all this happened to us?"* Gideon wondered where were the miracles of the past he had heard about? He and others felt abandoned, forsaken, beaten down.

The Angel of the LORD responded with His answers. 'Gideon, I want you to go as My representative. I'm sending you, in My strength and victory.' At that point, Gideon again spoke only of how he saw things and how he saw himself—'I am the youngest of the least, the least of the least.' The Angel gave him words of hope and confidence—*"Surely I will be with you, and you shall defeat Midian as one man."* Though the Midianites were as *"numerous as locusts"* with so many camels, *"as numerous as the sand on the seashore,"* for Gideon, the Lord promised it would be like a one-on-one fight and he would win (Judges 6:16; 7:12).

Gideon wanted a sign of some sort; he went to prepare an offering. When he placed the offering on a rock, the Angel of the LORD touched it with His staff, and the offering was consumed in a blaze of fire. Then, the Angel of the LORD vanished. Of course, Gideon was speechless and frightened. Immediately he cried out to the Lord. The Lord responded with words of peace—much like the resurrected Lord Jesus did with His disciples when they saw Him that Resurrection Sunday (John 20:19). Gideon responded worshipfully by building an altar to the Lord, naming it *Yahweh-Shalom*—"The LORD is Peace."

WORD STUDY
Yahweh-Shalom

After the Angel of the LORD appeared to Gideon, giving him his assignment, Gideon built an altar and named it *Yahweh-Shalom*, translated "The LORD is Peace." This name is more than a name or label. It is a message about the peace Gideon experienced when he met, conversed with, and received direction from the Angel of the LORD. The altar represented the peace Gideon had and the fact that he had not perished having seen the Lord face to face. The word *Yahweh* or *Jehovah* refers to the Lord and is often translated in the Old Testament as LORD, appearing in small capitals. The Hebrew letters in English are *YHWH* (Strong's #3068), referring to the Lord as the Eternal, Self-existent God (always being—the word rooted in *hayah*, "to be" (Strong's #1961)). The Hebrew word *shalom* (Strong's #7965) is most often translated "peace" but refers to far more than simply peace. It means "safe" or "well." It refers to multi-levels of well-being, touching every dimension, mental, emotional, and physical.

STOP AND APPLY—Who Are You?—Ever been overwhelmed with life or just with today or this week? Have you wondered what's going on? Have you had the thought— "I'm worthless, I don't blame God for leaving me"? Those are lies either from yourself, the world, the devil—or all three. Gideon felt worthless, the least and less. But God had a plan. He is willing to work with willing hearts. Victory does not depend on me or you, it depends on God. So, who are you? Place yourself in the Lord's hands, surrender to Him, and do what He says. He may stretch you, show you how weak you are, but He will never abandon you (Hebrews 13:5-7).

DAY THREE

TESTING TIME

God never tests us to find out what's in us; He already knows the hearts of all people (1 Kings 8:39; Psalms 11:4; Acts 1:24). He tests us so that we know clearly what's in our hearts. Sometimes, it is not too pretty. Sometimes, He does new things, gives new strength, leads in new ways, so that we come to know Him better. He stretches all of us to increase our capacity to know Him. He brings us from "thimble-full" to "juice cup" all the way to "gallon jug" to "55-gallon drum," even to "semi-truck" or "tanker ship." Why? So we know Him better and help others know Him better. Today, we will see several tests Gideon faced and how the Lord worked in Gideon's life.

 IN THEIR SHOES
Increasing Capacity to Know Him and Help Others Know Him

The Lord has His ways of stretching and growing each of us, and we know He wants us to grow (1 Corinthians 3:6–7; Ephesians 4:15–16; 1 Peter 2:1–3; 2 Peter 3:18). He wants us to know Him better, know His Word better, know ourselves better, all so that we can worship more fully and help others grow and know Him and His Word more fully. He continually increases our capacity to know Him more, not for mere "know-about" factual or theological knowledge, but for experiential, "here's-what-He-did-in-my-life/our-lives" knowledge. Read of His desires in Proverbs 3:5–6; Jeremiah 9:23–24; Hosea 6:3; John 17:3; Ephesians 4:13; Philippians 3:7–10. Often, He uses tests to do that, as in Deuteronomy 8:2–16; 2 Chronicles 32:31; John 6:5–6. He does this *"to do good for you in the end"* (for eternity, Deuteronomy 8:16).

📖 What did the Lord instruct Gideon to do in Judges 6:25–26?

How did Gideon respond, according to verse 27?

📖 Read verses 28–30. What reaction came from the men of the city? In verses 31–32, what response do you find from Joash, Gideon's father?

_____

_____

_____

The Angel of the LORD first came to Gideon to encourage him and to reveal Himself, then He spoke to lead Gideon in the first steps of doing His will. He gave Gideon very clear instructions: tear down the altar to Baal and the Asherah pole and with the timber, offer a burnt offering to the Lord. Gideon, none too brave, recruited ten men and did all this at night. The next morning the offended men of the city wanted to kill Gideon. Joash, his father, stopped them and wisely and boldly said, 'let Baal fight his own fights—if he is upset with Gideon, let him contend with him.' Joash even gave Gideon a new name (or perhaps a nickname)—Jerubaal, meaning "let Baal contend."

📖 Gideon faced many challenges and many enemies. The next test lay before him. He had his "marching orders" from the Angel of the LORD, but what steps should he take? Describe the situation and Gideon's response as found in Judges 6:33–35.

_____

_____

_____

Gideon did not have overwhelming confidence in himself or his fellow Israelites. He may not have been sure about God. What did he request of God in verses 36–40?

_____

_____

_____

_____

📖 God had another trust test for Gideon. What occurs in Judges 7:1–8?

_____

_____

_____

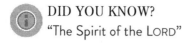

DID YOU KNOW?
"The Spirit of the LORD"

Seven times in the *Book of Judges* the phrase *"the Spirit of the LORD"* is used in relationship to four of the judges or deliverers. This Spirit clothed and empowered Othniel, Gideon, Jephtheh, and Samson for their assignments given by the Lord (Judges 3:10; 6:34; 11:29; 13:25; 14:1–4, 6, 19; 15:14).

How did God reassure Gideon, according to Judges 7:9–14? How did Gideon respond, according to verses 15–18?

_____

_____

_____

The Midianites, Amalekites, and others from *"the east"* came across the Jordan River and camped in the vast Jezreel Valley. What could anyone do? Probably not much, but God had clear plans. Judges 6:34 reads literally, *"so the Spirit of the LORD clothed Gideon,"* like putting a handy work-glove or suit of armor on him. Gideon then blew the ram's horn, calling his fellow Abiezrites to join him. Others came too, from the tribes of Manasseh, Asher, Zebulun, and Naphtali. This was good, but Gideon needed reassurance. He asked God to soak a wool fleece on the dry threshing floor that night. When Gideon woke up, the fleece was soaked. Once more, Gideon asked for the opposite—the ground soaked and the fleece dry. God kindly obliged. God was testing Gideon, and Gideon was testing God's orders. God gave His reassurances.

Gideon and his fellow soldiers camped at the spring of Harod at the southeast end of the Jezreel Valley. In God's sight, Israel's army was too big; they would be tempted to be proud if they won with their numbers. God ordered all who were afraid to go home—twenty-two thousand of the thirty-two thousand departed. The Lord said, *"still too many"* (7:4). He ordered a test for the ten thousand; He chose those who came to the spring and lapped the water like a dog. Only three hundred did that.

IN THEIR SHOES
Gideon's Three Hundred: Watchful or Worried?

The debates abound about whether Gideon's three hundred who lapped water like a dog were resourceful or extra weak. Were these being watchful, cautious, and therefore good for battle or were they the wary, worried ones, looking out for signs of trouble, actually worried and weak when it came to fighting this imposing horde? The text does not say. God works through our weakness, as Paul testified in 2 Corinthians 12:7–10. We may not know about Gideon's three hundred, but we can respond to what God asks of us with "Yes, Sir! . . . Where? . . . When? . . . I'm in!" knowing that even in our weakness, He can be seen and heard.

That night, at the edge of battle, God reassured Gideon by leading him to go down to the edge of the Midianite camp. There, they (since Gideon was afraid, he brought his servant Purah with him) heard a man relating his dream and giving the interpretation about Gideon's coming victory over Midian. When Gideon heard, he worshiped the Lord, returned to the camp and prepared the three hundred for their assault. His command? "*Do as I do!*" It was clear and simple. What would happen next?

STOP AND APPLY—Good Leadership—It is always good leadership to listen, learn from, and follow the Lord. Then, we can say as Gideon said, "*do as I do.*" The apostle Paul states in 1 Corinthians 11:1, "*be imitators of me, just as I also am of Christ,*" in Philippians 3:17, "*join in following my example,*" and in 2 Thessalonians 3:7–9, "*follow our example.*" That's good leadership.

Day Four

Doing Your Part

According to Romans 14:12, "*each one of us shall give account of himself to God*" for how we have followed Him, how we have or have not trusted and obeyed Him. Each of us has spiritual gifts given to us by the Lord and each of us has a part to play in the Body of Christ and in His mission (1 Peter 4:10–11; 1 Corinthians 12:4–7; Philippians 1:5, 27). You are responsible for you. The Lord will not allow me to stand before Him and say, "It's not my fault, it's them, or him, or her, or . . ."—whatever excuse we can come up with. As the Lord gives each of us a part, so He gave Gideon an assignment, along with the three hundred. How did they do?

📖 What occurs as recorded in Judges 7:19–25?

 IN THEIR SHOES
"*Weary Yet Pursuing*" (Judges 8:4b)

Don't ever give up on God, His Word, or His will. Don't ever give up dealing with sin, pursuing holiness, or praying with others (2 Timothy 2:22). Jesus told a parable about not giving in to evil, not giving up in prayer, never giving up on the Father (Luke 18:1–8). Gideon and his men did not give up. They continued "*weary yet pursuing.*" Jesus deserves all our praise, for He did the same and more on the Cross. He faced excruciating pain, agony, and loneliness, but He stayed and lived until He completed the Father's will and could cry out "*It is finished,*" and then He died (John 19:30).

📖 What kind of complaint do the men of Ephraim make, according to Judges 8:1? Read Judges 8:2–3. How does Gideon respond?

📖 What do you discover about Gideon and his men in Judges 8:4?

_____

_____

At around 10:00 p.m., under cover of night at the beginning of the second or *"middle watch,"* Gideon and his men struck. When they sounded the three hundred ram horns, broke the pitchers revealing the three hundred torches, and shouted, the hordes of Midianites, Amalekites, and others panicked. The enemy began fighting one another and running away from their campsites. Men from Naphtali, Asher, and Manasseh joined Gideon's 300 in pursuing the fleeing Midianites. The men of Ephraim captured and slew many, including two of the Midianite leaders Oreb and Zeeb.

When the men of Ephraim complained about not being called sooner, Gideon carefully reminded them that they had, in fact, captured two of the main leaders of Midian, Oreb and Zeeb. The anger of the men of Ephraim subsided when Gideon gave them the clearer picture of how well they had done in dealing with the Midianites.

DID YOU KNOW?
Where Did the Midianites Run to?

The Midianites ran southeast toward the Jordan River and crossed it, fleeing into the Transjordan territory. Judges 7:22, 24 mentions three towns—Beth-shittah near Zererah, Abel-mehola by Tabbah, and Beth-barah near the Jordan River. The location of these towns is uncertain, but they are likely in the Transjordan area. Involved in the pursuit in this area were Gideon, his three hundred, along with men from Naphtali, Asher, and both areas of Manasseh. They captured the two Midianite kings, Zebah and Zalmunna (perhaps leading kings) near the town of Karbor, further south and east of the Dead Sea—a lengthy but victorious pursuit.

Gideon and his men continued faithful in pursuit of the enemy hordes, seeking to rid the land of this menace. Even though they were weary, they came to the Jordan River, crossed it, and continued their mission, *"weary yet pursuing."*

📖 As the pursuit continued, how did the men of Succoth and Penuel respond to Gideon's plea for help? What did Gideon do in response to their refusals? Read Judges 8:5–9, 13–17 and record your insights.

_____

_____

_____

What do you discover in Judges 8:10–12, 18–21?

_____

_____

 What do you find out about Gideon in Judges 8:22–27? What are some things you learn about wealth?

_____

_____

_____

_____

In Judges 8:28, what is the result of Gideon's obedience?

_____

_____

Gideon kept leading his men. At times, not everyone wants to follow God or the leaders He raises up. Some want to do as they please and not be bothered by others' needs. The men of Succoth failed to connect with the purposes of God that day, even taunting Gideon. When he asked them for bread, simple help at a time of great need, they refused. This was not a mere battle for self-promotion; Gideon was seeking to restore order and peace by joining the Lord in ridding the land of pagan hordes. Gideon also sought help from the town of Penuel, but they too refused. He told them he would be back and deal with them. This refusal Gideon faced was an affront to the Lord.

Gideon executed the two Midianite kings, Zebah and Zalmunna (v. 21). When the battles were over, Gideon also chastened the men of Succoth and Penuel. Though the men of Israel urged Gideon to rule as a king, he refused, pointing them to the Lord, to follow His leadership. Gideon requested gold earrings (or nose rings) and received them, much wealth in gold. Wealth is neutral; it can be used for good or evil. Gideon's gold, in fact, brought a stumbling block as he made it into an ephod that became "_a snare to Gideon and his household._"

DID YOU KNOW?
What Is an Ephod?

The Hebrew Word _ephod_ means "covering" or "robe" (Strong's #646). It can refer to a cape, mantle, or robe. Israel's High Priest wore an ephod as part of his High Priestly garments. Gideon made his ephod of gold, perhaps a covering or sheathing for an idol, but apparently not to be worn. Many people came to Ophrah to consult the ephod or consult God by it, substituting it for the Lord Himself and a relationship with Him. This _ephod_ soon "_became a snare to Gideon and his household_" (Judges 8:27). Anything that substitutes for the Living God or hides Him is a fake god, an idol.

When all was said and done, we see that the Lord spoke to and led Gideon in dealing with the Midianite menace. He gave Gideon and his men victory. The "_land was undisturbed,_" and its inhabitants lived in peace for forty years. The Midianites, Amalekites, and others were gone.

STOP AND APPLY—Too Weary?—Are you weary doing God's will? Has He given you a tough assignment? Are you working with some uncooperative "believers" or unbelievers? What should you do? Written to believers, some of whom were off-focus, others who were out-of-tune, Galatians 6:9 urges, *"And let us not lose heart in doing good, for in due time we shall reap if we do not grow weary. So then, while we have opportunity, let us do good to all men, and especially to those who are of the household of the faith."* If you have become weary, keep on pursuing like Gideon and his men—*"weary yet pursuing."* Know that God is ever faithful.

DAY FIVE

WHOM WILL I FOLLOW?

The life and times of Gideon proved remarkable in many ways. He faced challenges, many because of Israel's sin. He faced costs to his time that proved to be an investment in the life of the people of Israel, at least in the life of those in central Israel, the territory of Manasseh and surrounding tribes. What can we learn from Gideon? There are at least five principles that come to mind when looking at the account of Gideon's life and exploits. Consider each one of these as you seek to follow the Lord and His leadership.

Take Sin Seriously. The people of Israel failed to do this and faced the chastening of the Lord because of it. This chastening came through the hordes of Midian, the Amalekites, and the *"sons of the east."* What does that matter to you or me? Ask the Lord to show you anything that is displeasing to Him. Confess that sin. Forsake it. Replace it—do what is right in place of what is wrong. Know or be assured of 1 John 1:9—the Lord is "faithful." That means He never errs, never lies, never stops doing His will. He promises to forgive and *"cleanse us from all unrighteousness,"* and He will do that. He is just or righteous. That means He is always right. He does not 'wink' at sin or chuckle over our missteps. Jesus paid the full price for every sin on the Cross—He died for us. How much will He forgive? He forgives us and cleanses us *"from all unrighteousness."* "All" means "all"—nothing missed, nothing left out, no 'oops' in His working, His forgiving, His cleansing. Now, talk to Him. Perhaps you will want to make a journal entry here or write a portion of Scripture. Make a memorial mark to remember this time with the Lord. Take sin seriously.

Take the Lord Seriously. The Angel of the LORD came to Gideon. He wanted Gideon to take Him seriously, and He patiently spoke with Gideon. He has not changed. He wants you and me to take Him seriously. He is God. He is ever Great, Good, Giving, and Guiding. He knows where each should go and what each should do. Take Him seriously. Talk to Him now. Is there something He wants to do in you or through you? Trust Him. Remember, He is always faithful. Perhaps you will want to make another journal entry or write a prayer or a memorable Scripture portion. Do whatever is needed. Take the Lord Seriously.

"This is My commandment, that you love one another, just as I have loved you. Greater love has no one than this, that one lay down his life for his friends"—John 15:12–13

Take His Word Seriously. The Lord gave clear directions to Gideon. He was willing to patiently wait and lead Him step by step in this assignment. He is our gracious God. He leads us, never herds us. He may call us to obey quickly, but He does not force His will. Nor does He tolerate us dragging our feet. He even says in Psalm 32:8 that He will guide us *"with My eye upon you."* He goes on to warn, *"do not be as the horse or as the mule which have no understanding, whose trappings include bit and bridle to hold them in check, otherwise they will not come near to you"* (Psalm 32:9). Don't rush ahead or lag behind but walk beside Him. Go to His Word every day. Listen and learn. Let Him lead you. What insights is He giving you from His Word? Write those here. Obey today. Take His Word Seriously.

Take Friends and Enemies Seriously. Gideon found that he had friends and enemies. We all do. Even Jesus had friends and enemies. What should we do about it? Obviously, we need to follow our Lord's lead. We find at least five facts about friends in Scripture. Read each of these and the scriptures for each. Record what the Lord is teaching you today about your situation. Remember also, sometimes the best way to treat an enemy is to make him or her your friend. Don't try to be "Mr. or Ms. Vengeance." Let God deal with that. For now, look at these Five Facts about Friends.

Best Friends—The best Friend anyone can know is Jesus Christ. In Scripture, Abraham is called *"the Friend of God"* (2 Chronicles 20:7; Isaiah 41:8; James 2:23). Jesus called His disciples *"My friends"* the night before He went to the cross to die a covenant death, showing Himself a true friend who laid down *"His life for His friends"* (John 15:13–15). Is Jesus your best friend? He can be. Talk to Him as friend to Friend. Let Him show you who He is, what He wants, and what part He wants you to play. Write any thoughts that you have about Him as your best friend and you as His friend.

Be a Friend—Show yourself friendly. Be kind to others. Scripture carefully instructs us to *"do good to all men, and especially to those who are of the household of the faith"* (Galatians 6:10). Read about how David and Jonathan were covenant friends in 1 Samuel 18:1–4. Write any insights the Lord gives you.

_____

_____

_____

_____

_____

Believe a Friend—It is important to be truthful to one another, even being a friend by *"speaking the truth in love"* so that each sees and knows what is true and real. This includes rebukes as well as blessings (Ephesians 4:15). Read Proverbs 27:5–6, 9–10 and note your insights.

_____

_____

_____

Beware of Fake 'Friends'—Not everyone who talks like a friend is really a friend. There are fake friends. When Judas came to betray Jesus in the Garden of Gethsemane, Jesus said, *"Friend, do what you have come for."* Matthew 26:50 in the original Greek translation records the word *hetairos* (Strong's # 2083) which means "friend," but points to one who is different from me (from the Greek word *heteros*—meaning "other," "different" (Strong's # 2087), "unlike another" (Matthew 26:50). It is a fake friend, one who is not in agreement with, not alike, one who uses another to get for oneself. That was Judas. King Saul proved to be similar, becoming jealous of David, willing to use him, but soon ready to kill him. Read about Saul and David in 1 Samuel 18:2, 6–9; 19:1. Note any insights you see.

_____

_____

_____

_____

Build Up Friends—In Scripture, we see several examples of people who built up others with words or deeds of encouragement. One example comes from the lives of David and Jonathan. Read 1 Samuel 23:15–18 and write your insights and how you could build up someone this week.

TAKEAWAYS
The Times of Gideon

There are nine takeaways from the Times of Gideon: 1) God never changes; evil is always evil, 2) Sin has consequences for the sinner and for others, 3) God tests hearts to show us our hearts and direct our lives, 4) God is patient, 5) God uses willing (available) hearts, 6) God gives far more good than we deserve, 7) Treat others as valuable, 8) Worship the Lord Jehovah as God and none other, 9) Always be grateful/show gratitude.

Take Your Part Seriously. You matter. Your obedience matters. God wants to use you in doing your part. There is no other person who can do your part. If you do not obey, certainly the Lord can raise up another—and He may. He will get His will done, but He wants to involve you and me. He wants each of us doing or saying what He commands. He always has the best plans, and He wants us to trust Him. What is He saying to you today? Record your thoughts or insights here and date them.

Lord, how creative You are in bringing deliverance to people. Thank You for the example and testimony of Gideon and how You worked in and through him. He was certainly far from perfect and not what most would think of as "leadership potential," but You as his Leader worked Your mighty works in him and through him. I am grateful for his example of *"weary yet pursuing"*—he did not give up on You, Your Word, Your will, or the job You gave him to do. Thank You. Give me eyes to see what I need to see about You and about Your will for me, what part I play, how, where, and when You want to work. In Jesus' Name, I pray. Amen.

NOTES

LESSON 4

DECEPTION—REBELLION—STUMBLING
THE FAILURE OF NOT FOLLOWING GOD

Deception hurts. It hurts God. It hurts people. In his poem "Marmion," Sir Walter Scott (1771–1832) of Scotland states correctly, "Oh what a tangled web we weave, when we practice to deceive!" More than once, that proved true in the days of the Judges. We will see this reality as we examine Judges 9–12. The scriptures do not paint a picture of perfect people or perfect leaders, but of very ordinary people and very human leaders. We need to see that today.

Judges 9–12 is filled with the errant ways of many. Some tried to lead, but not with an honest heart, and certainly not with a servant's heart. The people of Israel found themselves continually in need of better leaders, but those were hard to find. Therefore, some arose that fumbled and stumbled their way through Leadership 101, never truly helping anyone. Others led with some success, but never with the character of the Lord Himself. How desperately we need Him.

It becomes evident when we look in the *Book of Judges* and look around today, that while times and cultures change, people do not. The Lord works in the heart, from the inside out, and everyone needs His work as well as His wisdom to live and lead properly. There are some valuable lessons we can learn from the people and leaders of the times of the Judges.

DAY ONE

WHEN DECEPTION RULES

After the forty years of peace under Gideon, the people of God had not learned what God wanted. They did wrong again, and this time evil men took advantage of that. What can we learn about when deception rules? Nothing has changed among the nations of this earth. Deceptive people continue to lead others astray for their own benefit. What did the people do? Let's look in the *Book of Judges* and discover what occurred and what we can learn.

IN THEIR SHOES
What about Gratitude?

The people of Gideon's day proved ungrateful for the work he had done, and unthankful for how the Lord used him. They were ungrateful for the Lord Himself. Jesus faced ingratitude by others at times. When He healed ten lepers, only one returned to thank Him (Luke 17:11–19). That leper was a Samaritan, from the very region where Gideon once lived.

📖 Read Judges 8:33–35. What do you find about the people in Gideon's region after he died?

_____

_____

Who was Abimelech, according to Judges 8:30–31?

_____

_____

📖 What did Abimelech do, according to Judges 9:1–3? Look at Judges 9:4. How did the men of Shechem respond, and what did Abimelech do after this?

_____

_____

_____

_____

WORD STUDY
"Worthless and Reckless Fellows"

Judges 9:4 states, *"Abimelech hired worthless and reckless fellows"* who followed him and did his bidding. The term "worthless" is a translation of the Hebrew word *reyq*, meaning "empty" or "worthless" (Strong's #7386). This could point to being in debt or simply desperate. The word "reckless" is a translation of *pachaz*, meaning "to bubble up, froth" (as boiling water) (Strong's #6348). This could indicate being unstable or hot-tempered, even frivolous.

📖 What plans did Abimelech carry out in his father's (Gideon's) town of Ophrah, according to Judges 9:5? Based on the details in verse 6, how did the men of Shechem respond?

_____

_____

The people of central Israel revealed their forgetful and ungrateful hearts. They showed no honor for Gideon for "*all the good that he had done to Israel*," nor for the Lord "*who had delivered them*" from many enemies. Again, they began valuing and worshiping the Baals, various false gods of the Canaanites of that area. They focused on the local god, Baal-berith (translated, "lord of the covenant"), but not on Israel's covenant with the Lord nor His with them. Choosing to be deceived about the Baals, they were open to deceptions about their leaders.

Gideon had died, and now they looked for another king-like man. Abimelech put himself forward as the best choice (in his eyes). He was a son of Gideon by a concubine in Shechem and half-brother to Gideon's other sons. He sought kingship from his mom's hometown of Shechem, pointing out to the men of Shechem that he himself was "*your bone and your flesh*." They took the bait, gave him money, and he used that money to hire "*worthless and reckless fellows*" who followed him and did his bidding. They went to his father's town of Ophrah and there executed all but one of his seventy brothers. (One named Jotham escaped by hiding himself.) With Abimelech now assumed to be the sole descendant of Gideon, the men of Shechem made him their new king.

📖 What did Jotham do? Read and summarize Jotham's impassioned speech delivered from the hillside of nearby Mount Gerizim in Judges 9:7–21.

What occurred next? Read verses 22-29 and record what happened.

DID YOU KNOW?
The Cities of Shechem, Arumah, and Thebez

Shechem stood in the central part of Israel, near Mount Gerazim. Jacob purchased land there for one hundred pieces of silver (Genesis 33:19–20). The Israelites buried Joseph in Shechem (Joshua 24:32). The well there became known as "Jacob's well" and served as the meeting place between Jesus and the woman of the village of Sychar (John 4:4–12). For a time, Abimelech lived at Arumah, a small town near Shechem (Judges 9:41). Thebez, in the hills of central Israel, lay about ten miles northeast of Shechem. Abimelech died there.

📖 Zebul, Abimelech's "lieutenant" in Shechem, was angered over the words of Gaal and sent word to Abimelech about Gaal. What did Abimelech do? Read verses 30-41 and summarize the events recorded.

_____

_____

_____

_____

How did Abimelech respond to the actions of the people of Shechem, according to verses 42–49?

_____

_____

_____

What did Abimelech do after burning Shechem? How and why did he die? Record your insights from verses 50-57.

_____

_____

_____

_____

Jotham compared the words and ways of Abimelech to a lowly, fruitless bramble bush and contrasted that futility with images of a fruitful, beautiful olive tree, fig tree, or vine. The men of Shechem had chosen him to reign over them and failed to deal "in truth and integrity" with Gideon, his memory, or his family. Because of their payments to Abimelech, they too stood guilty of murdering Gideon's sons and dishonoring Gideon. Jotham called down a curse upon them and Abimelech, wishing that each would face judgment from one another. Jotham then fled.

Abimelech ruled as a tyrant king for three years over Shechem and nearby Arumah and Thebez. Distrust toward one another characterized the men of Shechem and Abimelech. In their disloyalty to him, they began robbing whoever passed nearby; no longer would Abimelech receive revenue from traders coming near or to the city. Gaal, son of Ebed came to Shechem with his brothers, stirred up the men against Abimelech, and sought to become their new leader. Zebul, Abimelech's lieutenant or governor over Shechem, angry about Gaal's words, urged Abimelech to come back and deal with these men. He did, fighting with Gaal, wounding many, and the next day killing many warriors and people of Shechem. He destroyed the city, scattered salt on it, and finally burned the tower or *"inner chamber"* of the temple (or house) of El-berith. All who took refuge there died. The name El-berith (or Baal-berith, "god of the covenant") reveals their idolatry toward Baal.

IN THEIR SHOES
What Is an *"Upper Millstone"*?

The *"upper millstone"* mentioned in Judges 9:53 was part of the hand-mill of a home. It served to crush grain such as wheat or barley to make flour. Possibly made of hard basalt rock, the round stone would have been ten to twenty inches in diameter, a weighty stone, but able to be carried. Most homes would have a millstone for crushing grain, and a woman (perhaps a maid servant) would have been responsible for this regular chore (Exodus 11:5; Isaiah 47:1–2; Jeremiah 25:10; Matthew 24:41). Because of the regular need for crushed grain and bread, the law forbade taking an upper millstone as a pledge lest a family be unable to make bread (Deuteronomy 24:6). The household upper millstone would be turned by hand over the lower stone, crushing the grain for flour. A woman in Thebez threw her *"upper millstone"* from the tower and hit Abimelech in the head as recounted in Judges 9:53 and 2 Samuel 11:21.

Abimelech traveled to nearby Thebez and captured it. The people fled to the roof of the central tower, hoping to be protected there. When Abimelech came near to burn the tower as he had at Shechem, a woman threw down an upper millstone that cracked his skull. To avoid the disgrace of that day, being slain by a woman, he called for his armor bearer to kill him. The armor bearer obeyed. Abimelech died. Jotham's curse came upon the guilty people of Shechem and upon Abimelech.

STOP AND APPLY—No Longer Cursed—Galatians 3:13 says, *"Christ redeemed us from the curse of the Law, having become a curse for us—for it is written, 'Cursed is everyone who hangs on a tree' "* (Deuteronomy 21:23; Galatians 3:7–14). Each of us has done enough wrong to merit a curse on our lives. While on the cross, Jesus took the curse of our sin on Himself. Thank Him immensely for this sacrifice! Praise Him!

DAY TWO

NEEDS NEVER STOP

After Abimelech's tyrannical rule in the central part of Israel, the need for leadership loomed larger than ever. Who would lead? Who could help the people of Israel? Several judges arose in these days, each doing their part to *"save Israel."* What can we learn from these men? Let's explore what occurred and see what applications the Lord has for each of us today.

📖 Who arose as a judge after Abimelech, according to Judges 10:1?

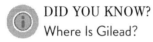 Where was Tola from? What did he do for Israel? Read verses 1–2 and note your answers.

According to verse 2, how long did Tola judge in Ephraim?

After Abimelech died, the Lord provided for a man named Tola to arise and judge Israel. Apparently, he gave leadership to people in the territory of Ephraim in central Israel. His birthplace and burial place were in Shamir, a town in the hill country of Ephraim, north of Judah and Jerusalem. Tola saved Israel, indicating the possibility of deliverance from some oppressor during this time—there were many Canaanite peoples still in the land. For twenty-three years, he gave leadership to the people in this region, providing stability and peace, perhaps helping them better know the heart of God through His Word.

DID YOU KNOW?
Where Is Gilead?

The territory of Gilead lay east of the Jordan River as part of the allotment of the half-tribe of Manasseh. In Genesis 31:25, it is called *"the hill country of Gilead"* and extends from east of the Sea of Galilee to the north end of the Dead Sea. It covers about 1,200 square miles (60 miles by 20 miles). Known for its fertile ground and abundant forests, the tribes of Reuben, Gad, and Manasseh requested this land when they came from Egypt, with most of it going to Manasseh (Deuteronomy 3:15–17). The Gileadites were part of the tribe of Manasseh.

Who arose after Tola, according to Judges 10:3?

Where was Jair from? What further facts do you discover about him in verses 4–5?

After Tola, Jair the Gileadite arose to judge Israel, probably ruling during some of the same years, but in Gilead several miles east-northeast from Ephraim. Jair was named after his ancestor Jair, son of Segub, a descendant of Manasseh mentioned as a great warrior in Numbers 32:39–41 and 1 Chronicles 2:22–23. Jair lived in Gilead on the east side of the Jordan River, part of the half tribe of Manasseh in that region. We discover from Judges 10:3 that he had thirty sons who rode on thirty donkeys, both indications that he had considerable wealth. Often Scripture speaks of kings riding on donkeys (see Genesis 49:11; Zechariah 9:9). Jesus Himself came into Jerusalem on a donkey hearing the messianic cries of the people, *"Blessed is the King who comes in the name of the Lord"* (Psalm 118:26; Matthew 21:1–11; Luke 19:29–40).

Jair and his thirty sons ruled over thirty cities known as Havvoth-jair, meaning "the towns of Jair," referring to his ancestor, Jair, son of Segub, who conquered several cities around 1406 BC (Numbers 32:41), some three hundred years earlier. Jair judged this area of Gilead for twenty-two years and died in the land.

What did the children of Israel do after Jair died, according to Judges 10:6? What false gods captured their attention and worship?

 Look at verse 7. How did the Lord respond?

What did the children of Israel have to deal with, according to verses 8–9?

DID YOU KNOW?
Who Were the Philistines?

The Philistines, also known as the "people of the sea," immigrated from the island of Crete (also known as Caphtor, Genesis 10:14; Deuteronomy 2:23; Amos 9:7) and other islands and lands around the Mediterranean Sea. They first invaded Egypt before the fourteenth century BC, then settled on the coast of Canaan. Eventually they established five city-states (Ashdod, Gaza, Ashkelon, Gath, and Ekron). The Philistines proved strong militarily with their iron technology, unknown to that extent among the Israelites. The people of Israel often fought them under the leadership of several, including Samson, Saul, and David. Their region or territory became known as Philistia, which, in later years formed the basis for the term "Palestine" (from the Assyrian *philistu* via the Hebrew *phelesheth* (rooted in *phalash*, "to roll," thus rolling or migratory). Their idolatrous religion centered on the false god Dagon. Though sometimes seen as a fish god, it was regarded as the father of Baal and known as the grain or agricultural god.

 Based on Judges 10:10, how did the children of Israel respond to this season of oppression? What was the Lord's response in Judges 10:11–14?

📖 What answer did the children of Israel give to the Lord? Read Judges 10:15–16.

_____

_____

_____

After Jair died, the people of Israel in the region of Gilead again worshiped the Baals and Ashtaroth with heart attitudes and practices very *"evil in the sight of the LORD."* The Israelites followed many false gods, including the gods of Aram (Syria), Sidon (on the coast), Moab (the god Chemosh), the sons of Ammon (the god Milcom, also called Molech), and the Philistines (the god Dagon). The *"anger of the LORD burned against Israel,"* like a deep heart pain. So, He allowed the Philistines and the Ammonites to afflict, crush, and shatter them for eighteen years.

The people cried out to the Lord, and He responded, reminding them of how He had delivered them from others who had oppressed them (the Sidonians, the Amalekites, the Maonites). That was then, but now they had forsaken Him once again. He chided them, *"go and cry out to the gods which you have chosen."* He knew and, most likely, they knew that would do no good. Those gods are dead, lifeless, cannot hear, cannot speak, cannot save, or satisfy in any way. The people of Israel knew they had sinned and cried out for the Lord to *"please deliver us this day."* Then they showed genuine repentance and changed their actions. They *"put away the foreign gods from among them."* The Lord responded with compassion. What would happen next?

STOP AND APPLY—Anything Clouding Your Thinking?—The people of Israel often faced clouded thinking, even deception from others. Most of the time (possibly every time), sinful choices precede and follow certain kinds of cloudy thinking. That can happen to you or me today. When we read less and less of God's Word, spend less and less time with Him, fail to interact with Spirit-filled people, we get more and more cloudy, fuzzy, or foggy in our thinking. Stop for a moment and ask the Lord to show you anything that may be clouding your thinking, confusing your perspective, hampering your choices. Any idols standing in the way of you seeing God clearly? Any distractions keeping your attention away from the Lord? Deal with them now. Clean the windshield of your heart now. The Lord will show you where to wash next. Take it one step at a time. You'll find Him clearing your vision and your thinking.

DAY THREE

NO, MAYBE, YES

Which way do we go? What should we do? Those were questions the people of the Gilead region were asking in Judges 10 and 11. How did God lead them? They were not sure about what to do or which way to turn, but God was faithful. They had a long way to go, to be all He wanted them to be, but it was a start. What about your walk, your future, your direction in life? Look at the lives of the people of Gilead, the life of Jephthah and ask God to show you what you need at this crossroads, at this turn. Let's explore some more of this wilderness that Israel had gotten itself into.

 DID YOU KNOW?
Who Were the Ammonites?

The Ammonites descended from Ammon, the incestuous son of Lot and his younger daughter (Genesis 19:38). Deuteronomy 2:19 speaks of them as the children of Lot. They often oppressed Israel. Their idolatrous worship focused on the false god Milcom (also called Molech) and sometimes included child sacrifice. This *"detestable idol"* proved to be one of many stumbling blocks in Solomon's corruption (1 Kings 11:1–5).

📖 What situation confronted the people of Gilead, according to Judges 10:17–18? Also, according to Judges 10:7–8, what had the Gileadites been dealing with for several years?

_____

_____

_____

📖 What options did they see before them? What choices did they make with these options, according to Judges 11:1–2?

_____

_____

_____

What happened in Jephthah's life after he fled from Gilead to Tob, according to 11:3?

_____

_____

_____

The people of Gilead had faced the Philistines and the Ammonites for eighteen years (Judges 10:8). Now the opposing forces of the Ammonites encamped against them, apparently ready to conquer and rule over them. The leaders of Gilead did not know what to do, except to try and figure out some way to fight the Ammonites. Jephthah was one of their number with a reputation as a *"valiant warrior."* He was also a Gileadite, but there was a problem; he was the son of a prostitute, with Gilead as his father. Because of this, his half-brothers drove him away. Jephthah went to Tob, about fifteen miles east of Ramoth-Gilead. There, he became the leader of a band of *"worthless fellows*" (literally, "empty"), possibly men in debt or discontent, all of them looking for a way to make ends meet. These men, along with Jephthah, moved about in the area, likely becoming a noteworthy fighting force.

IN THEIR SHOES
God Uses All Kinds of People

When Jephthah's half-brothers forced him to leave their area, he fled to Tob. There, several others teamed up with him who, like him, could have faced rejection from others, perhaps family and former 'friends.' Judges 11:3 calls them "*worthless fellows,*" using the Hebrew word *req* (Strong's #7386), meaning "empty." Apparently, they were lacking in some way (perhaps in debt), or their lives were spent in some other way. They traveled around with Jephthah and likely became a significant fighting force that later joined with Jephthah in dealing with the oppressive Ammonites in the territory of Gilead. While very likely not in the "Who's Who" of Israel at that time, God used Jephthah and his friends to do His will.

📖 According to Judges 11:4, what did the people of Gilead have to deal with? What did they decide to do and why? Search verses 5–6 and note your findings.

_____

_____

_____

_____

_____

Describe the interactions between the men of Gilead and Jephthah, based on what you find in Judges 11:6–10. According to Judges 11:11, what resulted?

_____

_____

_____

During this time, the Ammonites began fighting the men of Gilead, and apparently the Gileadites were losing ground. Therefore, certain leaders traveled to find Jephthah and see if he would lead them in this conflict. If he would, they would make him their "*chief*" (Hebrew, *qatsiyn*—leader, captain) and ruler, judge, or "*head*" (Hebrew, *rosh*—implying first in rank or order) like a king. They went from "No" to "Maybe" to "Yes," asking him to lead them. He agreed, and at Mizpah the people made him "*head and chief over them,*" as Jephthah "*spoke all his words before the LORD,*" indicating his wholehearted decision to follow the Lord and to be their leader.

📖 Read Judges 11:12–27. What did Jephthah do? How did the Ammonite king respond, according to verse 28?

_____

_____

_____

_____

What do you find about Jephthah in verse 29?

_____

_____

_____

According to verses 30–33, what occurred? In light of what the Lord did and based on the text, is there any indication that Jephthah's vow was necessary? Did the Lord require that of Jephthah?

_____

_____

_____

_____

Read verses 34–40 and summarize what occurred.

_____

_____

_____

When Jephthah took the reins, he immediately sent messengers to the king of the Ammonites asking why he came to fight. The king responded that Israel had taken land from the Ammonites when they came from Egypt (three hundred years earlier). That was not true, and Jephthah clearly pointed out that Israel had left Edom and Moab undisturbed. The land they won in battle at that time was under Sihon, king of the Amorites— Amorite land, not Ammonite land. The Ammonite king disregarded everything Jephthah said. Then, "_the Spirit of the LORD came upon Jephthah._" He marched through the territories of Gilead and Manasseh to the Ammonites. "_The LORD gave them into his hand._" He subdued the Ammonites, capturing twenty cities "_from Aroer_" to "_Abel-keramim._" Thus, Israel controlled a stretch of land spanning fifty-plus miles, from the Jabbok River, east of the Jordan River, to the Arnon River, east of the Dead Sea.

Jephthah had made a vow that if the Lord delivered the sons of Ammon into his hand when he returned home, the first one to come out of his house to meet him would be offered up as a burnt offering. Of course, that first person to come out the door to greet him upon his return would be his young daughter. Much debate has ensued, and much ink has spilled over what actually happened. Did his vow mean he then offered his daughter as a burnt offering or did he simply consign her to a celibate life before the Lord? We may not be sure, but it appears that Jephthah's vow was unnecessary. *"The Spirit of the LORD"* came upon him to equip him before the battles with the Ammonites and before his vow. There appears to be no need for his vow, nor command from the Lord for such a vow.

STOP AND APPLY—Do What You're Told!—Sometimes we decide we should do something based on faulty reasoning, on misunderstanding God, on not properly evaluating the circumstances facing us, or on lack of a true understanding of His Word. There is no indication God required Jephthah to make a vow. It appears he did that on his own, and the consequences came with his choice. Someone has wisely stated, "We can make whatever choices we want, but we cannot choose the consequences." How true that is! Make sure, as much as you can, to only do what you're told, what Scripture says, what God has clearly led through His Word, His Spirit, and His Spirit-filled people.

DAY FOUR

CONFLICTS CONTINUE

After Jephthah's victory over the Ammonites, the men of Ephraim came complaining. They questioned him about why he did not call them to help fight the Ammonites. Sometimes people disagree with what we have done or the way we have done it. What should we do? What did Jephthah do? We will continue looking at him and his life, along with some others who faced days that needed conflict resolution. Let's explore what we can learn from them.

IN THEIR SHOES
When Brothers Disagree

Sometimes brothers disagree. God desires for brothers (all of us) to live in harmony. He cares about what happens as seen in Genesis 4:9–12, when Cain uncaringly asked, *"Am I my brother's keeper?"* The answer is "yes." God delights to see brothers *"dwell together in unity"* (Psalm 133:1–3). The descendants of two brothers, Manasseh and Ephraim, fought and killed one another as Jephthah dealt with the matter (Judges 12:4–7). In addition to over eighty "one another" Scripture commands, Jesus gave clear guidance for reconciliation (Matthew 18:15–35; Galatians 6:1–5).

How did Jephthah handle the conflict with the men of Ephraim, according to Judges 12:1–6?

What do you discover about Jephthah in verse 7?

_____

_____

The men of Ephraim came to Jephthah with their complaints about not being called to help in the battle against the Ammonites. They were so upset, they threatened to burn down his house. They would not be appeased by Jephthah's explanation, so he gathered the men of Gilead and fought them, soundly defeating them. This civil war pitted the tribes of Ephraim and Manasseh against one another; descendants of brothers from Joseph. Through a strange set of circumstances, the men of Gilead used the Ephraimites' inability to pronounce _Shiboleth_ with the "sh" sound as a means to condemn them. Thousands of Ephraimites died in this conflict. After judging Gilead for six years, Jephthah died in the land of Gilead.

Conflicts continued. The people of Israel still needed judges. Likely, the judges who came after Jephthah overlapped in their times of judging, as they judged different regions of the land. Who arose next to judge the people of Israel, according to verse 8? Where was he from?

_____

_____

_____

📖 What do you discover about Ibzan in verse 9? What does this tell you about Ibzan?

_____

_____

_____

How many years did Ibzan judge the people of Israel, according to verses 9–10?

_____

Ibzan likely judged in the territory of Zebulun, since there was a Bethlehem there not labeled "Bethlehem of Judah" (Joshua 19:15, Judges 17:7–9). Ibzan had thirty sons and thirty daughters, strongly implying that he had great wealth and doubtless several wives. Notably, he gave his daughters away in marriage to sons-in-law outside his local town (perhaps outside the tribe of Zebulun) and "brought in" brides-to-be for his thirty sons. Since most in Israel married within their tribe, this could be an indication of how rare this was in Israel at this time. After Ibzan judged his region for seven years, he died and was buried in his hometown of Bethlehem.

DID YOU KNOW?
Two Bethlehems?

Joshua 19:15 mentions a town named *"Bethlehem"* in the territory of Zebulun in the north central portion of Israel, while Judges 17:7 speaks of *"Bethlehem of Judah,"* south of Jerusalem. Town names usually were descriptive; *Bethlehem* means "house of bread," a likely name for any town in a farming or grain-growing region. It is probable that the judge Ibzan came from Bethlehem in Zebulun and judged in that area.

According to verse 11, what tribe did Elon come from?

How long did Elon judge in his territory, according to verses 11–12?

Since Ibzan and Elon came from the tribe of Zebulun, it is likely that Elon arose after Ibzan to judge in that territory. He did so for ten years, perhaps around 1066 to 1056 BC. No indication is given in the *Book of Judges* who the oppressor could have been, but in this period it is likely that one or more of the Canaanite peoples proved to be *"as thorns"* and a *"snare"* in the lives of the people of Israel (Judges 2:3).

Where did Abdon come from, according to verse 13? Based on verse 15, what tribe was he a part of?

What do you discover about Abdon in verse 14?

What Canaanite people group does it appear Abdon may have dealt with, according to verse 15?

How long did Abdon judge in the territory of Ephraim, according to verse 14?

DID YOU KNOW?
Who Were the Amalekites?

The Amalekites descended from the line of Esau through his son Eliphaz and the concubine Timna (Genesis 36:12). Amalek became a chief among his people, and the Amalekites developed significant military might. They *"did not fear God"* and proved to be underhanded thugs (see Deuteronomy 25:17–19). After Joshua led the battle against Amalek, Exodus 17:16 notes, *"the LORD will have war against Amalek from generation to generation."* As Amalek was continually a menace and force to be dealt with during the period of the Judges (Judges 3:13; 6:3, 33; 7:12; 10:12; 12:15), the Lord ordered Saul to execute the Amalekites, but he did not (1 Samuel 15:2–3, 8, 13–29, 32–33). The people of God dealt with them in the days of David and Esther (see 1 Samuel 30:1–18; Esther 3-7).

Abdon came from Pirathon in the territory of Ephraim, likely his tribe. He *"had forty sons and thirty grandsons, who rode on seventy donkeys,"* an indication of his extensive wealth as well as his multiple wives. It is possible that Abdon dealt with remaining Amalekites or their infectious influence from people in *"the hill country of the Amalekites"* within the territory of Ephraim. The Amalekites proved to be a perpetual enemy to Israel (see Exodus 17:8–16; Deuteronomy 25:19; 1 Samuel 15:2–3). Abdon judged the people of Israel in Ephraim for eight years (perhaps around 1070–1062 BC).

STOP AND APPLY—What Can You Do?—Ibzan, Elon, and Abdon served in the territories of Zebulun or Ephraim where they lived. Like Shamgar, little is known about each one, but each one did what he could with what he had where he was for the good of the people in his area and in the will of God. It is likely the Lord called each to judge the people around him and deal with Canaanite oppressors. How does this apply to us today? Where each is, each can call on the Lord to guide in His will for these days. He will give His grace sufficient, His wisdom adequate, time enough, and power appropriate to do His will, wherever He places each.

DAY FIVE

WHOM WILL I FOLLOW?

The practical definition of "God" is "The Placer," How so? The Greek word for "God" is *theos*, similar to the ancient Greek word *theteres*, meaning "placers." Whoever puts things in place is, by definition, God in that situation. From the beginning of time, the Lord put all in place. From the first with Adam in Genesis 2:15, to the redeemed mentioned in Revelation 22:3–5, 14, 17. Each of us is in place on purpose. How does that matter and what applications from the *Book of Judges* can we see?

The statements made about Shamgar can be applied to each of the judges of Israel— Each did what he could, with what he had, where he was, when he lived, for the good of the people, and the glory of God. We can learn certain principles from them. There are at least four application points for daily life. Having been put in place on purpose, look through these and see how you can live.

> *"A new commandment I give to you, that you love one another, even as I have loved you, that you also love one another." (John 13:34)*

Your Place(s) Matters. Think of your times and places. It is significant that the Apostle Paul, speaking in Athens to several philosophers and city leaders, focused them on *"the God who made the world and all things in it, . . . [who] gives to all life and breath and all things"* (Acts 17:24, 25). He created each of us and places each one of us where we live for a certain time period in that place. Consider what further words Paul stated. He spoke of the Lord, *"having determined their appointed times and the boundaries of their habitation."* Each of us is in place on purpose. Your place, my place matters to God and to others. Talk to the Lord about this. It may be helpful to make a journal entry here or write a portion of Scripture. Make your mark about these matters.

Your Period of Time Matters. Paul noted the *"appointed times"* of everyone. When and how long each of us lives matters to God and to others. Consider each of these scriptures and record your insights.

Deuteronomy 32:29—What is the Lord's concern as expressed through Moses' words?

Psalm 90:12 (a psalm of Moses)—What is Moses' counsel to you and me?

Job 14:5—What is Job's counsel?

Psalm 39:4–7—What applications to your life do you find from David?

Psalm 139:16—What else do you learn from David?

_____

_____

_____

Thank the Lord for the period of history He has placed you in. Ask Him to direct you for these times and to give you understanding of "the times" to know what to do, like "the sons of Issachar" (1 Chronicles 12:32).

_____

_____

_____

_____

_____

What more is God saying to you? Pause and listen carefully, perhaps re-reading the above verses. Remember, He never says "oops" or "I didn't think about that." His love, holiness, and faithfulness are impeccable. Use the small space here for a journal entry or "note to self." Do what you need to do. Your period of time on this planet matters!

_____

_____

_____

_____

_____

_____

People Matter. Every person matters in some way. The Lord continuously showed His care and gave His wisdom and power for many different people groups across Israel (for example, Zebulun, Ephraim, Manasseh). People matter. There are over eighty "one another" commands in Scripture. That's significant. You matter and others matter. Ask the Lord to show you how best to help others. He will empower you to love others. He will answer prayer. Spend some time talking to Him about yourself, your place, your time, and those people (or that person He has brought to mind) all around you.

TAKEAWAYS
Abimelech, Jephthah, and Others

A look at certain "leaders" in the *Book of the Judges* yields eight takeaways: 1) Ingratitude is never good, 2) Corrupt power brings corrupt fruit, 3) God uses all kinds of people to accomplish His will, 4) Surface decisions often yield useless results, 5) Never try to impress God, 6) Do what God says, not what you or others assume, 7) Trust God with who you are where you are, 8) What matters to God is what matters.

The Person and Purposes of God Matter. Read these verses and note any applications to daily life you see.

Psalm 16:1–2, 11. What is David's plea?

_____

_____

_____

Psalm 73:25–28. What is the testimony of Asaph?

_____

_____

_____

What matters to God? All these factors. Consider each one again. Look them over. Think about what each means. Then, in worship and obedience, walk with the Lord in each area.

Lord, You never abandoned Your people. (Although, I probably would have—they were a mess!) Thank You that You have not abandoned me, for, in reality, I, too, am a mess too much of the time. Thank You for raising up judges who cared and did what they could by Your strength and wisdom. They were certainly not perfect, but they mattered where they were, when they were, according to who they were. May I do the same in my place, for this time, with who I am (and who You are making me to be). In Jesus' name, I pray. Amen.

LESSON 5

BEHIND THE SCENES
WHEN WE CANNOT SEE ALL GOD IS DOING

So many times, we wonder what is going on around us or in a certain situation, but Scripture reveals there is often more going on than we first thought. God is working behind the scenes more than we ever realized. He is active with His plans, using people we never would have thought He would use, orchestrating circumstances in more detailed ways than the most famous composer or orchestra conductor ever could.

When we turn the pages of the *Book of Judges* to the events of Samson's life and times, we enter some of the most unique behind-the-scenes movements in Scripture. The Lord's ways are many times far from understandable. What Samson did, his ways, his faults, successes, and failures flow together in a unique way—something is going on, or better still, Someone is at work that we simply cannot see at the moment. Let's explore the life and times of Samson and discover more of the ways of God in the times of the Judges.

DAY ONE

FAITHFUL LORD

Throughout the *Book of Judges*, we read a repeated fourfold cycle of sin—oppression—crying out—deliverance—except in the case of Samson. There is no record of people crying out about the Philistine oppression in that day. That does not mean people were not praying. It simply means we have no record of them praying. Today, sin is rampant in many ways, and many are crying out to the Lord.

The events of Samson's day occurred around 1099–1059 BC, over two hundred years since the people of the local tribe of Dan had migrated north, conquered the city of Laish (or Leshem), and there rebuilt the city of Dan. Some from the tribe of Dan, including Samson's parents, remained in their allotted territory in the hill country of central Israel, between the tribal allotments of Judah and Ephraim.

The Philistines ruled the day in this territory, stretching from the hill country to the Mediterranean coast. Their corrupt worship of the false god Dagon proved a menace and poison to the people of Israel, but God did not remain passive or inactive. We discover some of His activity around the person of Samson.

Zorah is located in the hill country of central Israel, about fifteen miles west of Jerusalem, situated on a hillside overlooking the Valley of Sorek in the region originally allotted to the tribe of Dan. It was the birthplace and burial place of Samson. Eshtaol is just over a mile northeast of Zorah, also in the hill country. Timnah is located in the lower hills of central Israel, about four miles west of Zorah. Known to be dominated by Philistines, Samson went there seeking a woman as his wife. An ancient city, Gaza lay on the Mediterranean coast about thirty-six miles from Zorah. It served as the Philistine capital and home to one of the temples of Dagon. The Philistines imprisoned Samson there and forced him to grind grain in the prison. Along with many Philistines, Samson died in Gaza.

Read Judges 13:1. What occurred among the children of Israel?

_____

_____

_____

While we have no record of the people crying out to the Lord over the Philistine oppression, we find the Angel of the LORD very active. What did He do, according to verses 2–5?

_____

_____

_____

The children of Israel once again "*did evil in the sight of the LORD,*" and He put in place the Philistines for forty years of chastening. Always, it is what the Lord sees that matters, that's accurate. What seems right in a person's sight is sometimes evil. Even In Isaiah's day, some 350 years after these events, he spoke of people calling good evil and evil good—"*Woe to those who call evil good, and good evil, who substitute darkness for light and light for darkness; who substitute bitter for sweet, and sweet for bitter!*" (Isaiah 5:20). The times of the Judges were such times. Into that very dark, bitter time, the Angel of the LORD came to Manoah's wife with words of miraculous hope.

What details do you discover in the Angel's conversation with Manoah's wife? Read Judges 13:3–5 and summarize what you find.

_____

_____

What would be this child's job, according to verse 5? What did 'Mrs. Manoah' tell her husband, according to verses 6–7?

According to verse 8, how did Manoah respond?

How did the Angel of the LORD respond to Manoah's plea? Read verse 9 and note your answer.

WORD STUDY
"Manoah Entreated the LORD"

The word "entreat" is a translation of the Hebrew word *athar* (Strong's #6279) which means "to burn incense." The idea is an intense cry for an answer or for deliverance. It carries with it the idea of intensity in prayer, with a heart of worship and submission.

What interactions do you discover in verses 10–20?

Read verses 20–23. How did Manoah and his wife respond to the actions of the Angel of the LORD?

📖 What significant facts do you find in verses 13:24–25.

_____

_____

_____

_____

The Angel of the LORD came to Manoah's wife who lived with her husband Manoah in Zorah. They had no children, for she was barren. The Angel appeared to her and told her she would "*conceive and give birth to a son.*" This son would be very special, a Nazirite from the womb. Therefore, she was "*not to drink any wine or strong drink, nor eat any unclean thing.*" In addition, no razor should ever come on to her son's head, but his hair was to grow long. This child would be used of God to begin delivering the children of Israel from the Philistines.

Manoah's wife told her husband about the "*very awesome*" appearance of the Angel of the LORD and all He had told her. She did not know His name or where He came from. Manoah cried out to the Lord, entreating Him earnestly. He wanted this "Angel" to teach them what to do for this boy. God heard, and "*the Angel of God*" came to his wife again. She ran to get her husband. Manoah asked Him to tell them what "*mode of life*" and "*vocation*" the boy should have.

STOP AND APPLY—Obey in the Details—Someone has wisely stated, "partial obedience is total disobedience." What part matters? All of it. When the Lord says to do something, He wants us to follow Him in the details, trusting Him for all He has said. Manoah and his wife sought to do that throughout Samson's life. Jesus once spoke a parable or illustration of true obedience. He asked if a father tells a son to go and do something, and the son says, "*I will,*" but doesn't, and then this same father tells his second son to go and do something, and he says, "*I won't,*" but does, which one "*did the will of his father*"? The second son (Matthew 21:28–31). It's about the details. Obey in the details!

Day Two

Questionable Samson

S amson grew into a strong young man but proved unwise in many ways. He showed himself to be lustful and strong-willed. Even though his father and mother urged him to not seek a Philistine bride, he wanted as his bride a girl from Timnah who "*looks good to me.*" Nothing wrong with physical attraction, but something very wrong with spiritual defection.

Samson's calling seems questionable; how could God use someone like Samson? God was working behind the scenes, true to His Word and to His covenant with Abraham. He would not leave His people to perish, even if it meant having to put up with someone like Samson. What can we learn from these days in Samson's life?

📖 Read the account in Judges 14:1–7. What do you learn about Samson and his parents? What do you learn about the Lord?

_____

_____

_____

_____

What significant details do you discover about Samson in verses 5–6?

_____

_____

_____

What occurs in verses 8–9? Does this relate to Samson's status as a Nazirite? How?

_____

_____

_____

Samson grew up. When he traveled to the town of Timnah, about five miles west of Zorah, he saw a young girl who "*looked good*" to him. Literally, the translation is "was right in Samson's eyes." Again, we see the focus on what one thinks is right in one's own eyes. Samson's parents spoke against him marrying a Philistine girl, but Samson proved headstrong. We also note that Samson experienced the empowering of "*the Spirit of the LORD*" enabling him to kill a rushing young lion, something his parents did not see, nor did he tell them. Perhaps they had gone on ahead for some business purpose or to make necessary arrangements for the upcoming wedding feast. Samson talked to the young girl in Timnah, then returned home to Zorah. Apparently, some weeks later, on a return trip from Timnah, he ate some of the honey harvested from a beehive in the lion's carcass. A Nazirite should never touch a dead person. This was not a dead "person," but the touch of death nonetheless; Samson was none too cautious during this time.

📖 Read Judges 14:10–14. What occurred at Samson's wedding feast?

_____

_____

What pressures came from the thirty Philistine young men, according to verse 15?

_____

_____

📖 According to verses 16–18, what happened next?

_____

_____

📖 How did Samson respond to the words of the thirty men? Where did he go? What involvement do you find from the Lord in these events? Read Judges 14:4 and 19 and record your answers.

_____

_____

_____

_____

DID YOU KNOW?
Where Are Ashkelon, Etam, and Lehi?

The city of Ashkelon, in Philistine territory, lay on the Mediterranean coast, about fifteen miles northeast of Gaza (also on the coast) and over twenty miles southwest of Timnah. Etam lay in the territory of Judah, in the hill country about fourteen miles southeast of Zorah and about three miles southwest of Bethlehem of Judah. Scripture notes Samson stayed _"in the cleft of the rock"_ there, perhaps a secure cave. This place served as a retreat location for him. From there, the Philistines took him captive to Lehi, about three miles southeast of Zorah. There he easily snapped his ropes and then slew about a thousand Philistine men with a fresh jawbone of a donkey. The literal name of this place is Ramath-Lehi, meaning "the Hill of the Jawbone," probably named after this incident.

Samson's father, perhaps reluctantly, arranged a typical seven-day wedding feast for his son. At the feast, Samson offered a riddle and a reward if they could guess the riddle. If not, he would receive a reward. They could not figure out the riddle, but behind Samson's back, pressured and threatened his bride-to-be into finding the answer. Samson told her, and she told the thirty men, which angered Samson. Working behind the scenes, the Lord continued putting things in place to deal with the ruling idolatrous Philistines. In this situation, _"the Spirit of the LORD"_ came on him, he traveled to Ashkelon, there slew thirty Philistines, then gave their clothes to the thirty men at the feast. He then went back to his home in Zorah, seemingly leaving his bride-to-be 'at the altar,' so to speak.

📖 What happened next? What details do you discover in Judges 14:20 and 15:1–2?

_____

📖 How did Samson respond to losing the wife he thought he had, according to Judges 15:3–5?

_____

_____

_____

How did the Philistines respond to the devastation of their crops, according to verse 6?

_____

_____

📖 Read verses 7–13. What occurred next?

_____

_____

According to verses 14–17, what did Samson do, and how was the Lord involved?

_____

_____

_____

What further details do you discover about Samson in verses 18–20?

_____

_____

_____

IN THEIR SHOES
Anyone Thirsty?

Several times in Scripture, we find the Lord supernaturally providing water. He quenched the thirst of Hagar and Ishmael in the desert (Genesis 21:15–19). Years later, He sweetened the bitter water of Marah for the children of Israel (Exodus 15:22–25). He gave water from *"the rock at Horeb"* for the Israelites traveling from Egypt to Mount Sinai (Exodus 17:1–7) and again months later in the wilderness (Numbers 20:10–11). When Samson prayed, the Lord opened a new spring of fresh water for him at Lehi (Judges 15:18–19). Jesus spoke to the woman at the well near Sychar about Him giving *"living water"* for the deeper spiritual thirst (John 4:10–14). Jesus also issued a call at the Feast of Tabernacles in Jerusalem; anyone who thirsts could come to Him and find abundant living water from Him (John 7:37–39). Even today, His invitation is open for anyone who thirsts to *"Come . . . let the one who wishes take the water of life without cost"* (Revelation 22:17). Forever, His own will never thirst, but find His *"water of life"* ever abundant and refreshing (Revelation 7:16–17; 21:6).

Samson decided to go back to Timnah to his supposed new bride. However, her father had given her to Samson's *"friend"* (Best Man), who married her. As a result, Samson, again angered, burned Philistine grain fields, vineyards, and groves using torches tied to 300 foxes' tails. Because of this, the Philistines went to Timnah and burned the man and his daughter. In anger, Samson slew them for their vengeance and went to Etam near Zorah. Three thousand men of Judah, apparently compromising and fearful of the ruling Philistines, willingly catered to their current rulership, spoke to Samson, then turned him over to them.

With shouts of victory, the Philistines took Samson to Lehi. Suddenly, *"the Spirit of the LORD"* came upon Samson once again, he broke the ropes binding him, then slew a thousand Philistine men with the jawbone of a donkey. Then, his thirst overpowered him, and he cried out to the Lord for water. God graciously and supernaturally provided water. Refreshed, Samson celebrated by naming the new spring *"En-hakkore,"* which means "the spring of him who called." Judges 15:20 gives a summary statement about Samson judging Israel for twenty years, during the Philistine occupation.

> *Longing for the Lord and His Word is part of growing, like a plant ever in need of water and nourishment. Augustine said it well, "Be always displeased with where thou art, if thou desirest to attain to what thou are not: for where thou hast pleased thyself, there thou abidest. But if thou sayest—'I have enough'—thou perishest. Always add—always walk—always proceed. Neither stand still, nor go back, nor deviate."*

[Charles Bridges, *An Exposition of Psalm 119* (Carlisle: The Banner of Truth Trust, 1827, 1974), p. 341, footnote, quote of Augustine.]

STOP AND APPLY—Thirsty?—Samson had many more issues in his life than mere thirst. God still showed His care in providing water for him at Lehi. Each of us have issues in our lives—the greatest need is to believe and know the Lord Jesus in a personal relationship, to have His *"water of life"* active in our lives. How can we walk each day, living 'unthirsty' lives and helping others find the true source of *"living water"*? At least two essentials: First, daily admit dependence on the Lord, the need of His ongoing quenching in life (Psalm 36:9; 42:1–2). Don't get caught trying to drink from a "broken cistern" that holds no water. Many tried that in Jeremiah's day. It never works, never quenches (see Jeremiah 2:13). Second, daily drink from the Scriptures, depending on the Holy Spirit to lead, teach, and supply Jesus' quenching wisdom, grace, and power (Psalm 119:131; Ephesians 5:26).

DAY THREE

DECEPTIVE DELILAH

Samson continued his headstrong ways. What would he do next? He continued an ongoing conflict with the Philistines and their idolatry, but also seemed to like some of the Philistine ways. Today, we will see him dealing with a deceptive woman named Delilah from the Sorek Valley, near Zorah. What can we learn from Samson and his ways and from this relationship?

📖 What choices did Samson make? Read Judges 16:1 and record your observations.

_____

_____

_____

What did the Philistines in Gaza attempt to do, according to verse 2?

_____

_____

What did Samson do in Gaza, according to verse 3?

_____

_____

IN THEIR SHOES
What Does It Take to Carry City Gates?

In what appears to be a feat of incredible strength, at midnight Samson took Gaza's city gate doors, their posts, and the bars away from the gate area and carried them to a hill or mountain between Gaza and Hebron. From the descriptions of Samson, it appears his strength did not come from himself, but from the Lord when needed.

Samson let his passions and lusts rule his life at times, even going into a prostitute in Gaza. Several of the Philistine men saw this as an opportunity to ambush and kill him the next morning and planned to do that. Samson decided to depart in the middle of the night. At midnight, he went and tore off the doors of the city gate along with two posts and *"the bars."* He then carried them to a mountain between Gaza and Hebron.

📖 What occurred in Samson's life after the Gaza events, according to Judges 16:4?

_____

_____

How did the *"lords of the Philistines"* respond to this new detail in Samson's life? Read verse 5 and note your insights.

_____

_____

_____

📖 What kind of interaction did Samson and Delilah have in this season, according to verses 6–14? Record your insights about this interaction.

_____

_____

_____

_____

Samson appears to stay focused on what he wants, rather than seeking the Lord. He met a woman named Delilah from the Sorek Valley, very near Zorah. Samson began to spend time with her. He loved her. This relationship caught the attention of the *"lords of the Philistines,"* wealthy leaders who wanted Samson out of the way. Judges 3:3 informs us about *"five lords of the Philistines,"* possibly referring to the leader-kings of the five key city-states of Philistia. Each of them offered Delilah 1,100 pieces of silver, a vast sum of wealth (perhaps 5500 pieces!).

Delilah began prying into Samson's life, seeking to find the source of his *"great strength."* Samson toyed with her, tricking her with his riddles, one, two, three times. Each time she tried to bind him and hand him over to the Philistines, but each time he escaped quite easily. She became increasingly frustrated; she was more interested in silver than in Samson or his well-being.

 DID YOU KNOW?
How Much Wealth Is 5500 Pieces of Silver?

When the *"lords of the Philistines"* came to Delilah they sought a deal; if she could *"see where his great strength lies and how we may overpower him,"* then *"we will each give you eleven hundred pieces of silver"* (Judges 16:5). Judges 3:3 mentions the *"five lords of the Philistines."* That means she could have received 5500 *"pieces of silver,"* about 140 pounds of silver, the equivalent of perhaps 550 years of wages for a common laborer—a fortune!

STOP AND APPLY—True Riches—It became evident in the story of Samson that Delilah was interested in silver more than anything else. She believed the lie that money brings meaning to life or that more riches bring more satisfaction. That is simply not true. Money can be a wonderful tool, but it is an awful idol; the kind of idol that can destroy a life. Jesus said not even when a person has an abundance does his or her life consist in possessions (Luke 12:15). Led by the Spirit, Paul wrote to pastor Timothy to focus himself and others on contentment. Those rich in this world's goods should never *"fix their hope on the uncertainty of riches, but on God"* (1 Timothy 6:6–10, 17–19). Be ready to give generously, *"to be rich in good works,"* storing up what matters *"for the future"* in order to *"take hold of that which is life indeed."* True riches are not found in 'stuff' that quickly fades, wears out, or breaks, but in God-honoring relationships that last forever.

DAY FOUR

FROM FRAIL SAMSON TO FOCUSED SAMSON

We learn from the account of Samson's life, that the Philistines captured him, gouged out his eyes, and bound him to the grain mill in the prison. There he labored, grinding grain for the Philistines. They thought they had won. During this time, Judges 16:22 notes that *"the hair of his head began to grow."* It appears that Samson's spiritual sensitivity also began to grow. Perhaps now, though physically blind, his spiritual sight and insight began to grow as never before. Let's trace his steps, his stops, and how God used him in these days.

 DID YOU KNOW?
What Could Hold Samson?

The *Book of Judges* records five attempts to bind Samson. Different materials and methods were used; first, *"new ropes"* which he easily broke at Lehi (Judges 15:13–14), then three with Delilah—*"seven fresh cords,"* which he easily broke (Judges 16:7–9), then, *"new ropes"* (16:10–12), then, weaving his hair in a web with a pin of a loom (16:13–14). He easily escaped (Judges 16:14). Finally, *"bronze chains,"* which did bind him because his hair was gone. It was not the chains, but the absence of the Lord and His strength (Judges 16:20–21). What could hold Samson? Lack of humble dependence on the Lord.

📖 How did Delilah respond after the third trickery by Samson? Look at Judges 16:15–19. What seems to be going on in Samson's thinking and feeling during this time? Summarize what occurred.

📖 What was the key to Samson's strength, according to Samson's own words in verse 17?

_____

_____

What do you discover about Samson's spiritual sensitivity in verse 20?

_____

_____

WORD STUDY
Lords of the Philistines

The five *"lords"* of the Philistines are mentioned in Joshua 13:3; Judges 3:3; 16:5, 8, 18, 23, 27, 30; 1 Samuel 5:8, 11; 6:4, 12, 16, 18; 7:7. The word "lord" is a translation of the Hebrew word *seren* (Strong's #5633a) which means "lord" or "ruler." The word *seren* is of foreign origin and is likely a Philistine loan word. Many see it linked to the Greek word *tyrannos* and translate it "tyrant" or "lord." Each of these lords ruled over one of the five city-states of Philistia and their rule is sometimes noted as tyrannical. *Seren* is used years later of the Philistine lords who opposed David and his men in 1 Samuel 29:2, 6; 1 Chronicles 12:19. It is certain these lords never followed the God of Israel, nor His Word, substituting instead the deceptive ideas and corrupt practices of the worship of the false god, Dagon.

Samson ignored the warning signs of Delilah's continued questions and inquiries about his *"great strength."* Why should this matter? What did it have to do with their relationship? After the third trickery of Samson, Delilah intensified her interaction, her questions, accusing him with words like *"your heart is not with me."* It appears that Samson was getting weary with her persistence—*"his soul was annoyed to death"* (16:16). So, he told her his strength was tied to his being a Nazirite, which was linked to his long hair.

Here may be one of the most revealing truths found in Samson's life. From reading Samson's story, it becomes clear that Samson's strength was a gift from God, not a part of some kind of superior physical makeup. This becomes evident in the events Samson faced in Gaza. His Nazirite hair was cut off and when he woke up *"he did not know that the LORD had departed from him"* (16:20). Apart from the Lord, Samson was a very ordinary man, not a strong man. The same is true for each of us; we must daily die to self and depend on the Lord for His strength, grace, and wisdom.

In Samson's day, Delilah thought she had won. She could get her silver now. She quickly called for the *"lords of the Philistines"* and told them what he had said—they paid her off. While Samson slept, she had his hair cut and then awoke him as before, saying, *"The Philistines are upon you, Samson!"* This time was different. This time, Samson was weak; and *"he did not know that the LORD had departed from him."* He presumed upon God one time too many and now he was a prisoner of the pagan Philistines.

📖 What did the Philistines do to Samuel, according to Judges 16:21? What else do you discover in verse 22?

_____

_____

_____

Describe the Dagon worship celebration given in verses 23–27.

_____

_____

_____

What did Samson do in the midst of this pagan taunting, according to verse 28?

_____

According to verses 29–30, what action did Samson take in this house? What resulted?

_____

_____

_____

_____

What do you discover in verse 31?

_____

_____

_____

Samson disclosed his secret to Delilah, and the Philistines easily captured the now weakened and frail Samson; they bound him and blinded him, gouging out his eyes. Then, they took him to prison in Gaza where they put him to grinding grain. When they gathered for a Dagon worship celebration, they decided to bring in Samson for 'entertainment.' Taunting him, they reveled in their apparent success, but the Lord and Samson saw things differently. Samson's spiritual sight became 20-20. He prayed to the Lord to give him this opportunity to deal with these false worshipers.

IN THEIR SHOES
Samson in Prayer

In the *Book of Judges*, we read of Samuel praying two times, each very instructive of his walk with the Lord. The first time is found in Judges 15:18. Samson had won a great victory at Lehi but was very thirsty and apparently had become weary. He called on the Lord (Yahweh), the covenant God, to quench his thirst. Verse 19 speaks of God (*Elohim*) answering, providing a fresh spring in the rock at Lehi. Samson named it *En-hakkore*, "the spring of him who called" (Judges 15:18–19). The second time he called on the Lord (*Yahweh*), seeking strength to deal with the Philistines in vengeance. God answered, giving him strength to bring down the house of Dagon on all those present (Judges 16:28–30).

With God-given strength, Samson pushed the load-bearing pillars of the house, and it came tumbling down, killing Samson and the hundreds of Philistines there. His brothers and other relatives came, took his body and buried him with his father Manoah in the family tomb near Zorah. Samson's worship had been hit-or-miss, at best, but in this event, he surrendered himself and his life to the honor of the living Lord.

STOP AND APPLY—True Worship—The Philistines worshiped a false god, Dagon, the grain god and what some called the "fish god." They thought he brought rain and crops and success to them, but they were deceived. The Lord had spoken through His people about true worship, but most would not listen. At the time Joshua and the Israelites entered Canaan, the stories of the Red Sea Crossing, the Jordan River Crossing, and other events were the topic of the day. In Jericho, Rahab mentioned these things that everyone knew, but she and her family were the only ones to take them and Israel's God seriously. She had become a worshiper of the one true God. Most would not, even refusing to worship the Lord in favor of one of the Baals or, as in the case of the Philistines, Dagon. How is your worship? Is the living God your God?

DAY FIVE:

WHOM WILL I FOLLOW?

Certainly, Samson is no example of pristine leadership. He lacked self-control and needed more Spirit control and much more focus on the Lord rather than himself. Herbert Wolf has summarized his life and his end very insightfully, "Unable to conquer himself, he was ruined by his own lusts. He stands as a tragic example of a man of great potential who lacked stability of character. Still, God in his sovereignty used him."[2] As someone has observed, "Often God uses crooked sticks to hit straight licks," but that does not absolve us from doing and saying what is right or obeying what the Lord has said.

---

2. *Judges*, in Frank Gaebelein, ed., *The Expository Bible Commentary*, vol. 3 (Grand Rapids: Zondervan Publishing House, 1992), p.479.

The secret to walking with God is the same today as it was in Samson's days as a judge. Jesus said to His disciples, *"I am the Vine, you are the branches; he who abides in Me, and I in him, he bears much fruit; for apart from Me you can do nothing"* (John 15:5). He did not say we could do only certain things, or only a few things, but *"nothing"* apart from an ongoing abiding relationship with Him. The apostle Paul knew he had *"received from the Lord"* forgiveness of sins, justification, spiritual life, spiritual gifts, even the ministry he had—all from the Lord (Acts 20:24). He told the Corinthian believers the same thing—*"what do you have that you did not receive?"* (1 Corinthians 4:7). That's why Paul testified, *"I have been crucified with Christ; and it is no longer I who live, but Christ lives in me"* (Galatians 2:20a). When he spoke of his 'successes' in ministry, he quickly noted, *"for I will not presume to speak of anything except what Christ has accomplished through me"* (Romans 15:18a). What Samson had and did are grounded in who the Lord is and what He did—He should receive the praise, glory, and thanks. Without Him, Samson or any of us—nothing.

God may use someone to accomplish His purposes, because He is faithful to Himself and to His Word, but just because He uses someone does not mean that someone is "right" in that moment. Very often, perhaps most often, if not all the time, God is working in His mercy and grace. The apostle Paul noted that God does much good in and through believers, and he personally testified that he was who he was *"by the grace of God,"* by what God had given and done (Romans 15:14–18; 1 Corinthians 15:10).

Samson, though forceful, was more often self-motivated than Spirit motivated; more marked by the fruits of *"the flesh"* than the Fruit of the Spirit. He is an example of one who paid too much attention to *"the lust of the flesh . . . the lust of the eyes . . . [or] the boastful pride of life"* (1 John 2:16).

As a start to strengthening your walk, pray through Colossians 1:9–14 for your life (and perhaps for someone else God brings to mind). Here is a prayer based on those verses.

Father-God, I come to You and ask that I *"may be filled with the true knowledge"* of Your will *"in all spiritual wisdom and understanding,"* so that I may *"walk in a manner worthy of the Lord,"* to please You *"in all respects, bearing fruit in every good work and increasing in the knowledge"* of You, my God. May I also be *"strengthened with all power according to Your glorious might, for the attaining of all steadfastness and patience."* May I ever be *"joyously giving thanks"* to You, Father, who has qualified me *"to share in the inheritance of the saints in light"* and delivered me *"from the domain of darkness and transferred"* me *"to the kingdom"* of Your beloved Son. Thank You for the price You paid for my redemption and the forgiveness of sins. Amen.

📖 Next read 1 John 2:16–17. How can we deal with those three problem areas today and avoid being like Samson (and many others)? Consider each of these and pray for your life in each area.

"The lust of the flesh." The "*flesh*" refers to everything about me or you that is not like Jesus. Romans 8:5–14 says that one who lives "*according to the flesh*" is not a genuine believer—To live according to the flesh means a total lifestyle of only paying attention to the "flesh," to what I want when I want it. After a person comes to Christ, the Spirit of God comes to indwell and guide the believer to daily put to death the deeds of "*the flesh.*" The flesh and anything done in the flesh can never please God. It is always unlike Him, never in agreement with Him. It is the "self" apart from God's control. This is sensualism—an emphasis on how I feel, what I want, all that appeals to me sensually—the senses (touch, smell, sight, sound, taste). The only place for the flesh is the Cross—counted dead, not influencing me. Look at the counsel of the Lord in the verses given here and record your insights and applications. You may want to use the space after these verses for a Journal Entry or a prayer for yourself or someone else.

Luke 9:23

Galatians 2:20; 5:16–24 and 6:14

Romans 6:5–14

Romans 12:1–2

For all that is in the world, the lust of the flesh and the lust of the eyes and the boastful pride of life, is not from the Father, but is from the world. And the world is passing away, and also its lusts; but the one who does the will of God abides forever. (1 John 2:16–17)

"The lust of the eyes." This refers to what I see, feel, sense, all that appeals to my sight. It is sometimes associated with materialism, the desire and delight in 'stuff' and 'more stuff'—more than I need or what I do not need or what I should not have in any case.

Genesis 3:6

Joshua 7:20–21

Luke 12:13–21

TAKEAWAYS
The Life of Samson

Walking through the life of Samson gives us six takeaways: **1)** God takes the initiative in leading us the right way; **2)** God often works behind the scenes to accomplish His will; **3)** God is patient with people; **4)** God has boundaries for everyone, even the ones He uses for His purposes; **5)** God hates fake gods and false worship because it is wrong and hurts people; **6)** Often our setbacks are God's setups for His bigger work, His fuller mission.

"The boastful pride of life." This refers to my pride. What I think, without humility (and, at times, without honesty). My way. My ideas. I-Me-My-Mine with ME at the center, rather than the Lord at the center. It is "me-ism"—worship of me. God's Word speaks to this.

Proverbs 6:16–17a

James 4:6–7

1 Peter 5:5–10

Lord, Thank You for the way in which You used Samson, giving Him Your supernatural strength to deal with Philistine people who had rejected You, rebelled against You and Your ways, and followed a fake god to help then in following their faulty ideas. Thank You for Your work to rid the land of those who continually brought corrupting and deadly ideas and influences into the lives of the people of Israel. May I be like Samson in those times when he sought You seriously—admitting my need, but never like him in being self-centered and self-motivated. Instead, may I be God-centered and Spirit-motivated. Show me any ways I am presuming on You, any ways that are in the "flesh," anything displeasing to You. Give me insight in Your Word—may the realities of Colossians 1:9–14 grow fuller and richer in my life each day. In Jesus' name, I pray. Amen.

LESSON 6

GOING ASTRAY
FOLLOWING THE WRONG WAY

The *Book of Judges* records a time when the entire nation was asking "who will lead us?" There were seasons when the people settled for bad leadership or simply followed whatever way each thought was right in his or her own sight. Many see the theme verse for the *Book of Judges* in the last verse of the last chapter, "*In those days there was no king in Israel; everyone did what was right in his own eyes*" (Judges 21:25). That is certainly true in the events of Judges 17—21. Based on the thoughts, words, and deeds of people in those chapters, everyone was going astray, not following the true and living God, but following whatever each person thought or maybe what a neighbor thought. That was usually following the wrong way.

Going astray? In the New Testament, Jude spoke of false teachers and apostate unbelievers as being like "*wandering stars for whom is reserved the blackness of darkness forever*" (Jude 13). Many in Israel in these days walked in their personal darkness, ignorant of or ignoring the Word of God, and leading others in that darkness. There is much to learn in watching someone do something the wrong way. For one thing, we do not have to fail in that way. One does not have to make the same missteps and mistakes someone else makes. We can learn from others. That is one good reason to look at and consider the events of these people and this period of time.

 DID YOU KNOW?
Two Appendices

Judges 17–21 present two appendices to the *Book of Judges*—Judges 17—18 and Judges 19—21. The events they describe occurred early in the history of the Israelites in the land of Canaan, not long after Joshua died. Most likely the events of Judges 19–21 occurred first, and the events of Judges 17—18 came soon after. The chapters have two "bookend verses," both saying the same thing, summing up what was true of the people in those days: "*In those days there was no king in Israel; everyone did what was right in his own eyes*" (Judges 17:6; 21:25).

Chronologically, the events of Judges 17—21 occurred early in the times of the Judges. To get the best chronological view, it is most accurate to see the events of the Benjaminites in chapters 19—21 as occurring first, then the events of Micah and the Danites in chapters 17—18 as occurring next, with the events of the early judges occurring after Dan had settled in the north. For this Scripture adventure, we will follow the path presented in the *Book of Judges*, looking first at Micah and Dan, then the matters of Gibeah and the tribe of Benjamin.

DAY ONE

MICAH'S MISSTEPS

Micah committed a host of sins, failing to follow God's Word in a number of ways. We do not have to blunder our way through life; we can learn from other's blunders. We can learn some things about how not to live.

Characterize the relationship between Micah and his mother found in Judges 17:1–2.

_____

_____

_____

What occurred in verses 3–5?

_____

_____

How does this line up with what God told His people in Exodus 20:4–6; Deuteronomy 4:15–19; 5:8–10 or more recently in Joshua 24:11–13?

_____

_____

_____

Micah and his mother had a strange relationship. He was willing to steal from her but was afraid when he heard her place a curse on whoever the thief was. When he admitted his theft of the silver and gave it back to her, she turned around and blessed him for admitting his theft, even speaking of being blessed "*by the LORD.*"

When Micah returned the 1,100 pieces of silver, she oddly declared, "*I wholly dedicate the silver from my hand to the LORD for my son to make a graven image and a molten image.*" Interestingly, after this, she took 200 of the 1,100 pieces of silver, gave it to a silversmith and asked him to make "*a graven image and a molten image*" (perhaps one image with part of it molten and part graven) which were (or was) placed in his house.

Through Moses, God spoke the words of Deuteronomy 4:15–19 and repeated the Ten Commandments just a short time before Israel entered Canaan under the leadership of Joshua. Joshua's words in Joshua 24 would have been spoken no more than twenty years before. How quickly we forget (or fail to listen in the first place)! These were not difficult words to understand, any more than saying "Don't drink the poisoned water." Micah and his mother had stopped paying attention to what Moses or Joshua or God said.

📖 What does the writer of the *Book of Judges* think of this time in Israel's history, according to Judges 17:6?

📖 Read verses 7–13. Summarize the story of the Levite of Bethlehem. How does it relate to the statement of verse 6?

 IN THEIR SHOES
What Is a Levite?

The Levites were descendants of Levi, the third son of Jacob. In the incident of the Golden Calf, the Levites rallied around Moses, becoming part of the chastening force of the Lord dealing with this idolatry (Exodus 32:19-29). Because of that, instead of each firstborn son being a priest to his family and the nation, the tribe of Levi would serve in that ministry (Numbers 3:5-10, 44-45; 8:14-19, 24-26; 18:1-6). In Canaan, the Levites' responsibilities centered around the Tabernacle at Gilgal, then Shiloh, and later at Gibeon and Jerusalem, until Solomon built the Temple (966–959 BC) (Numbers 18:4).

Marked by "*no king,*" no leader of the nation, this period of the Judges saw the people of the land doing what each considered right in his or her own sight. This became a time of independent choices, most made against what God had said was right in His sight. One example occurred early in this period. A Levite left Bethlehem and began looking for a place of better provision and possible "ministry," which he found at Micah's house. Micah hired him as his own private Levite, complete with newly made idols. This stood against God's Word, and Micah mistakenly thought the Lord would "*prosper me*" for this arrangement. The Hebrew word *yatab*, translated "prosper," focuses on being well, happy, successful. Though compromising God's Word and His clear instructions for the work of a Levite, this man from Bethlehem agreed to serve Micah and his household.

STOP AND APPLY—God Following Me or Me Following God?—Sometimes we act like Micah in Ephraim, assuming (or presuming) that God will agree with our thinking or what we want. We want God on our side, when it is much more important (and biblical) to make sure we are on God's side, following Him and His Word. We assume, like Micah, that now "*the LORD will prosper me,*" when, in fact, the Lord may need to chasten us. Pause. Pray. Ask the Lord for His insight into your life. Make sure you are following Him.

Day Two:

The Wayward Tribe of Dan

Micah seemed to have his "religion" in order with his new idols and a newly installed priest who was a Levite. It seemed right in his sight but failed to follow what God had said and how God saw things. It was wrong in God's sight. What would happen next?

📖 How well did the Danites do in conquering the Canaanite clans in the territory allotted to them (see Joshua 19:40–46), according to Judges 1:34–36?

The Amorites proved obstinate and forceful against the Tribe of Dan. It is possible the Danites lost many men battling the Amorites and Philistines, since their territory encompassed part of Philistia, especially cities like Aijalon and the coastal lands. At some point early in the times of the Judges, most of the Danites decided to stop fighting the Amorites and Philistines and look for a better place, hopefully an easier battle.

📖 What does Judges 18:1–2 say about the Danites? What idea did they come up with?

The Danites traveled a few miles north of their territory into the territory of the Tribe of Ephraim and came to Micah's house. What occurred there, according to verses 3–6?

What did the five "spies" find in Laish in northern Israel? Summarize what you discover in verse 7.

📖 Read verses 8–10. What did the "spies" tell their fellow Danites when they returned?

What did the Danites decide to do, according to verses 11–13?

The Danites decided to seek another place to settle in the land of Canaan. They sent five spies to search the land of Canaan. When they came to the house of Micah in the hills of Ephraim, they recognized the voice, perhaps the accent, of the Levite. The Levite told his story, and they asked him to "*inquire of God*" about their plans. He told them to "*go in peace,*" presuming and assuring them that God would give them success. When the men came to the city of Laish (or Leshem) in the north, they found it a rich, well-watered land and an easy place to conquer. They returned south to the area of Zorah southwest of Jerusalem and encouraged their fellow tribesmen to go and conquer the city of Laish, promising a place of abundance for the Tribe of Dan. Six hundred warriors departed for the north and came to Micah's house.

📖 What did the Danite warriors do at Micah's house, according to Judges 18:14–17?

According to verses 18–20, how did the Levite respond to what the Danite warriors did?

Micah and some additional men chased the Danites, seeking to retrieve the idols and Micah's private priest. What happened on the road out of Ephraim, according to verses 21–26?

DID YOU KNOW?
"From Dan to Beersheba"

The phrase *"from Dan to Beersheba"* or a similar phrase is found several times in the Old Testament. It is a way of referring to the entire nation of Israel from the north (Dan), near Mount Hermon to the far south (Beersheba), in the Judean wilderness or Negev.

Based on verses 27–31, summarize what the Danites did next? What kind of worship focus did the Danites adopt?

_____

_____

_____

The six hundred Danite tribesmen traveled to the hill country of Ephraim. The spies led them to Micah's house and to his idols. There they stole the idols and forcefully persuaded the Levite to come and be the priest for their tribe. The Levite was *"glad"* to go, apparently to a better, seemingly more significant place. He readily took Micah's idols and left with the warriors. Micah and his men chased them but found it useless to try and recover the idols or their priest. Far outnumbered, they went back home. The Danites continued north where they attacked and destroyed the city of Laish. They rebuilt it, renamed it Dan, and set up their tribe, along with their priest, who we discover is Jonathan, the son of Gershom and grandson of Moses.

WORD STUDY
The Jordan River

The Jordan River is most often referred to simply as "the Jordan." The word "Jordan" is a translation of the Hebrew word *Yarden* (Strong's #3383) rooted in *yarad*, which literally means "to come down," "go down," or "descend." The Jordan River descends "from Dan" or "out of Dan," because the Jordan River's headwaters are in the region of the city and tribal area of Dan in the north. They flow down into the Sea of Galilee and from there into the Dead Sea.

Most of the tribe of Dan led by an idolatrous, opportunistic Levite continued in this idolatry until *"the captivity of the land,"* likely the Assyrian campaign against the ten northern tribes of Israel that ended in 722 BC. The Lord had given clear instructions about Israel gathering and worshiping at one place (see Deuteronomy 12:1–14). Instead, the Danites, led by Jonathan (and later his descendants) were doing *"what was right"* in their own eyes, but very wrong and corrupting in God's eyes.

STOP AND APPLY—Leave or Stay?—Sometimes we decide based on our own wisdom to look for an easier battle, rather than seeking the Lord for His wisdom and strength for the battle before us where we are. The Lord had told the Israelites that He would be the one to lead them in conquering Canaan, but many did not rely on Him; they often turned to other gods, looking for what they thought might be a better option. God wants us to look to Him. Period. He and His will are always Best. Sometimes God says to leave as He did to the apostle Paul in Jerusalem (Acts 9:30; 22:17–18). At other times, He says to stay as He did to Paul in Corinth (Acts 18:9–11). Leave or Stay? The key is seeking the Lord and following Him and His direction.

DAY THREE:

THINKING WRONG AND CALLING IT RIGHT

The people of the tribe of Dan were not the only ones doing what they thought was right in their own eyes. This mindset pervaded the entire nation, from the north near Mount Hermon to the Judean wilderness in the south, from the east beyond the Jordan River to the Mediterranean Sea on the west. Judges 20–21 bring us yet more examples of thinking wrong but calling it right.

Throughout the *Book of Judges*, we read a repeated cycle of sin—oppression—crying out—deliverance. The saturation with sin and leaderless living is very well described in the events of the town of Gibeah and the internal war that erupted against the tribe of Benjamin. This likely occurred in the fourteenth century BC, sometime after Joshua's death.

📖 God revealed His intention for marriage in Genesis 2—one man and one woman married to one another, faithful to one another for life. In Matthew 19:5, Jesus quotes Genesis 2:24, describing God's original intent for marriage. What did the Levite of Ephraim do, according to Judges 19:1?

What did this concubine, this 'second' wife servant do, according to verse 2?

📖 Read verses 3–10 and summarize what occurred.

WORD STUDY
Describing Wrongs

The Hebrew words describing the actions of the men of Gibeah help explain their choices and actions. Judges 19:23: "*Act of folly*" (*nebalah*; Strong's #5039 [foolishness]), 19:25: "*abused*" (*alal*; Strong's #5953 [maltreat thoroughly, impose pain]), 20:6: "*lewd*" (*zimmah*; Strong's #2154 [bad plan or heinous crime]), 20:6: "*disgraceful*" (*nebalah*; Strong's #5039 [in context refers to foolishness, wickedness, or villainy]), 20:10: "*disgraceful*" / "*vileness*" (*nebalah*; Strong's #5039 [in context meaning wickedness]), 20:13: "*wickedness*" / "*evil*" (*ra*; Strong's #7451 [bad, harmful]).

📖 What did the Levite decide to do, according to verses 11–15?

A certain Levite who lived in the hill country of Ephraim decided to add a concubine to his household. While this may have been accepted by many in that day and in that culture, it was never what God intended. He wanted a man and woman to marry and remain faithful to one another for life. This Levite did what he thought was right in his sight. The concubine proved unfaithful to him, then went back to her father's house in Bethlehem. Four months later, the Levite traveled to Bethlehem seeking to bring her back to his home. He stayed there receiving the hospitality of her father but decided on the fifth afternoon to travel back home. They bypassed Jebus because of the possible Canaanite influences of the Jebusites there and perhaps wanting to find what they assumed would be a more hospitable place. When they arrived in Gibeah, they planned to stay in the town square just inside the city gates.

📖 From Judges 19:16–21, summarize what first occurred in Gibeah.

IN THEIR SHOES
The Impact of the Men of Gibeah

In the early days of the period of the judges, the immoral actions that occurred in Gibeah impacted the entire nation, especially the tribe of Benjamin. Over five hundred years later, Hosea wrote about depravity and iniquity in referring to the men and their actions in Gibeah (Hosea 9:9; 10:9).

📖 What happened as these ate supper, according to verses 22–24? Read Judges 19:25–26. What did the Levite do? What did the men of Gibeah do?

_____

_____

_____

_____

📖 What happened next, according to verses 27–28? Read also verses 29–30. Summarize what the Levite did when he arrived at his house.

_____

_____

_____

_____

WORD STUDY
"Worthless Fellows"

The men of Gibeah who approached the old man's house and sought immoral relations with the Levite are called "*worthless fellows*" or "*perverted men*" in Judges 19:22; 20:13. That is a translation of the Hebrew words *beliyyaal* and *ben*, (Strong's #1100 and #1121), literally translated "*sons of Belial*." Belial refers to that which is base, worthless, wicked, or ungodly and can mean "without profit." The word Belial came to be used in the New Testament of the evil of the devil and as one of his names (2 Corinthians 6:15).

An older man temporarily staying in Gibeah welcomed the Levite, his concubine, and his servant into his home, providing food and hospitality for their donkeys and them. As they ate supper, some "*wicked men*" or "*worthless fellows*" came seeking to have immoral relations with the Levite. The old man tried to stop them, offering his own daughter and the concubine instead. They repeatedly raped the concubine that night, and she died the next morning. The Levite loaded her on one of the donkeys and took her body to his house in Ephraim where he proceeded to cut her body into twelve pieces. He sent a piece to each of the Tribes of Israel. What was the response? "*All who saw it said, 'Nothing like this has ever happened or been seen from the day when the sons of Israel came up from the land of Egypt to this day. Consider it, take counsel and speak up!'*" (Judges 19:30). Something had to be done to right this wrong. We will discover what they did in Day Four.

STOP AND APPLY—Wrong Thinking, Wrong Choices—When people hear or read faulty words, foolish ideas, or false reasoning, often believing lies and deception, their choices can be very wrong and potentially very harmful. Such was the case in Gibeah. Wrong theology—wrong thinking (or no thinking) about God led to wrong choices, wrong actions, and ultimately to a deadly war. As someone has stated, "Sow a thought, reap an action, sow an action, reap a character, sow a character, reap a destiny." Wrong thinking and wrong choices led to destruction for most of the tribe of Benjamin. What is your source of ideas? TV, the internet, social opinions, or the Word of God. Think carefully, Choose wisely, Live holy.

DAY FOUR:

TRYING TO RIGHT WRONGS

What happened in Gibeah is nothing less than wicked and tragic. Everyone involved in these events were filled with wrong thinking but considering it right. The Levite should never have added a concubine to his family. The concubine should not have gone with him. The old man of Gibeah had a wrong solution to the wrong thinking of the men of Gibeah. Those men sinned grievously against the concubine and against the Lord. As a result, the woman died, and the Levite sought vengeance.

 DID YOU KNOW?
Where Are Gibeah, Mizpah, Shiloh and Bethel?

Judges 20:1 informs us that soldiers from eleven tribes gathered at Mizpah about two miles from Gibeah to deal with the horrendous events that had occurred in Gibeah. Gibeah is about four miles north of Jerusalem (Jebus). During this period, Gibeah and Mizpah were part of the territory of Benjamin. Mizpah lies about eight miles north of Jerusalem (Jebus). Shiloh, part of the territory of Ephraim, lies about nine miles north of Bethel, which is about eight miles from Gibeah (Judges 20:26-27).

How did the people of Israel respond to the immoral actions—this wickedness/wicked deed—in Gibeah, according to Judges 20:1–3?

_____

_____

_____

What did the Levite tell the men of Mizpah in verses 4–6? Based on verse 7, what did he request?

_____

_____

_____

Read verses 8–11. How did the men respond?

_____

_____

📖 Based on verses 12–14, what did the men of Israel do first?

_____

_____

How did the men of Benjamin respond, according to verses 14–16?

_____

_____

IN THEIR SHOES
Slinging Stones

Judges 20:16 speaks about the seven hundred left-handed men of the tribe of Benjamin who "*could sling a stone at a hair and not miss.*" These stones could be deadly, traveling at a speed of 80-90 miles per hour.

The tribes of Israel drew the battle lines—Benjamin's twenty-six thousand men versus the four hundred thousand of the other eleven tribes (verses 15–17). What occurred in the first battle according to verses 18–21?

_____

_____

📖 What do you find in verses 22–23? What happened?

_____

_____

_____

When each of the tribes of Israel received one of the portions of the concubine's body, they responded with shock and rage. They gathered at Mizpah about two miles from Gibeah. There they heard the Levite's story about the events in Gibeah, the rape and death of his concubine, and his actions after her death. He sought the "*advice and counsel*" of the men of Israel for this "*lewd and disgraceful act.*" The men of Israel decided to go against Gibeah to deal with the men there. The men of the tribe of Benjamin chose to defend their fellow Benjaminites, even in the face of their wickedness. The men of Israel traveled to Bethel, where the Ark of the Covenant rested and where Phinehas, the grandson of Aaron served as High Priest (verses 27–28). They "*inquired of God,*" seeking His will. Judah must lead. In the first battle, twenty-two thousand men of Israel died.

📖 What happened on the second day, in the second battle? Read verses 24–25.

How did the men of Israel respond to their second day of defeat, according to verses 26–27?

What direction did the Lord give through Phinehas the High Priest, according to verse 28?

📖 Read verses 29–43. What happened next?

Who fought the errant men of Benjamin, according to verse 35?

How many men of Benjamin fell in battle, according to verses 44–46?

⊙ DID YOU KNOW?
Where is the "Rock of Rimmon"?

The Rock of Rimmon sits about four miles east of Bethel. There, six hundred men of Benjamin fled and lived in the cave-filled hills for four months. The men of Israel sent them a proclaimed peace, and they came to Shiloh (Judges 20:47; 21:13).

📖 What did six hundred fleeing men of Benjamin do, according to verse 47?

What do you discover in verse 48?

After inquiring of the Lord again, the men of Israel went into the second day of battle. About eighteen thousand men of Israel fell that day. The men of Israel went to Bethel, wept before the Lord, and offered burnt offerings, actions meant to symbolize their surrender to the Lord and desire to do His will. Many were ready to quit, but Phinehas the High Priest gave them the Lord's clear direction—fight on. The men of Israel set up an ambush, defeating the Benjaminites, and capturing and destroying the city of Gibeah. While the Israelites fought, it was the Lord using them to strike the tribe of Benjamin over this wickedness. After destroying the city, the men of Israel pursued many of the men of Benjamin, killing seven thousand more, bringing the total slain in Benjamin to around twenty-five thousand. On that day, the men of Israel burned and destroyed several more cities of the tribe of Benjamin. Spiros Zodhiates has wisely stated, "You can choose your sin, but you cannot choose the consequences." Six hundred men of Benjamin fled to the Rock of Rimmon, cave-filled hills about four miles east of Bethel. They stayed there four months.

How did the men of Israel respond to the events of this civil war in Israel, according to Judges 21:1–4?

_____

_____

_____

What do you discover in verses 5–9?

_____

_____

_____

> *Spiros Zodhiates wisely stated, "You can choose your sin,*
> *but you cannot choose the consequences."*

According to verses 10–12, what occurred next?

_____

_____

_____

Fast forward four months. What communication did the men of Israel send to the six hundred men of Benjamin at the Rock of Rimmon, according to verse 13?

_____

_____

 Based on verses 14–23, how was this 'problem' solved? What happened?

_____

_____

What do you find about Israel in verses 24–25?

_____

_____

When the men of Israel had thoroughly defeated the men of Benjamin, they *"wept bitterly"* before God at Bethel concerning the near extinction of the tribe of Benjamin. The consequences of sin were serious. The men took an oath that none would give a daughter for marriage to a man of the tribe of Benjamin. Their sin of immorality was too serious. The next day, they built an altar and sought an answer concerning this near-extinct tribe. They decided to take vengeance on the people of Jabesh-gilead for not coming to Mizpah to help deal with this horrendous evil.

A fighting force of twelve thousand men of Israel went to Jabesh-gilead and executed the people, except for four hundred virgin young women whom they brought back as wives for the men of Benjamin. There were six hundred men, so, in addition, they decided to go to the festival at nearby Shiloh and instructed the other two hundred men of Benjamin to steal a wife from the unmarried young women at the festival. The six hundred men returned to the tribal lands of Benjamin, rebuilt cities, and settled into life there. The men of Israel each went to their respective territories and continued with life.

DID YOU KNOW?
The Festivals of Israel

God instructed the men of Israel to go up to His chosen place of worship (eventually the Temple in Jerusalem) three times a year (Passover Week, Pentecost, the Fall Feast of Tabernacles). The yearly *"feast of the LORD"* at Shiloh near Bethel was either the Passover or more likely the fall Feast of Tabernacles that celebrated the harvest, including the grape harvest of the late summer and fall.

Obviously, leaderless living marked most of this period of the "judges," as each person continued to do *"what was right in his own eyes."* They needed a leader who would follow the Lord and His Word. Years later, kings came, but ultimately, that leader named Jesus would come as the Son of David, Israel's greatest king. He is (and will one day show Himself as) the King of kings and Lord of lords, the leader of all leaders, the One to listen to and follow!

STOP AND APPLY—Dealing with Wrongs—One of the hardest choices in life is admitting one's wrong, saying, "I was wrong" or "I have sinned." It requires honesty, humility, and the choice to do what is right. Sometimes the admission is to the Lord alone, because He knows the hearts of all. He is willing to forgive and cleanse any and all sin (1 John 1:9). At other times, the admission must be to the wronged person(s), which is sometimes more difficult. What if the wronged person responds with unforgiveness or anger? You cannot change that, but you can love, pray for, and seek God's best for that person. You are responsible for you, not for someone else's response. What if someone wrongs you? Never take your own vengeance but give it to God for Him to deal with (Romans 12:17–21; 2 Corinthians 2:5–11; Galatians 6:1; Ephesians 4:30–32).

Day Five:

Whom Will I Follow?

How well did the people of Israel follow their God in the times of the Judges? Not too well. How well did the judges follow? Sometimes very well, sometimes in stumbling fashion. For today, how well are we doing? How can we follow more closely? In 13th century England, Richard of Chichester (AD 1197–1253) wrote a hymn entitled "Day by Day," which has come down to us in some hymn books, even entering the contemporary music scene. It is a very good statement and exhortation for each of us:

"Day by Day,

Dear Lord, of Thee three things I pray

To see Thee more clearly, Love Thee more dearly, Follow Thee more nearly,

Day by day."

"See . . . Love . . . Follow . . ."—a good prayer and a good song for the thirteenth century or any century. Each group of Israelites could have focused more fully on following the Lord and His Word. The lack of surrender to Him led to false and faulty worship of false gods, which, in turn, poisoned their decision making and their lifestyles. The lies they believed led them to much more sin, rebellion, and self-centeredness, along with mental and moral corruption.

How can we apply those truths? It comes down to genuine worship, whether in the days of the judges, the days of Richard of Chichester, or today. Jesus stated to the woman at the well near Sychar, *"the true worshipers shall worship the Father in spirit and truth, for such people the Father seeks to be His worshipers"* (John 4:23). True worship really matters. It is crucial. That was the issue during the times of the Judges; worshiping the one true and living God versus worshiping fake, dead gods. What about today? It still matters. It is still very crucial. We need genuine worship in our lives and in our church gatherings. This relates to what we have seen in this period and to what Richard of Chichester prayed and sang over six hundred years ago.

 DID YOU KNOW?
True Worship

Some people narrowly define "worship" as simply singing songs or uttering praises to God or about God. While singing and praising can be a part of worship, true worship is not about the songs one sings or the statements one makes, but about the heart that sings the songs or makes the statements (Romans 12:1–2; Colossians 3:16–17). It is about surrender to the Lord as the one living and true God. If no surrendered heart, then no full and genuine worship.

The first time the word "worship" is used in Scripture came from the lips of Abraham as he and his beloved son Isaac prepared to ascend Mount Moriah. Abraham told his servants *"we will worship and return"* (Genesis 22:5). On Mount Moriah, the Angel of the LORD encountered (and interrupted) Abraham and spoke of his genuine worship. When Abraham was about to sacrifice Isaac, the Angel stopped him and spoke of three things Abraham revealed—**1)** he feared God only, **2)** he gave wholeheartedly, **3)** he obeyed promptly. That matches the prayer to "see . . . love . . . follow" and shows us what the people of Israel could have done and what each of us should do "day by day." Let's consider these three matters.

Fear God only and always. That was true of Abraham—*"now I know that you fear God."* In that heart attitude and mindset, we will "see Thee more clearly." How are you doing in this area? Proverbs 9:10 states, *"The fear of the LORD is the beginning of wisdom, and the knowledge of the Holy One is understanding."* Someone marked by *"the fear of the LORD,"* regards Him highly, places ultimate value on Him and what He says. That means one worships Him from the heart, in spirit and truth, not with mere externals; no deception, lies, false images, or faulty imaginations like the religions of the world have. That worship surrenders to Him, as Romans 12:1 exhorts. Consider these scriptures about the fear of the Lord and how people can come to "see Thee more clearly." Note your insights and application points.

Exodus 14:31

_____

_____

_____

_____

Joshua 4:19–24

_____

_____

_____

_____

Jeremiah 10:1–16

_____

_____

Romans 12:1

When we give wholeheartedly, *"withholding nothing,"* that is what it means to "love more dearly" as God desires. How is your love of the Lord? How is your giving? Is it whole-hearted, half-hearted, no-hearted, or somewhere in the mix? Consider each of these scriptures as you think about this.

Deuteronomy 6:1-5. What is God's priority?

Matthew 22:35-40. What did Jesus consider of first importance?

Luke 6:38. What did Jesus say about giving?

Micah, Danites, and the Benjaminites

There are three takeaways from the people of Judges 17–21: **1)** Ignorance of God's Word or Ignoring God's Word leads one astray, **2)** Substitute gods are no substitute for the Living God, **3)** God uses many things to get our attention, then focus our attention, so that we pay attention to Him and His Word—what's right in His sight.

2 Corinthians 9:6-15. What did the apostle Paul say to the Corinthian believers about giving? What principles of giving did he include? (In this context, he was writing about helping some other believers in need.)

1 Timothy 6:13–19. In his first letter to Timothy—1 Timothy ('How to Do Church God's Way')—what wise counsel did Paul give to Pastor Timothy and the believers in Ephesus?

When we obey promptly what God has said, what He commands, we will "follow more nearly" in His wisdom. Abraham certainly did that. The Angel of the LORD stated, *"you have obeyed My voice"* (Genesis 22:18).

Deuteronomy 6:6-9. What follows loving God?

John 14:15, 23. What further word did Jesus state about what matters to Him?

Lord, You are worthy of worship, perfect, loving, holy, and wise. May I honor You as my King and truly worship You in spirit and truth, from an honest and truthful heart. Show me anywhere I am not walking in *"the fear of the LORD,"* not giving wholeheartedly, giving with a stingy heart or failing to obey You promptly and fully. I pray my life will be daily (hourly, moment-by-moment) focused on You as the Living Lord, that I will see, love, and follow You as a faithful and loving child. In Jesus' name, I pray. Amen.

NOTES

LESSON 7

THE LIFE OF ELI
FINISHING WRONG

In the life and times of Eli, we enter the final years of the judges in Israel. Eli served as High Priest at Shiloh during the twelfth century BC (lifespan, 1192-1094 BC). He also served as a judge for forty years (1 Samuel 4:18). Most likely his years as High Priest spanned the time from about 1162-1132 BC, about 30 years, handing over that duty to his son Phinehas and continuing as a judge until his death in 1094 BC. When he died at age 98, he had served the last forty years as one of Israel's judges (1 Samuel 4:18).

When viewing the Times of the Judges, we see a time when the entire nation was asking "Who Will Lead Us?" That reality continued in the times of Eli and his successor Samuel, before the first kings ruled in Israel. Most of the people continued to settle for bad leadership. Though some began to request that Israel have a king, the judges no longer met the peoples' needs or desires. Nor was it a time of faithfully following God or His Word. Most continued to simply follow whatever way each thought was right in his or her own sight.

DID YOU KNOW?
Where Is Shiloh?

Located about nine miles north of Bethel and twenty miles north of Jerusalem, the city of Shiloh served as the central worship location for Israel from around 1390 BC to the time of Samuel, almost three hundred years. The events of 1 Samuel 1–3 occurred at the Tabernacle located at Shiloh. People journeyed there to celebrate the Feasts, especially the Feast of Tabernacles after the fall harvests. Around 1390 BC, Joshua and the Israelites moved the Tabernacle from Gilgal to Shiloh and established Shiloh as the new location for the Tabernacle and Israel's worship (1 Samuel 18:1). The Tabernacle complex was destroyed in the 11th Century BC (likely between 1094 and 1050 BC). Psalm 78:56–64 refers to the sin of the people provoking the Lord, thus incurring His wrath, the defeat of Israel, the captivity of the Ark, along with His abandonment of Shiloh (see also Jeremiah 7:12, 14; 26:6, 9).

Day One

Knowing "About" Something Is Not All—Eli's Ministry

Born around 1192 BC, most likely Eli began serving as High Priest at the Tabernacle at Shiloh around 1167-62 BC, perhaps as early as age 25 or at the age of 30 (see Numbers 4:3 and 8:23–25). It appears that he served beyond the age of 50. This place and position of ministry meant much to the people of Israel. At the Tabernacle stood the Bronze Altar, where offerings made could link people to God's forgiveness and peace, followed by worship and celebration. How well did Eli serve there? What can we learn from this descendant of Aaron?

We are first introduced to Eli the priest in 1 Samuel 1:9? What was Eli doing at this time?

WORD STUDY
"Shiloh"

Not only was the town of Shiloh the location of the Tabernacle, Jacob first mentioned the word while blessing his son, Judah. He stated, *"The Scepter shall not depart from Judah, nor the ruler's staff from between his feet, until Shiloh comes, and to him shall be the obedience of the peoples."* Shiloh means "to whom it is" or "to whom it belongs," and the word also became a Messianic title linking the future Messiah with the Tribe of Judah. He would one day rule with the scepter, and to Him would belong obedience and worship. One can easily see the vital link between the name Shiloh and the place called Shiloh, both focusing on worship and obedience to the one true and living Lord, the God of Israel. Jesus came as the God-Man, the Messiah, the *"Lion that is from the Tribe of Judah"* and Shiloh, to whom belongs worship and obedience (Revelation 5:5–14).

Read 1 Samuel 1:9–14. (To see the full picture, you may want to read 1 Samuel 1:1–8 as well.) What does Eli's comment to Hannah reveal about others Eli may have seen worshiping or praying at the Tabernacle?

What kind of discernment did Eli show in this incident with Hannah? Review verses 12–16 and record your insights.

WORD STUDY
"Worthless Woman"

The words translated "worthless woman" or "wicked woman" in 1 Samuel 1:16 are from the Hebrew words *bath* and *Belial* (Strong's #1323 [rooted in *ben*; Strong's #1121, "son"] and *beliyyaal*; Strong's #1100), meaning "daughter of Belial." *Belial* can mean "worthlessness," "base," or "wicked." The *Brown, Driver, and Briggs Hebrew-English Lexicon* resource notes its meaning rooted in the idea of "without worth, use, or profit," "good for nothing." Some consider it to be rooted in *bala* (Strong's #1104), "to engulf" or "to swallow down" as in swallowing life like death or the grave. Hannah wanted to assure Eli that she was not drunk, but grieved or "*oppressed* (literally, "severe") *in spirit*," crying out to the Lord "*out of my great concern and provocation*" (1 Samuel 1:16).

📖 How did Hannah respond? What do you see about her in her response to Eli?

_____

_____

_____

_____

What further insights do you see about Eli in his words in verse 17 and Hannah's words in verse 18?

_____

_____

_____

Eli had served as High Priest at the Tabernacle in Shiloh most likely for over thirty years. He continued as a priest for many more years. He had seen many worshipers come and go. Dutifully, he supervised the Levites and worshipers there. During these years of the judges, a time when most people did "*what was right in* [their] *own eyes*" (Judges 21:25), doubtless Eli saw many people acting like those at the various altars of the Baals where drunkenness could have been common. Here, at Shiloh, he had probably seen some under the influence of too much wine. That was his first thought in seeing Hannah's lips move but hearing no sound—she's probably drunk. This also showed something of his lack of discernment.

Eli accused Hannah of being drunk. She objected immediately and strenuously, noting that she was only expressing her deep grief in prayer. She was "*oppressed in spirit*." Clearly, she declared, "*I have poured out my soul before the LORD.*" Then humbly she pleaded with Eli, "*do not consider your maidservant as a worthless woman.*" Graciously and wisely, Eli spoke with words of comfort and blessing, "*Go in peace; and may the God of Israel grant your petition that you have asked of Him.*" She received those words as words of "*favor*" and went her way "*no longer sad.*"

WORD STUDY
Peace and Prayer

When Eli responded to Hannah's impassioned words, he spoke of her going in *"peace,"* a translation of the Hebrew word *shalom* (Strong's #7965). *Shalom* is much more than mere "peace." It is rooted in *shalam*, (Strong's #7999), meaning "to be safe" or "completed," with the idea of security and friendliness. It points to multi-level well-being. Eli also noted her *"petition"* (Strong's #7596, *shelah*, rooted in *sha'al*). She asked God for a son. The key Hebrew word is *sha'al* (Strong's #7592), meaning "to ask," "to inquire," thus "to request." It shows honesty and humility to ask of God, who alone could grant such a request.

STOP AND APPLY—Seeing Beyond the Outside—As we walk with God, it is vital to make sure we are not merely knowing "about" something, but knowing by experience, knowing the reality before us. Eli based his comments to Hannah on the outward picture and perhaps what he had seen from certain others. He knew a lot "about" the Tabernacle, the priesthood, the Scriptures, as well as many of the ways of certain 'worshipers,' but he did not know everything. He could not see on the inside of Hannah's heart, but assumed she was drunk. In fact, she was crying out, *"oppressed in spirit."* Perhaps Eli should have first gone to the Lord in prayer and then spoken or asked questions of Hannah, to know how best to minister in this situation. We need to do the same: Pray first, Speak or Act second. Ask questions where we can. See beyond the outside—How? First, talk to the Lord who always knows what's on the inside.

Day Two

The Wicked Sons of Eli—Hophni and Phinehas

At the time of Eli's encounter with Hannah at the Tabernacle, Eli was about 85 years of age, having served in the Tabernacle over 50 years. His sons, Hophni and Phinehas served as priests, also being descendants of Aaron and of the tribe of Levi. They probably had served there over thirty years. Josephus the Jewish historian informs us that Phinehas served as High Priest during these days, having been given that responsibility by his father Eli (Josephus, Antiquities of the Jews, Book 5, Chapter 11.2). What do we learn from their lives and their service? How did they live during this time when so many were doing what was *"right in* [their] *own eyes"* rather than seeking the Lord and His Word for what He wanted?

📖 Read 1 Samuel 2:12–17. What was the spiritual atmosphere around the Tabernacle?

What do you discover about Hophni and Phinehas?

_____

_____

_____

What did their attitudes and actions reflect about their view of the Lord, His Word, or the offerings made to Him?

_____

_____

_____

_____

DID YOU KNOW?
Tabernacle Tools

First Samuel 2:13–14 speaks of a "*three-pronged fork*" as well as a pan, kettle, caldron, and pot, all used for the sacrifices. In addition, priests used several other items at the Tabernacle—Furnishings included the Bronze Altar, Bronze Laver, Table of Shewbread, Lampstand, Golden Altar of Incense, the Ark of the Covenant, bronze spikes/pegs, gold-covered boards and poles, bronze and silver sockets, and several kinds of coverings and curtains (animal skins and linen cloth). Tools or Utensils included firepans for hot coals, golden bowls for incense, plates for unleavened bread, gold snuffers for the lamp wicks and other utensils (Exodus 25:10–40; 26–27; 30:1–21; 35:10–18; 36:8–38; 37–38: 39:33–40).

Hophni and Phinehas, the sons of Eli, are termed "*worthless men*," literally "sons of Belial," who "*did not know the LORD*" nor the right ways a priest should act and work. They knew some things about God, His Word, His Tabernacle, but did not have a heart-to-heart relationship with Him. They proved themselves gluttonous, always seeking more for themselves, and negatively influencing the priest's servant to take more for them, even "*by force.*"

📖 What further insights do you glean from 1 Samuel 2:22–25? What do you discover about Hophni and Phinehas?

_____

_____

_____

_____

_____

What do you discover about Eli?

_____

_____

Hophni and Phinehas showed no spiritual sensitivity to the Lord, His Word, or the people at the Tabernacle. They followed their lusts, committing immorality with the women who served at the Tabernacle (see Exodus 38:8). They acted like many at the various altars to Baal marked by immorality as part of worship. The word spread. Eli heard what his sons were doing at the Tabernacle. He showed a measure of concern for the wayward and wicked actions of his sons, calling what they did _"the evil things."_ He focused their attention on the Lord Himself, but they paid no attention to their father, nor to the Word of the Lord. God's hand of judgment would fall on them for their choices, their sins.

📖 What did the _"man of God"_ say about what God had done, according to 1 Samuel 2:27–28?

_____

_____

What further words did he say about the sins of Eli, Hophni, and Phinehas? Read verse 29.

_____

_____

Read verses 30–34. What did he say about the coming consequences of their sin?

_____

_____

What further word of promise did this _"man of God"_ speak for the Lord, according to verses 35–36?

_____

_____

A certain _"man of God"_ came with a clear message from _"the LORD."_ He focused attention on how God had revealed Himself to the Israelites, especially the house of Aaron, even while still in Egypt. He noted that God had chosen the tribe of Levi as _"My priests,"_ and promised to provide everything they needed. With those privileges, now Eli and his sons were disdaining _"My sacrifice"_ and _"My offering . . . in My dwelling."_ Eli was, in fact, honoring his sons above the Lord, with each one (including Eli) *"making yourselves fat"* with the *"choicest"* or first/finest offerings of the people of Israel.

Eli and his sons chose to err. God chose to revoke His promises to their specific family; after these three died, all would die before reaching an old age. Grief would come; Hophni and Phinehas would die on the same day. However, God would remain faithful to Himself and His Word; He would raise up *"a faithful priest."* This was later fulfilled in the line of Zadok of the family of Eleazar, whose line would walk before the Messiah (*"My anointed"*; Ezekiel 44:15).

STOP AND APPLY—Honor or Despise?—In various ways, the Lord has proclaimed or promised *"those who honor Me I will honor, and those who despise Me will be lightly esteemed"* (1 Samuel 2:30). In Hannah's prayer, she spoke of the Lord bringing *"low"* and that *"He also exalts;"* He gives to some a *"seat of honor"* (1 Samuel 2:7b, 8d). Proverbs 29:23 states, *"a man's pride will bring him low, but a humble spirit will obtain honor."* Speaking to the multitudes about the proud Pharisees, Jesus said, *"Whoever exalts himself shall be humbled; and whoever humbles himself shall be exalted"* (Matthew 23:12; see also Luke 14:11; 18:14; James 4:10). Peter declares, *"Humble yourselves, therefore under the mighty hand of God, that he may exalt you at the proper time"* (1 Peter 5:6). Honor the Lord and His Word; never despise Him or what He says. It matters!

DAY THREE

GOD MEANS WHAT HE SAYS

What would happen to Eli, Hophni, and Phinehas? God is true to Himself and to His Word. He allows each person a measure of freedom—each can choose which way to go, but, as someone has wisely stated, *"One can choose his or her sin, but one cannot choose the consequences."* What would happen at the Tabernacle and in Israel? We will explore those matters in the Scriptures.

The Lord called to and then appeared to Samuel (probably around age 12). What further revelation did He give to Samuel regarding Eli and his sons, according to 1 Samuel 3:10–14?

_____

_____

_____

_____

According to verse 13, what did God say that Eli had done?

_____

_____

📖 Review verse 13. What had Eli's sons, Hophni, and Phinehas, done to themselves?

_____

_____

📖 What further insights do you discover in Leviticus 24:15–16 and Deuteronomy 17:12?

_____

_____

_____

_____

IN THEIR SHOES
God's Word

The phrase "*the word of the LORD*" appears over 250 times in the Bible, while the phrase "*thus says the LORD*" is found over 1,900 times in the Old Testament. He has made Himself, His mind, and heart very well known. When He speaks, He is to be taken seriously; He says what He means and means what He says.

The Lord made it clear He was about to carry out the judgment He had promised through the "*man of God.*" It would be so significant and evident that "*both ears of everyone who hears it will tingle.*" Eli's house would face judgment for the iniquity of his sons which he knew but did not rebuke. They "*brought a curse on themselves,*" even the death penalty for showing disregard for the priesthood, dishonoring and disobeying their father, and "*sinning against the LORD*" (1 Samuel 2:12, 17, 22–25; Leviticus 24:15–16; Deuteronomy 17:12).

📖 What did Samuel do with what the Lord told him, according to 1 Samuel 3:15?

_____

_____

What do you discover about Eli in verses 16–17?

_____

_____

What further insights do you glean from verse 18?

_____

After this serious revelation of judgment from the Lord, Samuel "*lay down until morn-ing*"—perhaps he slept, perhaps not. When morning came, he was filled with fear, not wanting "*to tell the vision to Eli*." Eli knew enough to know that the Lord had probably spoken to Samuel the night before—whatever He may have said mattered very much. He inquired about what the Lord had told Samuel, warning him not to leave out one word. Samuel recounted the message. Eli listened and, apparently with somber foreboding, yielded to the Lord and His message; Eli knew that God means what He says.

IN THEIR SHOES
God's Warnings

Throughout Scripture, God warns of the consequences of sin before the sin occurs (as in Genesis 2:17). He tells of judgment on evil before the evil happens. He often sends warn-ing "signals" to people as part of calling them to repentance—He desires to show mercy rather than judgment. The Lord says in Ezekiel 18:23 and 32 that He has no "*pleasure in the death of the wicked*" or of anyone. Micah 7:18 overflows with heartfelt compassion, "*Who is a God like You, who pardons iniquity and passes over the rebellious act of the remnant of His possession? He does not retain His anger forever, because He delights in unchanging love*" (Hebrew, *chesed*, [Strong's #2617], covenant mercy, lovingkindness). Lamentations 3:22–23 states, "*The LORD's mercies/lovingkindnesses indeed never cease, for His compas-sions never fail. They are new every morning; great is Your faithfulness.*" Thank Him and heed His warnings—"*repent and live*" (Ezekiel 18:32).

STOP AND APPLY—What Do the Scriptures Say?—The most important thing anyone can do is to listen carefully, seriously, and readily to God's Word. He says what He means and means what He says. His Word reveals that He is always interested in "worship" in spirit and truth and "faith" or trust that leads to loving obedience. He wants people to walk in a close, loving relationship with Him (Deuteronomy 6:1–5; Matthew 22:36–38). Jesus pointed this out in John 5:39–40; the central issue is not what the Scriptures say, but what one does with what the Scriptures say—does one come to Jesus to know Him, walk with Him, worship and obey Him, and experience His eternal life or just know about Him? He repeated this core issue of knowing the Father and Him in His prayer to the Father in John 17:3. How is your Scripture time? Your walk with the Lord? Pause, Pray, Obey.

DAY FOUR

WHEN JUDGMENT COMES

What would happen next? In the ensuing time, judgment came to Eli's sons, to Eli, to the nation of Israel, and even to the Philistines. The sins of Eli, Hophni, and Phinehas brought severe chastening from the Lord on His people. What can we learn from these events? What is God saying today with this record of events from over three thousand years ago? While times and cultures have changed, God and people have not changed. His honor and His word still matter.

DO YOU KNOW?
Where Are Philistia and Aphek?

The Philistine kingdom known as Philistia covers the coastal plains territory from Gaza in the south to Aphek in the Plain of Sharon in the north. In addition, the Philistines controlled much of the hill country in central Israel south and southwest of Jerusalem. Aphek lay along the main north-south trade route known as the *Via Maris* ("Way of the Sea"). It is about twenty-one miles west of Shiloh and about eleven miles east of the Mediterranean Sea. In New Testament days, it was a key city on the road from Jerusalem to Caesarea by the Sea and was known as Antipatris (Acts 23:21), named by Herod the Great for his father Antipater (Josephus, Jewish Wars, 1:147).

The Philistines came into Canaan sometime before 1200 BC and settled into what became known as Philistia, the coastal region southwest of Jerusalem. With their idolatry, coupled with superior military might, they proved to be a continual menace to the Israelites. In these days (around 1095 BC), they came to Aphek and set up to battle the Israelites at Ebenezer about two miles away.

What occurred, according to 1 Samuel 4:1–2?

_____

_____

How did the leaders of Israel respond to this defeat? Read verse 3 and record what you discover.

_____

_____

_____

What solution did they propose? What did they think would happen by using the Ark of the Covenant, according to verse 3?

_____

_____

_____

When the Philistines first battled the Israelites, the Philistines were victorious and around four thousand Israelites died in battle. The Israelites gathered at their camp and the leaders of Israel began asking "why?" They proposed bringing "*the Ark of the Covenant of the LORD*" from Shiloh to their camp at Ebenezer near Aphek (location of Antipatris, New Testament). They ran to Shiloh, and Hophni and Phinehas led those bringing the Ark of the Covenant twenty-one miles to the camp, about two miles from Aphek. The leaders and the Israelite soldiers made the assumption that if the Ark itself was with them it would "*deliver us from the power of our enemies*." Their assumption was, in fact, presumption and superstition; just because the Ark resided with them did not mean the Lord would work for them.

📖 Read 1 Samuel 4:4–9. Summarize what happened next.

_____

_____

_____

How did the Israelites respond to the presence of the Ark of the Covenant? How did the Philistines respond?

_____

_____

_____

_____

📖 What happened in the battle? Read verses 10–11 and note what happened to the Israelites, the Philistines, and to Eli's sons, Hophni and Phinehas.

_____

_____

_____

_____

When the Ark of the Covenant came into the Israeli camp, the men "*shouted with a great shout.*" The Philistine camp about two miles away heard the shout and wondered what could be happening. When they realized the Ark of the Covenant had come into the camp, they became afraid. They knew much of the history of the Israelites, including many details of how Israel's God delivered them out of the hands of the Egyptians hundreds of years before. The Philistine leaders urged their troops to fight as hard as possible, lest they "*become slaves to the Hebrews.*" The Philistines fought with great zeal and defeated the Israelites; thirty thousand Israeli foot soldiers died. The Philistines captured the "*Ark of God,*" and Hophni and Phinehas perished in the battle. (For further info, see the Chart "The Glory Cloud..." at the end of this lesson.)

IN THEIR SHOES
The "Glory"

The Glory of God, sometimes referred to as "the Shekinah Glory"—the Hebrew word *shekinah* meaning "dwelling"—appeared in the Pillar of Fire at night and in the Pillar of Cloud by day when the Israelites left Egypt (see Exodus 13:21-22). The Angel of God, the Very Presence of God, was in the "*pillar of cloud*" protecting and leading them (Exodus 14:19; see Numbers 9:15). He guided them in this way for almost forty years.

The "*glory of God*" appeared again at the Temple of Solomon (1 Kings 8:10-11), but when the Babylonians destroyed the Temple in 586 BC, the prophet Ezekiel spoke of "*the glory*" departing from the Temple (Ezekiel 10:3–5, 18-19; 11:22–23). No glory for over five hundred years, until the Birth of Messiah (Jesus) when Angels declared to some simple shepherds, "*Glory to God in the Highest*" (Luke 2:14). Today, we "*fall short of the glory of God*" (Romans 3:23), but Colossians 1:25–27 assures us of "*Christ in you, the hope of glory,*" and Revelation 21:22–23 pictures eternity with Christ in "*the city*" where "*the glory of God*" illumines all.

📖 Read 1 Samuel 4:12–18. What news did Eli hear? What part of the details most affected Eli—what caused the greatest reaction from him?

What occurred when Eli heard that the Ark of God had been captured?

A "*man of Benjamin*" ran the twenty-one miles from the battlefield near Aphek to Shiloh with news of what happened. His appearance told the story—"*his clothes torn and dust on his head.*" The Philistines had defeated the Israelites; thirty thousand died, including Eli's sons Hophni and Phinehas, two of the priests who had taken the Ark of God into the battle. Then, blind, aged Eli heard the worst words he could imagine—"*the Ark of God has been taken.*" That shock caused him to fall backward, breaking his neck, and he died. The Philistines triumphantly took the Ark from Ebenezer and traveled to Ashdod.

When God gives His *shalom*, His peace, it comes as multi-level well-being. Often, when He sends His judgment, it too is multi-level. That proved true in the case of judgment coming to Israel. At Shiloh, Phinehas' wife was pregnant and soon to give birth. What occurred, according to 1 Samuel 4:19?

📖 Read verses 20–21, how did she respond to the birth of her son and the events of those days?

WORD STUDY
Ichabod

Phinehas' wife heard her husband and father-in-law (Eli) had died and the Ark of God had been taken by the Philistines. She went into labor and gave birth to their son whom she named "*Ichabod*" (Strong's #350), which literally means "no glory." She stated, "*the glory has departed from Israel, for the Ark of God was taken*" (1 Samuel 4:22). This reality could get no worse. This presence of the Lord served as more than a mere national treasure. This was their very life, the heart and soul of their covenant relationship, His covenant promises; all rested on His presence with them. No judgment could be worse than this.

📖 Note her words in 1 Samuel 4:21–22. How did she see these events? What significance do you see in the name she gave to her son?

Pregnant and very near the time to give birth, the daughter-in-law of Eli and wife of Phinehas heard the news of the death of her father-in-law and her husband. More significant than the deaths of the men closest to her, was news of the Ark in Philistine hands. Four times we read, "*the ark of God was taken.*" The Ark of the Covenant took preeminence over everything else in Israel; it stood at the center of national life, the center of their worship and the center of their covenant relationship with God, because with the Ark was the glory of God, His very life and life-giving presence. This news was devastating, so much so, that she went into labor.

The women helping her in the birthing process sought to comfort and encourage her with news that she had given birth to a son, considered a great blessing. All she could think about was the ark being taken and her husband and father-in-law dying. Before dying after this birth, she named her son "*Ichabod*," literally meaning "no glory." She declared, "*the glory has departed from Israel, for the ark of God was taken.*" All considered the Ark to be the Throne of the Lord and the touchpoint for prayer (see 1 Chronicles 13:6). This was serious beyond words and a judgment beyond imagination.

STOP AND APPLY—Go toward the Lord—When Phinehas' wife heard news about the Ark of God, she spoke of "*the glory departing from Israel.*" God wants His children to go the other way, not away from Him and "the glory" but come closer, trusting the Spirit of Christ even now in any struggles and battles. He is transforming us "*from glory to glory*" (2 Corinthians 3:17–18). How? Through pressures and trials, God is working more of the death of Jesus in us, so that the life of Jesus is more clearly seen—"*. . . though our outer man is decaying, yet our inner man is being renewed day by day. For momentary, light affliction is producing for us an eternal weight of glory far beyond all comparison, while we look not at the things which are seen, but at the things which are not seen; for the things which are seen are temporary, but the things which are not seen are eternal*" (2 Corinthians 4:16–18). Go toward the Lord and His Word. Seek Him.

DAY FIVE

WHOM WILL I FOLLOW?

In the days of Eli, Hophni, and Phinehas, the people of Israel continued to do many things according to their own opinions and views. For many, Judges 21:25 still proved true: *"In those days there was no king in Israel; everyone did what was right in his own eyes."* God allowed many Canaanites to remain in the land, including the Philistines. This reminds us of the stern lessons of Judges 3:4, *"and they [the Canaanites] were for testing Israel, to find out if they would obey the commandments of the LORD, which He had commanded their fathers through Moses."* Tests do not make us uninformed or deficient; they reveal where we are uninformed or deficient. It was true for Israel, as it is true today. Consider what the people of Israel faced in that day. What applications can we find for today?

📖 Read 1 Samuel 4:1–11 again and summarize the situation.

DID YOU KNOW?
"The Hand of the LORD"

A person's hands reveal what kind of work they do. When referring to the Lord, the hand speaks of His sovereign power. When the Philistines had taken the Ark of God, they thought they had won, but they quickly changed their minds. The account in 1 Samuel uses the word for the hand of the Lord nine times—each time as a cause for concern and fear by the Philistines and for the assurance of the Lord's preeminence for His people (1 Samuel 4:8; 5:6, 7, 9, 11; 6:3, 5, 9; 7:13). They placed the Ark of God in the Temple of Dagon. After the second night, Dagon's hands were literally *"cut off"* (1 Samuel 5:3, 4). After the children of Israel led by Joshua crossed the Jordan River, Joshua 4:23–24 (noting the drying up of the Red Sea and the Jordan River), states, *"that the peoples of the earth may know that the hand of the LORD is mighty"* (see also Psalm 89:13).

Israel continued to deal with the Philistine menace and once again faced warfare with them. During these final days of Eli and his sons, the Israelites foolishly thought they could use the Ark of the Covenant as a military weapon—as some sort of token of blessings or almost as a 'good-luck' charm, presuming it gave them a strategic advantage in battling the Philistines. However, they found that one cannot use God.

News of the Ark coming into the Israeli camp cheered the Israelis but frightened the superstitious Philistines. They had heard of the mighty deeds of the Lord in delivering Israel out of Egypt. They mustered their courage and fought for their lives. God allowed Israel to be soundly defeated; thirty thousand Israeli foot soldiers died, the Ark was taken, and Eli's two sons Hophni and Phinehas died. Concerning the journeys of the Ark from the battlefield into Philistine territory and back to Israel, Adrian Rogers has wisely noted four valuable lessons we must keep in mind. The first lesson is that God will not be used. Israel sadly discovered this when they tried to use God via the Ark of the Covenant, seeking to gain victory over the Philistines.

📖 When the Philistines captured the Ark of the Covenant, what happened in the land of the Philistines, according to 1 Samuel 5:1–12 and 6:1–18?

_____

_____

_____

What did the Philistines learn about 'capturing' the Ark of the Covenant?

_____

_____

_____

The Philistines carried the Ark first to Ashdod, one of the locations of a house of their god, Dagon, where they placed the Ark. That night, the idol fell face-first before the Ark. They set it aright and the next morning, the idol had fallen again, and the head and hands of Dagon were cut off—how did that happen? In some way, the Lord cut off the hands of Dagon, apart from any human hand at work! The lifeless 'fish god' Dagon, the supposed 'god of grain' was no match for the living God of Israel. The citizens of Ashdod faced severe illness. _"The hand of the LORD was heavy on the Ashdodites, and He ravaged them and smote them with tumors."_

The Philistines next took the Ark to Gath where _"the hand of the LORD was against the city with very great confusion and He smote the men of the city, both young and old, so that tumors broke out on them."_ Then, they sent the Ark to Ekron where the people cried for fear and dread. The city was struck with great confusion and _"the hand of God was very heavy there."_ So, the Philistines sent the Ark back to Israel—to the city of Beth-shemesh near Ekron. A second lesson from Adrian Rogers: The Philistines discovered that God cannot be captured or imprisoned.

When the Philistines returned the Ark to Beth-shemesh, they used a cart pulled by two milch cows (milking cows, or "cash cows"). The people of Israel rejoiced and immediately used the wood of the cart for a sacrificial fire and offered the cows as a burnt offering to the Lord (1 Samuel 6:1–16). In the midst of the joy of having the Ark back in Israel, the people learned a sobering lesson. Some of the men looked inside the Ark, and the Lord struck several men dead (1 Samuel 6:19–21). A third lesson: The Lord will not be trivialized.

"God will not be used, captured, trivialized, or ignored."

—Adrian Rogers

Several years later, David and his men learned a vital lesson—the fourth lesson: God's Word and God's Ways cannot be ignored—They tried to move the Ark on a cart (like the Philistines) instead of being carried on the shoulders of God-appointed priests as His Word directed. When the Ark was almost upset by the oxen, Uzzah reached out his hand to steady the Ark and God struck Him dead (2 Samuel 6:1–19). God will never bow to Philistine theology, nor honor Philistine methodology or ever agree with Philistine philosophy—not then, not now, not ever.

STOP AND APPLY—How Is It Between You and the Lord?—Israel found out that God will not be used. The Philistines found out God cannot be captured. The Israelites discovered that God cannot be trivialized. Later David and Israel discovered God and His Word cannot be ignored. How about you and me? Are we guilty of any of these things?

Are you facing some "Philistines" in your life, things that rob you of joy, or peace, or time? Deal with any of those "Philistine" enemies according to the Word of God. You may want to write a prayer or insight here.

Have you tried to use God like a "good-luck charm"? Or have you tried to capture God or box God in to your scheme of things? Pray. Ask God to lead you to know and walk in His ways (Psalm 25:4-5; 37:5).

Is there any area in which you have trivialized God? Take Him and His Word seriously. Make any personal notes here.

_____

_____

_____

_____

_____

TAKEAWAYS
The Life of Eli

There are four takeaways from the lives of Eli and his sons: **1)** Know the Lord, **2)** Know His Word, **3)** Worship the Lord—it's about a relationship with Him, **4)** Walk in His Word—take one step of obedience at a time.

Is there a point(s) where you have ignored God and His Word? Are you seeking Him for what's going on in your life now?

_____

_____

_____

_____

_____

Lord, show me any way in which I am presuming on You or Your Word (Psalm 19:13-14) or any ways I have been trying to use You, capture You, trivialize You or ignore You. Thank You for not giving up on me or on Your plans for me. Thank You for being eternally faithful and true—You do not change (Revelation 19:11; Hebrews 1:12; 13:8). Lord, sometimes I become battle-weary because of the "Philistine" enemy elements I face in my life. I look to You to show me how to deal with those elements, to die to my "self" and to walk in Your ways, in Your Word. Thank You also for Your strength, for Your indwelling Holy Spirit; may I walk true to Your character and ways by the power of Your Spirit. In Jesus' Name, I pray. Amen.

The Glory Cloud of the Lord and the Fire of God

The Manifestations of the Presence of the Lord—The Shekinah Dwelling on Earth

Scripture	Event	Place
Genesis 1:26–27; 2:7, 22–23; Psalm 8:5; Hebrews 2:7	The Lord created the Man and the Woman in His "*Image*" and "*Likeness*," marked by "*glory and majesty.*"	Garden of Eden
Genesis 3:8–21	Some manifestation of the Lord occurred in the Garden of Eden, perhaps the Angel of the LORD. He sought Adam and the Woman who knew He was there and talked with Him.	Garden of Eden
Genesis 3:24	The Cherubim and a flaming sword guarded the way to the Tree of Life.	Garden of Eden
Genesis 11:31; 12:1–4; Acts 7:2–4	The Lord of glory appeared to Abram in Mesopotamia (Ur).	Ur of the Chaldeans
Genesis 15:7–21 (verse 17)	The Lord entered into Covenant with Abram and appeared in a cloud of smoke (like a smoking oven) and a flaming torch.	Hebron
Exodus 3:2–6	The Angel of the LORD appeared to Moses in a burning bush that was not consumed by the supernatural fire.	Mount Horeb (Mount Sinai)
Exodus 13:17–22	The Lord led the people of Israel out of Egypt with a Pillar of Cloud by day and a Pillar of Fire by night.	Egypt and in the Wilderness
Exodus 14:19–20	The pillar of the presence of the Angel of the LORD shielded the Israelites from the Egyptian army.	At the Red Sea
Exodus 14:21–31	The Lord confused the army of Egypt and brought the waters of the sea upon them.	Through the Red Sea
Exodus 16:4–12	The Glory of the Lord appeared in the Cloud, and the Lord gave them meat in the evening and manna in the morning.	Wilderness of Sin
Exodus 19:1–25	The Lord came down on Mount Sinai in smoke and fire.	Mount Sinai

Exodus 20:1–21	The Lord spoke to the people from the fiery, smoke-covered mount.	Mount Sinai
Exodus 20:21–26; 21—23	The Lord spoke to Moses and gave him the various laws for His people.	Mount Sinai
Exodus 24:1–11	Moses went up to meet the Lord with Aaron, Nadab, and Abihu along with seventy elders of Israel.	Mount Sinai
Exodus 24:12–18	Moses and Joshua went up to the mountain. After seven days, Moses entered the midst of the cloud on the mountain to receive the stone tablets of the law and the instructions for the Tabernacle (Exodus 25-31).	Mount Sinai
Exodus 33:7–11	Moses often met the Lord at the Tent of Meeting, and the "pillar of cloud" would descend and rest there. The Lord spoke with Moses face to face.	Outside the camp of the Israelites.
Exodus 33:12–16	Moses prayed for the presence of the Lord to go with them on the journey.	Mount Sinai
Exodus 33:17-23; 34:6-9	Moses prayed to see God's glory and the Lord revealed His glory "passing by" Moses.	Mount Sinai
Exodus 34:29-35; (2 Corinthians 3:7–18)	Moses' face shone temporarily from being in the presence of the Lord.	Mount Sinai
Exodus 25:8, 22; 29:42–46; 40:34–35; Numbers 9:15	The Tabernacle fulfilled the purpose for which the Lord commanded it be constructed. It was the dwelling of the Lord with His people.	Mount Sinai
Exodus 40:36–38; Numbers 9:15–23	The cloud of glory rested on the Tabernacle by day and the pillar of fire by night. When the cloud was taken up the people followed the Lord wherever He led them.	Wilderness journey
Leviticus 9:1–24	The cloud of glory appeared and fire from the Lord consumed the sacrifices Aaron and his sons offered.	Mount Sinai

Numbers 12:1–15	The Lord came down in a pillar of cloud and dealt with the complaint of Miriam and Aaron against Moses.	Hazeroth in the Wilderness
Numbers 13–14	The glory of the Lord appeared when the Israelites grumbled in unbelief over entering the land of Canaan. The Lord sentenced them to die in the wilderness.	Wilderness of Paran at Kadesh
Numbers 16:1–40	Korah, Dathan, and Abiram rebelled against Moses and Aaron as God's chosen leaders and declared themselves as equal leaders. The glory of the Lord appeared, the ground swallowed the men and their families. 250 others offering incense were slain by the fire of the Lord.	The Wilderness
Numbers 16:41–50	The glory of the Lord appeared, and the Lord sent a plague to judge those who complained against Moses and Aaron	The Wilderness
Numbers 20:2–13	The Lord appeared when the people complained about no water at Meribah. Moses struck the rock and forfeited going into the land of Canaan.	Wilderness of Zin at Kadesh (Meribah)
Deuteronomy 4:32–33; 5:4-5, 22–33	At Moab, before the people crossed over into the land of Canaan, Moses recounted the times the Lord appeared and spoke out of the fire on the mountain, giving them the Law.	At Moab telling of Mount Sinai
Joshua 4:15-24; 5:1–15; 6:1–5	The priests carried the Ark of the Covenant into the Jordan and it dried up. The people marched through and camped at Gilgal where the "Captain of the Host of the LORD" appeared to Joshua giving him His battle plan for Jericho.	Jordan River, Gilgal, Jericho
Judges 6:11-24	The Angel of the LORD appeared to Gideon and caused fire to consume the offering he made.	Ophrah

Judges 13:1-24	The Angel of the LORD appeared to Manoah and his wife promising them a son and then ascended in the flame of the altar where they were offering a burnt offering.	Zorah
1 Samuel 3:10, 21	The Lord appeared at the Tabernacle at Shiloh where Samuel ministered as a priest and prophet.	Shiloh
1 Samuel 4:11-22; 5-6	The Philistines captured the Ark of the Covenant from Israel and God brought great turmoil and sickness to them. God cannot be captured.	Ebenezer, Ashdod, Gath, Ekron, Beth Shemesh
Psalm 26:8	David prayed, "O LORD, I love the habitation of Your house, and the place where Your glory dwells." [literally, "the place of the tabernacle of Your glory"].	Israel
Psalm 73:21–28	Asaph spoke of being in the presence of the Lord, of being received "to glory," and declared, "the nearness of God is my good."	Israel
1 Kings 8:1–11; 2 Chronicles 5:2–14; 6:1-2	In the reign of Solomon, the priests brought the Ark of the Covenant into the newly built Temple and the Cloud and Glory of the Lord filled the Temple.	Jerusalem
2 Chronicles 6:12–42; 7:1–3	When Solomon finished praying at the dedication of the Temple, the fire of God came down and consumed the burnt offering and the glory of the Lord filled the Temple.	Jerusalem
Ezekiel 10:1–4, 18–19; 11:22–24	Ezekiel saw the glory of the Lord depart from the Temple to the East Gate, then to the Mount of Olives.	Jerusalem Temple and Mount of Olives
Ezekiel 43:1–12	Ezekiel saw a vision of the glory of the Lord returning to a reconstructed temple.	Jerusalem
Isaiah 6:1–13; John 12:41	In the year King Uzziah died, Isaiah saw a vision of the Lord in heaven.	Heaven

Isaiah 40:5; 60:1–2; 66; Habakkuk 2:14; Zechariah 2:5	Several prophets spoke of the coming kingdom in which the presence of the Lord would be manifested in His glory being seen.	Israel and the earth.
Haggai 2:6–9	Haggai prophesied about the glory of the Lord appearing in the temple in the future.	Jerusalem
Daniel 7:9–10	Daniel saw a vision of the Ancient of Days in His glory.	Heaven
Daniel 7:13–14	Daniel saw a vision of the Son of Man coming in the clouds of heaven.	Heaven and earth
Luke 2:8–20	The glory of the Lord appeared to the shepherds in the fields outside Bethlehem at the birth of the Messiah Jesus.	Shepherds' fields near Bethlehem
John 1:1, 14	Jesus is "The Word"—"*And the Word became flesh, and dwelt among us, and we beheld His glory, glory as of the only begotten from the Father, full of grace and truth.*"	Before and in All Creation
Matthew 2:1–12	The magi followed "*His star*" to find the Christ child in Bethlehem. That star went before them and stood over the house where the Child was. Many believe that supernatural star which appeared and led these men was the Shekinah fire of God.	Bethlehem
Matthew 16:27	Jesus promised His disciples that one day He would come in the glory of His Father with His angels.	Earth
Luke 9:28–36; Matthew 17:1–8; Mark 9:2–8; 2 Peter 1:16–18; James 2:1; John 1:14	On the mount of Transfiguration Jesus' face and clothing changed, Moses and Elijah appeared in glory and the Father overshadowed them in a cloud. Peter, James, and John saw this.	The Mount of Transfiguration (possibly Mount Hermon)
Matthew 24:30, 26:64; Mark 13:26; 14:62; Luke 21:27 (Daniel 7:13–14)	First to His disciples and then later to the Jewish leaders at His trial before His crucifixion, Jesus promised that He would come as the reigning Son of Man in the clouds of heaven (a manifestation of His glory).	Heaven and earth

Acts 1:9–11	Jesus ascended in a cloud of glory forty days after His resurrection. The angel promised His return in the same way.	Mount of Olives in Jerusalem
Acts 2:1–4 (1 Corinthians 6:19; 2 Corinthians 6:16)	Tongues of fire rested on each of the believers gathered on the morning of Pentecost. These appear to be individualized pillars of fire resting on the new temples of the Holy Spirit. (Paul speaks of believers being the temple [Greek, *naos*, "inner sanctuary" or Holy of Holies] of the Holy Spirit.)	Jerusalem
Acts 6:15; 7:54–60	Stephen's face appeared as the face of an angel. When they were seeking to execute him, he saw the glory of God and Jesus standing at the right hand of God.	Jerusalem and Heaven
Acts 9:1-9; 22:3–16; 26:9–18	A very bright light from heaven, brighter than the sun, flashed all around Saul as he was on the road to Damascus and the Lord Jesus spoke to him.	Damascus Road
2 Corinthians 3:8–9	The ministry of the Spirit is marked by the glory of God.	Wherever
2 Corinthians 3:18	Believers in Christ are being transformed into the image of Christ *"from glory to glory."*	Wherever
2 Corinthians 4:3–6	God *"has shone in our hearts to give the light of the knowledge of the glory of God in the face of Christ."*	Wherever
2 Corinthians 4:16–18	An eternal weight of glory is being worked in us as God renews the inward man in the midst of the light affliction.	Wherever
Romans 8:18–21	We and the creation await the glory of the revealing of the sons of God.	The Creation
Colossians 1:27	Paul speaks of *"Christ in you, the hope of glory."*	Wherever
1 Thessalonians 4:17	Believers in Jesus will be caught up in clouds [of glory] to meet the Lord in the air.	Earth and Atmosphere
Hebrews 1:3	Jesus is the radiance or the outshining of the glory of God.	Heaven and earth

Hebrews 2:10	Jesus is bringing many sons to glory, to a life full of the Shekinah glory.	Heaven
Revelation 1:9–20	The Apostle John saw the Lord Jesus in His resurrected glory and received the Revelation of things to come.	Island of Patmos
Revelation 15:5–8	John saw the Temple in Heaven filled with smoke from the glory of God. This was in addition to the many manifestations of the Lord throughout the Revelation.	Temple in Heaven
Revelation 21:1–27; 22:1–5	The Tabernacle of God, the New Jerusalem, appears and the Lord and His people live eternally in the glorious presence and light of the Lord.	New Jerusalem, New Heavens and New Earth

<h1 style="text-align:right">LESSON 8</h1>

THE LIFE AND TIMES OF SAMUEL
FAITHFUL TO THE LORD

Samuel served as the last of the judges, and he anointed Israel's first and second kings, Saul, then David. He is listed among the prophets in Acts 3:24; 13:20, and Hebrews 11:32. Samuel served at a very tumultuous time when the Philistines controlled much of the coastland and exerted a strong and corrupting influence on Israel. The people continued to do what was *"right in his* [or her] *own eyes"* rather than what was right in the sight of God. The worship at the Tabernacle in Shiloh became more corrupt while Eli and his sons led there.

What was needed in Israel? What did a faithful follower of God and His Word face in these days? At such a time, the need for godly leadership became more important than ever. God was working. He chose to use a grieving, barren woman to bring Samuel into this world. What can we learn from her? What can we learn from Samuel?

 DID YOU KNOW?
The Tabernacle at Shiloh

Much of the setting of 1 Samuel 1–4 is the Tabernacle complex at Shiloh. This complex held several structures including housing for Eli and his family as well as for Hophni and his family, Phinehas and his family, and others who served there. Around 1395 to 1390 BC, it had been moved from Gilgal to that location after much of the land had been conquered in Joshua's days. Samuel was born around 1105 BC, so in Samuel's early years, the Tabernacle complex had been at Shiloh almost 300 years.

DAY ONE

THE BOY "SAMUEL"—"ASKED OF GOD"

Though Hannah appears to be the favored wife of Elkanah, she was barren. She faced ridicule and badgering from Peninnah, the "other" wife in the home. They lived in Ramah, and in their home Peninnah had several children while Hannah had none. It was not an easy time to live and not an easy place to live in. Grieved and oppressed in spirit, Hannah sought the Lord at the Tabernacle. What could God do?

📖 Summarize the home life of Hannah according to 1 Samuel 1:1–8.

_____

_____

_____

Characterize the spiritual life found in this family? What do you find about the ways of each one—Elkanah, Hannah, and Peninnah?

_____

_____

_____

_____

Elkanah and his two wives Hannah and Peninnah lived in the hill country of Ephraim in Ramathaim-zophim, also known as Ramah, about five miles north of Jerusalem. Elkanah was a descendant of Levi according to 1 Chronicles 6:22–28. Elkanah led his household to seek the Lord, regularly journeying to the Tabernacle at Shiloh for the yearly feast, most likely the Feast of Tabernacles celebrating the Fall harvests. It was the most joyous of the seven feasts. Elkanah showed his love for Hannah, probably his first and oldest wife, but barren. Tension in the home arose, because Elkanah's second wife, Peninnah, bore several children. She provoked Hannah, especially around feast times. This may reveal that her provoking ways focused on Hannah's barrenness, perhaps accusing her of being cursed by the Lord or harboring some hidden sin. Elkanah sought to comfort and cheer her, especially during the feast times, but Hannah's heart continued to grieve.

📖 What did Hannah do, according to 1 Samuel 1:9–10?

_____

_____

_____

What was at the heart of her prayer, according to verse 11? Based on the facts of verses 12–16, what characterized her praying?

_____

_____

_____

_____

📖 How did Eli respond at first? What words did he speak after she explained her oppression of spirit? How did Hannah respond to him after his words of peace? Read verses 17–18 and note your insights.

Hannah did the wisest thing she could do in light of the tension between her and Peninnah and even in regard to Elkanah; she sought the Lord in prayer. Marked by great grief and oppression, literally "severe in spirit," Hannah poured out her heart to the Lord. She vowed that if the Lord would give her a son, she would give him to the Lord for life as a Nazirite ("*a razor shall never come on his head*"). Because her lips moved with no sounds coming forth, Eli wrongly assumed she was drunk, but after hearing her heart, changed and said to her "*go in peace*" and pronounced a blessing—"*May the God of Israel grant your petition that you have asked of Him.*" Hannah responded with new hope, no longer sad, and joined in the feast.

📖 What happened in Hannah's life, according to 1 Samuel 1:19-20?

According to verses 21–23, what did she do with her new son?

What occurred after Samuel was weaned, according to verses 24–28?

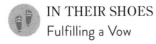

IN THEIR SHOES
Fulfilling a Vow

In Numbers 15:1–3, 8–10, the Lord gives certain regulations for fulfilling a vow. One should bring a young bull along with a grain offering (with olive oil) and a drink offering, to place on the altar at the Tabernacle. The burnt offering symbolized whole-hearted surrender, worship, and obedience—each element totally crushed and consumed in the holy fires. Scripture calls this a sweet aroma to the Lord. This picture certainly reveals the hearts of Hannah, Elkanah, and Samuel.

Hannah became pregnant and gave birth to a son. She named him Samuel, which means "name of God" and sounds like the Hebrew word *sha'al*, meaning "ask" or "request." Hannah knew her son was "asked of God." She kept Samuel in Ramah for the years of weaning him, to about age three. During these years, she doubtless spoke often to him about his birth, the Lord's work, the meaning of his name, and how he was an answer to prayer. Likely, she talked to him about the fact that a razor would never come on his head—he would be a Nazirite dedicated to the Lord for life. After being weaned, Samuel and the family traveled to Shiloh, where they offered the sacrifice befitting a vow, gave Samuel to Eli for service in the Tabernacle, and worshiped the Lord. Worship and surrender marked the hearts of Hannah, Samuel, and Elkanah.

At the Tabernacle, about four years since her barrenness prayer, Hannah prayed once again. This prayer also revealed her heart in many ways. Saturated with the Word of God, she focused on the Lord and His ways. She showed a God-centered heart, exalting Him for who He is and for His salvation. She knew that He knew her and all those who had spoken against her and against the Lord over the years. Hannah saw the bigger picture; God was working beyond what she could see in Ramah or in Shiloh. He was working to bring *"His king"* and *"His anointed,"* the Messiah, into Israel, and she rejoiced in what He would do. She could leave her son Samuel at Shiloh, confident that God would take care of him. The Lord would also bring in the fulness of His salvation.

IN THEIR SHOES
The Yearly Sacrifice

Exodus 34:23 states, *"three times a year all your males are to appear before the Lord GOD, the God of Israel"* and Deuteronomy 16:16–17 notes the need for each man to give *"as he is able"* (see also Exodus 23:14–17; Deuteronomy 16:1–17). These three times listed are Passover Week (Feasts of Passover, Unleavened Bread, First Fruits), the Pentecost Feast (seven weeks after Passover Week), and the Fall Feast of Tabernacles (immediately after the Feast of Trumpets and the Day of Atonement). In part, so they could worship worry-free, the Lord also promised to protect their property while they were gone to the place of the Tabernacle or later the Temple (Exodus 34:24). Elkanah's *"yearly sacrifice"* likely occurred at the Fall Feast of Tabernacles after all the harvests had been gathered in (1 Samuel 1:3, 21; 2:19; Deuteronomy 16:13-17).

Read 1 Samuel 2:1–10, Hannah's prayer.

What do you note about the spiritual condition of Hannah in these days? What might Samuel have learned from Hannah during those three or four years at home?

📖 Contrast the ways and works of Samuel with those of Hophni and Phinehas in 1 Samuel 2:11–26.

_____

_____

_____

_____

_____

What do you learn about Samuel in verses 11, 18–21, and 26?

_____

_____

_____

_____

📖 Compare verse 26 with Luke 1:80 and 2:52. Note your insights.

_____

_____

_____

_____

_____

Samuel grew physically as a young boy, but more importantly he grew _"in favor both with the LORD and with men,"_ much as we see occurring in the young years of John the Baptist and of Jesus. Unlike Hophni and Phinehas, Samuel focused on the Lord and what true worship should be. He could see the obvious difference between the yearly worship of his parents, Elkanah and Hannah, and the daily ways of the sons of Eli. Like John the Baptist and the child Jesus, Samuel matured physically, socially, and spiritually.

DID YOU KNOW?
Samuel's Clothing

In 1 Samuel 2:18, we read of Samuel _"ministering before the LORD"_ and _"wearing a linen ephod,"_ the garment of a priest (Exodus 29:8; 39:27, 41; 40:14–15). The linen ephod was a sleeveless, vest-like garment. Hannah also made him a new robe each year and brought it to him at the Tabernacle when Elkanah and she came to offer the yearly sacrifice (1 Samuel 2:19). Later in Israel's history, the Lord made it clear that the priests were to wear linen garments in the future Temple and never wear wool so that they would not sweat in their service (Ezekiel 44:15–19).

STOP AND APPLY—Giving Up—When we speak of "giving up" something to God, have we really thought how much the Lord has "given down" to where we are? Surrender is the heartbeat of heaven—even what we call "The Lord's Prayer" states, *"Your will be done on earth as it is in heaven"* (Matthew 6:10). How is God's will done in heaven? It is done worshipfully, humbly, promptly, quickly, gratefully, energetically, no whining, complaining, or disobeying. And, what do we have that we have not received?—the apostle asks in 1 Corinthians 4:7. The Lord has given so much. "Giving up?" Don't give up on God. Don't give up on prayer. Do give up your life to Him. Worship Him.

Day Two

Samuel, the People of Israel, and . . . "What about a King?"

Samuel's early years at the Tabernacle under the supervision of Eli proved very instructive. He saw the ways of Eli and his two sons, Hophni and Phinehas. Doubtless, he noted the various ways and attitudes of people 'worshiping' there. What do we learn from young Samuel? What would God say to you or me through this young man?

📖 According to 1 Samuel 3:1, what kind of spiritual atmosphere prevailed at the Tabernacle in Samuel's youth?

_____

_____

📖 Read verses 2–15. What occurred in Samuel's life?

_____

_____

📖 What kind of reputation did Samuel develop in these early years, according to 1 Samuel 3:19–21; 4:1a? What marked him, the place of Shiloh, and the land of Israel in these years?

_____

_____

_____

_____

DID YOU KNOW?

God's View of Samuel

The Lord saw Samuel as unique, a man for those times in Israel. Psalm 99:6–7 groups him with Moses and Aaron. He is noted as one who *"called on His name; . . . He spoke to them."* Samuel, like Moses and Aaron, knew the Lord and sought to lead the people as God and His Word directed.

When Samuel was a boy, the Tabernacle and ministries at Shiloh proved somewhat lifeless. *"Word from the LORD was rare in those days,"* and many groped in the darkness. *"Visions"* did not occur very often. Things began to change. When Samuel was probably about twelve years of age, the Lord called out to him in the night. Thinking it was Eli needing something, Samuel went to him two times. Eli discerned that something different was going on; the Lord Himself *"was calling the boy."* Eli told Samuel to respond with *"Speak, LORD, for Your servant is listening."*

Samuel returned to his bed, and the Lord returned, calling Samuel's name. He then told Samuel what He was about to do in judging Eli and his sons for their *"iniquity."* The next morning, Eli made Samuel tell the entire message, even though it was one of coming judgment. He obeyed. More words came from the Lord; Samuel proved faithful to speak them to the people of Israel. Everyone began to regard him as *"a prophet of the LORD"*—*"none of his words"* failed, the mark of a true prophet (Deuteronomy 18:22).

📖 After God's judgment on Eli and his two sons, on the people of Israel, and on the Philistines (who tried to capture the Ark and the God of the Ark), the people of Israel *"lamented after the LORD"* (1 Samuel 7:2). Samuel, then probably in his early thirties, spoke as a prophet to the people. Read 1 Samuel 7:3–11. What did Samuel do, and what did the people of Israel do?

_____

_____

_____

_____

What marker did Samuel put in place as a reminder of the Lord and His work, according to verse 12?

_____

Summarize what you discover in verses 13–14.

_____

_____

_____

_____

WORD STUDY
Ebenezer

After the Lord "*thundered*" against the Philistines and Israel routed them, Samuel put in place a stone marker "*between Mizpah and Shen*" as a reminder of His work and their victory. He named the place and the stone "*Ebenezer*," literally, "*Eben-ha-ezer*," meaning "stone of the help." This word combines two Hebrew words, *eben* (Strong's #68), meaning "stone," and *azar/ezer* (Strong's #5826, #5828), meaning "to surround," "protect," or "help." There, Samuel declared "*the LORD has helped us*." (1 Samuel 7:12).

📖 What marked Samuel's ministry, according to 1 Samuel 7:15–17?

_____

_____

Samuel focused the people on their personal relationship to the Lord, calling them to "*return to the LORD with all your heart*" and get rid of any and all idols. He told them, "*direct your hearts to the LORD and serve Him alone*," if they expected His deliverance from the Philistines. They obeyed. Samuel gathered the people at Mizpah in central Israel, near Shiloh and his home of Ramah. They offered sacrifices, Samuel prayed, and the people sought the Lord. Then, the Philistines marched against Israel, and the Israelites became afraid. Samuel and the people prayed more earnestly. The Lord answered and "*thundered*" against the Philistines, whom the Israelites then routed. Samuel led the people in marking the place, the day, and the event. From that point, the Philistines were not a menace in the days of Samuel. They would come back in the days of Saul and David.

DID YOU KNOW?
Where Are Bethel, Gilgal, Mizpah, and Ramah?

Samuel's circuit included three cities in addition to his home city of Ramathaim-zophim or Ramah, about eighteen miles north-northwest of Jerusalem. Bethel, originally named Luz, was the place where Jacob had his dream of a ladder connecting earth and heaven; Abraham also encamped there (Genesis 12:8; 13:3; 28:19). It lay twelve miles north of Jerusalem and about four miles southeast of Ramah. Gilgal, about fifteen miles northeast of Jerusalem and about one-mile northeast of Jericho, served as the first camp of the Israelites after they crossed the Jordan River (Joshua 4:19–20). The Tabernacle stood there during the years of the Joshua-led conquest, before being moved to Shiloh, some twelve miles northwest. Gilgal was about nine miles from Bethel. Mizpah (of Samuel) lay about fourteen miles south-southwest of Shiloh and about fourteen miles west of Gilgal. The journey from Mizpah back to Ramah in the territory of Ephraim was about fourteen miles northwest.

Samuel "*judged Israel all the days of his life*." To adequately judge the people in that region, he regularly traveled in a circuit to Bethel, Gilgal, and Mizpah. He also ministered in his hometown of Ramah where he built an altar to the Lord. Likely, he led a school of the prophets there, training men in the Word and ways of God (see 1 Samuel 10:10; 19:20, 2 Kings 2:3, 5, 7; 4:38–44; 6:1–7). These days proved beneficial for the people of Israel in that region as he helped them focus more faithfully on the Lord and His Word.

📖 Read 1 Samuel 8:1–3. What happened in Israel?

_____

_____

_____

What kind of judges were Samuel's sons, Joel and Abijah?

_____

_____

📖 Read Exodus 18:21. How does this compare with Joel's and Abijah's actions?

_____

_____

_____

Years passed; Samuel grew old, so he appointed his sons as judges. No one in Israel's past had appointed a judge; that was God's work. As they served miles away in Beersheba (Israel's southernmost point), Joel and Abijah showed a different ethic than their father: they "_turned aside after dishonest gain and took bribes and perverted justice._" Not good! The very character qualities mentioned over and over in past regulations were missing in Samuel's two sons. Hundreds of years before, Moses' father-in-law Jethro had given wise counsel about the "_able men_" who could help Moses; they were to be men who feared God and hated "_dishonest gain_" (Exodus 18:21–26). This proved so significant in Moses' eyes that he re-emphasized the story and the regulations almost forty years later, just before the nation went into Canaan (Deuteronomy 1:9–18).

📖 What did the older men of Israel say to Samuel at this time? Read 1 Samuel 8:4–6.

_____

_____

_____

📖 Do you see any significance in their request for a king "_to judge us like all the nations_"? What difference do you see in what God ordered in Deuteronomy 17:18–20?

_____

_____

_____

_____

_____

God wanted *"able men"* to lead His people, ever shunning dishonest gain, whether as priests, kings, prophets, or leaders in the tribes and families. He wanted them to be honest and just, doing what is right for rich or poor, whether they be well-known or unknown. Proverbs 6:16–19 lists seven things God hates; the first two are haughty or proud eyes and a lying tongue. He despises dishonesty. It is against His nature; He is *"the Truth"* (John 14:6); one of His names is *"Faithful and True"* (Revelation 19:11). Revelation 21:7 says the judgment of the lake of fire includes *"all liars"* (see also 21:27). Revelation 22:15 reports that those *"outside"* the City of God include *"everyone who loves and practices lying."* God hates dishonesty!

The older men came to Ramah and spoke to Samuel. They noted his older age and the ways of his sons not matching the ways of Samuel, especially in righteously judging the matters brought before them. They wanted a king *"to judge us like all the nations."* What is the problem with that request? It did not match God's heart desire that they have a king who judged or ruled by the Word of God. Paramount in God's order was the importance of the Word, so much so, that each king was to write his own copy of the Scriptures under the watchful eye of a priest. God wanted His Word known and obeyed. This was not simply a preference, like flavors of food, but vital to the life of the king and the life of the nation. How would Samuel respond?

STOP AND APPLY—Back to the Basics—Samuel did not come up with a new idea or way to worship God. He simply called the people to put away idols and place their heart focus on the Lord and His Word. That path has never changed. Jeremiah 6:16 speaks about the *"ancient paths,"* not antique, not antiquated, old-fashioned, out-of-date, or expired, but *"ancient"*—always true to the Lord and His Word and what it means to walk with Him. Hundreds of years later, the apostle John enjoined his readers, *"Little children, guard yourselves from idols"* (1 John 5:21). Idolatry is always a danger, close by. God or God's ways never change or get old—Ancient? Yes, but never outdated. A championship basketball team wins because they dribble, shoot, rebound, and pass better than another team—no 'secret sauce,' nothing magical, just "the basics." Pause and talk to the Lord about the "basics" in your life.

DAY THREE

SAMUEL, THE PEOPLE OF ISRAEL, AND SAUL

The people of Israel continued to clamor for a king. God knew and even planned for Israel to have a king. He spoke of kings coming from the descendants of Abraham and Sarah (Genesis 17:6, 16) and of Jacob (Genesis 35:11). The Lord even gave clear regulations about a future king (Deuteronomy 17:14–20). Having a king was not wrong, but in Samuel's day their motives for wanting a king were wrong. Samuel became grieved hearing their cries and realizing their hearts. What would he do? How could he deal with this? What can we learn from him and from the Lord during this pivotal time in Israel's history?

📖 How did Samuel respond to the older men? What do you find him doing in 1 Samuel 8:6b? Also read verses 7–9. What did the Lord tell Samuel?

What did Samuel tell the people, according to verses 10–18?

How did the people respond to Samuel's warnings and cautions, according to verses 19–20?

How did Samuel conclude the issue, according to verses 21–22?

DID YOU KNOW?
Where Is Gibeah?

There are several places labeled *Gibeah* (meaning "hill") in Israel. Saul's home was at Gibeah of Saul, also known as Gibeah of Benjamin, located three miles north of Jerusalem and four miles southeast of Mizpah where Saul was chosen by lot under the direction of Samuel (1 Samuel 10:17–26). Gibeah of God (*Elohim*), also known as Geba had a high place (worship center) and a Philistine garrison located there (1 Samuel 10:5). Gibeah of God (Geba) lay about four miles northeast of Gibeah of Saul, about five miles north-northwest of Jerusalem, and about eleven miles west-southwest of Gilgal. At Gibeah of God, Saul prophesied with a band of prophets (1 Samuel 10:10).

When the older men came to Samuel in Ramah asking for a king over them, Samuel became very displeased. The first thing he did was pray to the Lord. The Lord responded quickly, instructing Samuel to listen to them, to know that they were rejecting the Lord as king more than rejecting Samuel as prophet. The Lord saw their actions as forsaking Him to serve other gods, as their ancestors had done time and time again. The Lord also wisely guided Samuel in giving them a warning about having a king and what a king's procedures and ways would mean for the people.

Samuel obeyed the Lord, giving the people a multi-level warning. A king would require taxes and servants and an army. Those would come from their sons and daughters. They would pay for government services with their crops, their time, and their goods, so much so that it would cause them to cry out, but the Lord would not answer.

The people ignored Samuel's words of warning and still clamored and whined for "*a king over us*," thinking that a king would solve so many problems; he would "*judge us and go out before us and fight our battles*." Samuel listened, understood their words, and repeated them to the Lord in prayer. The Lord told Samuel to give them what they wanted. Samuel dismissed the people back to their towns and cities. What would happen next? [For further info see the chart "**The Lord is King and Judge**" at the end of this lesson.]

📖 What occurred in Israel, according to 1 Samuel 9:15–16? What did the Lord tell Samuel?

_____

_____

_____

What was to be the kings "job," according to verse 16?

_____

_____

Summarize the meeting between Saul and Samuel as recorded in verses 17–27.

_____

_____

_____

📖 What did Samuel do to Saul in 1 Samuel 10:1? Summarize what occurred as recorded in verses 2–16 of this chapter.

_____

_____

Saul went looking for his family's stray donkeys but could not find them. His servant and he then agreed to go to the "seer" (prophet) in Ramah, hoping to get information. The Lord told Samuel that Saul would come; he was the one the Lord had chosen to be the new king. His job would be to "deliver My people from the hand of the Philistines," likely now growing stronger and more oppressive in the land. Most likely, the people had cried out to the Lord again, probably in relation to the Philistine menace, the pattern often repeated when an oppressor arose in the period of the judges. Samuel invited Saul to eat with him and assured him his donkeys had been found. Samuel revealed "the word of God" to Saul; he would become the "ruler of His inheritance," so Samuel anointed Saul as king. After this, Samuel instructed him in what to do upon leaving Ramah.

IN THEIR SHOES
"The Spirit of the LORD"

In the Old Testament, the Holy Spirit did not permanently indwell believers; He "came upon" or clothed His servants like a cloak or a glove for their God-given tasks, as in the case of Gideon (Judges 6:34). When the "Spirit of the LORD" came upon Saul "mightily," he was empowered to rule and fight as king (1 Samuel 11:6). It appears that the Spirit stayed upon Saul in the first part of his reign, until his disobedience to Samuel and the Word of God (1 Samuel 15:28–29). Likely, the work of "the Spirit" continued in his reign until soon after this, when Samuel anointed David as the new king and "the Spirit of the LORD came mightily upon David from that day forward" (1 Samuel 16:13–14). Later, when confessing his horrendous sins (adultery and murder), David prayed that God would not "take Your Holy Spirit from me" (Psalm 51:11).

Saul traveled toward home in Gibeah. He met two men who assured him the donkeys had been found. Then, he met three men journeying to Bethel to worship who gave Saul two loaves of bread, perhaps sustenance for his journey. Saul then met a group of prophets, and "the Spirit of the LORD" came upon him, changed him, and he began prophesying. He told his uncle about Samuel, the word about the donkeys, but nothing else.

📖 What occurred at Mizpah, according to 1 Samuel 10:17–25?

_____

_____

_____

How was Saul chosen as king, according to verses 20–21?

_____

_____

_____

📖 Describe the interaction between Saul, Samuel, and the people, according to verses 24–27.

_____

_____

_____

_____

📖 What further word do you see about Saul becoming king in 1 Samuel 11:14–15.

_____

_____

_____

Samuel gathered the people of Israel (probably representatives from various tribes) at Mizpah. There, the people drew lots which pointed to the tribe of Benjamin, followed by the Matrite family, then Saul son of Kish. After finding Saul hiding by the baggage, Samuel revealed him as the Lord's choice as king. The people cheered, _"Long live the king."_ Samuel then explained _"the ordinances of the kingdom,"_ wrote them on a scroll, set them before the Lord, (possibly in the Tabernacle temporarily at Mizpah), then, sent the people back to their homes. Saul went to his home in nearby Gibeah. Certain _"valiant men whose hearts God touched"_ went with Saul, while certain _"worthless men"_ (sons of Belial) despised Saul, but Saul stayed silent about them.

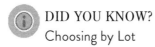

DID YOU KNOW?
Choosing by Lot

The people of Israel, led by Samuel, chose Saul as king at Mizpah _"by lot"_ (1 Samuel 10:17-21). This was not by chance, for they trusted the providential hand of God to superintend. Proverbs 16:33 assures, _"The lot is cast into the lap, but its every decision is from the LORD"_ (see also, Proverbs 18:18). The apostles used this method in selecting Mathias as Judas' replacement, praying and trusting the Lord in this matter (Acts 1:24-26). The testimony of the New Testament affirms the indwelling of the Holy Spirit in each believer to guide each believer to continually put _"to death the deeds of the body"_ (Acts 2:4; Romans 8:12–17; Galatians 5:16–25; Ephesians 5:18). He also teaches each (John 14:16-18, 26; 15:26; 16:13).

The people of Israel clamored for a king, and God allowed that. He chose Saul as king, and Samuel anointed him (1 Samuel 9:1–27; 10:1–16). From the people's perspective, they saw Saul selected _"by lot"_ at Mizpah (1 Samuel 10:17–21) and by public affirmation at Gilgal (1 Samuel 11:14–15). The people did so _"before the LORD,"_ with peace offerings indicating their desire to follow Him. All _"rejoiced greatly."_ Would this king be His kind of king?

STOP AND APPLY—What God Wants or What I Want?—When we come to prayer, are we seeking what God wants or seeking God for what we want? Psalm 37:4 speaks about delighting in the Lord and Him giving one the desires of the heart—some see that as God giving me whatever I want, whatever I desire. Not so. It appears that it is more about desiring the Lord Himself, what He wants, when He wants, how He wants. When I want what He wants, He gladly gives me what I want—because it is, in fact, what He wants to give for me and for His purposes. A friend once told me, "God needs to fix my 'wanter.'" This is a great opportunity for a "heart check": how are you doing, or how are you desiring? Is it His way or your way? Talk to Him and adjust where needed. After all, everyone must adjust in some way; His way, the best way.

DAY FOUR

SAMUEL FAITHFULLY FOLLOWED GOD

Samuel continually showed his concern for the people of Israel and their relationship with the Lord. He wanted them to follow the Word of God. When he gathered the people at Gilgal, Samuel focused their attention on his ministry and on the Lord and His Word along with God's desire for a king like God wanted.

📖 Samuel spoke to the people at Gilgal. What was his testimony about his own life and ministry, according to 1 Samuel 12:1–5? What counsel and caution did Samuel give to the Israelites in verses 1–16, especially verses 14–16?

📖 How did Samuel focus the people's attention about their wickedness, and how did they respond, according to 1 Samuel 12:17–21?

"Moreover, as for me, far be it from me that I should sin against the LORD by ceasing to pray for you; but I will instruct you in the good and right way. Only fear the LORD and serve Him in truth with all your heart; for consider what great things He has done for you."
(1 Samuel 12:23–24)

📖 What caution and encouragement did Samuel give in 1 Samuel 12:22–25?

_____

_____

Samuel asked the people, and they affirmed that he had a stellar testimony of ministry over the years, never cheating anyone, always seeking what is right. He recounted how God had been faithful to Israel over the years, focusing on the times since Egypt. Many times, the people *"forgot the LORD their God"* and then faced oppression. When people prayed, God answered and delivered, but most recently they clamored for a king, *"although the LORD your God was your king."* Then, Samuel pointed them to their new king Saul.

At the same time, with the idea of covenant blessing and curses, he assured them of his continuous prayer for them, cautioning and calling them to *"fear the LORD and serve Him,"* to obey His Word, not rebelling against Him or His Word. In part, as a precaution and, in part, to reveal to them their hearts in asking for a king, Samuel showed them how the wrath of God could be poured out as he prayed for unseasonal and unwanted rain and thunder on the wheat crop; the rains poured, and the people cried out, confessing as sin their insistence on asking for a king rather than being content to follow the Lord as their king.

Samuel continued exhorting them to fully follow the Lord, the faithful God. He would continue to pray for them and instruct them *"in the good and right way."* He concluded, urging them to fear and follow the Lord, not doing wickedly lest they and their king be *"swept away."*

When the Philistine menace escalated, Saul called Israel to fight. In 1 Samuel 10:8, Samuel called Saul and the people to meet at Gilgal to affirm his kingship. After that, Saul traveled to Gibeah, then back to Gilgal where he waited on Samuel. What did Saul do, according to 1 Samuel 13:8–9? What occurred just after Saul's burnt offering, according to 1 Samuel 13:10?

 IN THEIR SHOES
Waiting on God

Saul failed to wait on God; in his fear and impatience, he chose to disobey the word of the Lord given through Samuel. Just a few minutes more would have been obedience. Someone wisely said, "God often works two minutes till too late, but He is never late. He is always on time." His time and timing are always purposeful and useful. Waiting on God means trusting Him—Joseph had to wait in jail. While forgotten by the Egyptian cupbearer, he was never forgotten by the Lord (Genesis 40:23;41:1, 8–13). When confronted with what He knew would be wrong timing, Jesus said, *"My hour has not yet come"* (John 2:4; 7:6, 8, 30; 8:20), but then John 13:1 tells us, *"Jesus knowing that His hour had come"* followed His Father's plans—always on time, in the fulness of time (Galatians 4:4). As we wait, God is working what He knows is right, useful, purposeful, even beautiful.

📖 Saul and Samuel interacted over Saul's offering of the burnt offering and not waiting on Samuel. According to 1 Samuel 13:13–14, what did Samuel call Saul's actions? What were the consequences? What did God want in a king?

Samuel told Saul to go to Gilgal, wait seven days, and there Samuel would meet him and offer up burnt offerings and peace offerings as part of his new role as king (1 Samuel 10:8). Saul had led the Israelis in a victory over the Ammonites, showing his valor and leadership as king (1 Samuel 11:1–11). The people affirmed Saul as their new king, and Samuel addressed the people gathered at Gilgal (1 Samuel 11:12–14; 12:1–25). Soon after, the Philistines gathered at Michmash, about four miles northeast of Gibeah. Saul mustered the Israelis together, then went to Gilgal and waited for seven days. Then, fearful and impatient, he disobeyed Samuel and his word as a prophet of God. Saul chose to offer a burnt offering on his own, though unnecessary before going into battle against the Philistines. This was no small matter. Samuel arrived just as the errant burnt offering concluded.

When Samuel came, Saul began making excuses for why he did what he did. His offering was not necessary, but Samuel knew obeying the Lord was absolutely necessary. Two times Samuel mentioned "*you have not kept the commandment of the LORD your God*" (1 Samuel 13:13, 14). As a result, Saul's kingdom would not endure; instead, the Lord would appoint "*as ruler over His people*" a man with a heart for God, one who could trust, obey, and wait on God.

📖 Saul continued to reign but with a wrong heart. He failed more than once, but 1 Samuel 15 reveals the last straw. According to 1 Samuel 15:1–3, what judicial order did God give through Samuel?

What did Saul do? Read verses 4–9 and summarize what you discover.

IN THEIR SHOES
Saul at Gilgal

Three key events occurred in Saul's life at Gilgal—**1)** Israel affirmed Saul as king (1 Samuel 11:14–15), **2)** Samuel rebuked Saul for his impatience in not waiting on Samuel and offering the burnt offering and peace offerings himself, thus bringing the loss of his kingdom to another (1 Samuel 13:8–14), and **3)** For his disobedience in the matter of the Amalekites, Samuel confirmed the Lord's rejection of Saul as king (1 Samuel 15:10–29).

📖 What did Samuel do and say, according to verses 10–19?

_____

_____

_____

📖 How did Saul respond to Samuel's rebuke? Summarize the interaction between Samuel and Saul, based on what you read in verses 20–31?

_____

_____

_____

_____

📖 Read verses 32–35. What did Samuel do?

_____

_____

Samuel gave Saul orders from the Lord to deal judiciously with the Amalekites. The Amalekites had many opportunities to do what was right in God's sight, but consistently refused, even fighting the people of God and God's plans. The Lord ordered an execution; the Amalekite society was morally and spiritually bankrupt, filled with a sin-cancer of the soul. Spiritual gangrene had set in; they had gone beyond the limits of mercy. Like an amputation, the only solution in this case was execution; the Lord through Samuel sent Saul as executioner.

Saul gathered his troops and attacked. He warned the Kenites to leave and they did. Saul then defeated the Amalekites but spared their king Agag and "*the best of the sheep*" along with other healthy livestock. God knew; this was a heart issue, not a military matter. God spoke to Samuel about him; "*he has turned back from following Me, and has not carried out My commands.*" Though grieved, Samuel came early to Saul's camp at Gilgal with the question, *"what then is this bleating of the sheep?"* Saul tried to shift blame to *"the people"* for sparing the best livestock to *"sacrifice to the LORD your God."* Samuel then gave Saul God's verdict; Saul had done *"what was evil in the sight of the LORD"* (acting like the people of the period of the judges).

DID YOU KNOW?
Samuel's Torn Robe

At Gilgal, when Saul reached out to stop Samuel from walking away, he tore *"the edge of his robe"* (1 Samuel 15:27). How did that happen? It is very likely that what Saul grabbed, and tore is one of the four corner cords sewn on each Israelite garment (Numbers 15:37–41; Deuteronomy 22:12). The tassel served as a continual reminder of *"all the commandments of the LORD, so as to do them and not follow after your own heart and your own eyes,"* a problem for people in the days of the judges and in Samuel's day (see Judges 21:25). It seems that Saul disregarded the tassel cord, symbolic of the Word of the Lord, like he disregarded the Word of the Lord in his life.

Samuel focused the matter: *"Behold, to obey is better than sacrifice."* Saul had *"rejected the word of the LORD, He has also rejected you from being king"* (1 Samuel 15:23b). When Samuel began walking away, Saul grabbed *"the edge of his robe,"* likely the corner tassel sewn on as a reminder of the Word of the Lord (see Numbers 15:37–41). Like the corner tassel torn from Samuel's robe, so God had *"torn the kingdom of Israel"* from disobedient Saul and given it to his *"neighbor."* Samuel obeyed the Lord and slew Agag the Amalekite, then returned to his home in Ramah where he *"grieved over Saul."*

📖 What did God instruct Samuel to do next, according to 1 Samuel 16:1? How did Samuel respond? Note what he did in 1 Samuel 16:2 and then in 16:3–5?

📖 Read verses 6–10. What did Samuel learn about how God sees people?

What did Samuel, Jesse, and his sons discover that day? What do you find in verses 12–13?

The Lord questioned Samuel's ongoing grieving over Saul. He commanded him to go to Bethlehem and anoint God's *"selected"* king from one of the sons of Jesse. Samuel had questions which God answered. Samuel obeyed. When he arrived in Bethlehem, the older men met him with fear and foreboding. He told them he came in *"peace"* to *"sacrifice to the LORD"* at Jesse's house. Samuel looked at each son, one by one, as the Lord said, in essence, "not this one," emphasizing that He looks at the heart, not a person's outward appearance.

After seeing seven sons, Samuel asked if there were any more. One more, *"the youngest . . . tending the sheep."* When David came in, the Lord said to Samuel, *"Arise, anoint him; for this is he."* With Jesse and all the brothers standing around, Samuel anointed David as the next king, and *"the Spirit of the LORD came mightily upon David from that day forward."* Samuel returned to Ramah.

The record about Samuel from this point is sparse. He continued his ministry as judge about another fifteen years. Early in David's escapes from Saul, he fled to Ramah and told Samuel all that had occurred between him and Saul (1 Samuel 19:18–24; 20:1). At that time, David and Samuel stayed in nearby Naioth in Ramah, which may simply refer to the *"dwellings"* of the school of the prophets in Ramah, for those prophets are who Saul and his men encountered (four times) when they sought to capture David there. After this, David departed.

 IN THEIR SHOES
Samuel Prayed

Samuel lived a life of praying for others. His oft quoted words in 1 Samuel 12:23 reveal this: *"Moreover, as for me, far be it from me that I should sin against the LORD by ceasing to pray for you."* Other verses that show him in prayer or speak of his praying, include 1 Samuel 7:5, 8–9; 8:6, 21–22; 12:18–19, 23; 15:11 as well as Psalm 99:6 and Jeremiah 15:1.

First Samuel 25:1 records the death of Samuel (probably around 1014 BC, age 91, with David about age 27) and his burial in Ramah. Many mourned. The next time we hear of Samuel occurred in the strange encounter of Saul with the medium or witch of Endor (1 Samuel 28:1–20). Saul saw Samuel or some manifestation like him and heard the judgment against him for his disobedience. Much debate has arisen around this incident. Whatever occurred, Saul showed his heart, even disobeying the Word of the Lord in this (Deuteronomy 18:10–14). The next day, he died in battle with the Philistines (about 72 years of age).

STOP AND APPLY—Whom Will I Follow?—The Lord wants true worship and trusting obedience from the heart. What does that look like? Consider the ways of Samuel, Saul, and David. Think about the Word of God given to each of them. What might a heart of following look like in your life? Consider the Scriptures in **Day Five: "Whom Will I Follow?"** Spend some personal time with the Lord and His Word.

DAY FIVE

WHOM WILL I FOLLOW?

S amuel was born at a time when people continued to do *"what was right in his own eyes,"* rather than following the Lord and His Word. Samuel ministered in that toxic spiritual atmosphere and brought the Word of God to people who either had never heard, had forgotten what they heard, had ignored what they heard, or opposed what they heard. The same is true today—some have never heard, some have forgotten what they heard, some have ignored what they heard, and some have purposefully opposed God and His Word, at least, the parts they have heard (or heard about). How are we to live in a day like today?

The Lord is the best leader and wants us to worship, follow, and obey Him. He knew His people would always need good leaders. He longs to be the leader of each of His children but also provides for leadership His way. One of the first instances of His clear principles for leadership came in the days of Moses.

📖 Read Exodus 18:13–26 and record the guidelines God gave for the *"able men"* who could serve alongside Moses.

 IN THEIR SHOES
Words for Leaders' Lives

The Scriptures place major importance on leaders following God and His Word. God gave very clear guidelines for leaders in several passages. A sample includes Exodus 18:17–26; 23:1–9; Deuteronomy 1:9–18; 16:18–20, and 1 Samuel 12:3–5.

📖 Note any further insights from Deuteronomy 16:18–20.

📖 Read Deuteronomy 17:6 and 19:15–21. What do you find about the necessity for honest witnesses and just trials?

God knew people would follow various leaders, some wicked, some foolish, some better, even some honest and righteous. The Lord had very clear guidelines for the leaders who would lead the people of Israel.

📖 Read Deuteronomy 17:14–20. What guidelines for leadership do you find there? Also, list the basic elements of leadership God gave for the future kings of Israel

_____

_____

_____

_____

_____

📖 When Solomon ruled as king, he wrote many songs and proverbs. One of those passages related to being a king, a leader over the people. Read Proverbs 31:1–9 and note this Spirit-directed advice under the name King Lemuel (perhaps another name for Solomon), which means "belonging to El (Almighty or Strong One), to God." What should a king do and not do?

_____

_____

_____

_____

Moses wanted God's best for the people of God. He sought to give them God's Word and wise counsel for their daily decisions as well as for disputes that might arise. Disputes, conflicts, differences of opinion did arise, and it was about to wear out Moses. His father-in-law Jethro saw this and told him so. He gave Moses wise advice: listen to me, take this to the Lord and, if He so directs, apply it. He told Moses he needed "*able men*" to come alongside him to help lead the people, to settle disputes, to bring better order and harmony among God's people. The advice was simple: install men of character in place of leadership. Character counts. What does that mean? The leaders must be those who "*fear God,*" who are "*men of truth*" and who "*hate dishonest gain*"—no bribes, no miscarriage of justice. Such leadership would enable disputes to be settled, and the people could have what (almost) everyone wanted: each could "*go to their place in peace,*" having received a good hearing and applying wise advice from the Word of God.

IN THEIR SHOES
Postures in Prayer

There are several postures in prayer in Scripture and in church history. Ezra prayed in great anguish with his robes torn, on his knees with hands "*stretched out*" to "*the LORD my*

God" (Ezra 9:5). Daniel prayed three times a day, "*kneeling on his knees*" at his open window facing west toward Jerusalem (Daniel 6:10). In John 17:1, Jesus prayed "*lifting up His eyes to heaven*" (see also Matthew 14:19) and then, in the Garden of Gethsemane, Jesus "*fell on His face,*" prostrate on the ground, praying in great agony (Matthew 26:39; Mark 14:35; Luke 22:41). Paul told Timothy in Ephesus, "*I want the men in every place to pray, lifting up holy hands*" (1 Timothy 2:8). The picture of a person kneeling with hands folded is modeled after one kneeling before a king in a medieval homage ceremony. Whatever the outward posture, the inner person is what matters, an honest, humble, holy, surrendered heart is crucial—"*Your will be done!*" (Psalms 51:6; 145:17–19; Matthew 6:10).

When Israel chose a king, as the Lord knew they would do one day, that king must be a fellow Israelite whom God Himself chooses. He was not to "*multiply horses,*" a common practice for building one's military might. The might of Israel would be the Lord, His "*right hand*" and "*arm*" at work (Psalm 44:1–8). He wanted none of the ways of Egypt in His people, nor a king having many wives, another common practice among leaders of that day. His focus must not be wealth, but the Word of God, even writing his own copy in the presence (and careful eye) of the priests so that he wrote it accurately and understood it fully. This would lead to the essential fear of "*the LORD his God,*" obedience to Him and His Word, and humbly walking before Him and before the people. No king should drain his strength with immorality or cloud his judgment with wine or strong drink. He should seek justice for everyone, especially the poor who could never repay.

📖 Have times changed? Yes. Have people changed? No. What counsel do you find for leaders in 1 Timothy 2:8? What further advice do you find in 1 Timothy 3:1–13 and 6:6–19?

📖 Some things are "*good and profitable for men,*" for all men and women (Titus 3:8). Record your insights about these "*good and profitable*" things in Titus 1:5–16; 2:1–15 and 3:1–11.

A heart without "wrath and dissension," but rather marked as "holy" is part of the recipe for every man, especially leaders. This is God's will. Those who would be leaders in a local church must be men of character —proven as to their past, predictable as to their future actions, however, understandably not perfect in the present. The qualities of 1 Timothy 3 and Titus 1 are for any man, but certainly needed in any leader. A leader must show self-control, a mark of being Spirit-controlled, never out of control or going astray due to the influence of alcohol or any other substance, nor because of pride and its hidden, but deadly dangers.

TAKEAWAYS
The Life and Times of Samuel

In Samuel's life, we can see at least four takeaways: **1)** 'Prayer First' is consistently the right choice, **2)** Faithful obedience to the God of the Word and the Word of God is His choice, **3)** Life is meant to be a Journey of following God, trusting Him step by step, **4)** God is faithful to Himself and His Word.

These principles and precepts are true for the personal life, for marriage, for family life, and for business and community life. Being an example to others starts in the home and ripples out from there like ripples in a pond. Of prime importance is one's personal relationship to Jesus, our Blessed Hope and Savior who has changed us (and is changing us) from the inside out—we are to be always growing, learning, knowing how to better relate to the Lord and others, until Jesus returns. This is certainly "good and profitable" for all of life, for every season of life.

STOP and APPLY—How About You?—In looking over the leadership advice from Jethro, Moses, and Paul, do you see any applications to your life? Note how many different cultures and times these truths passed through. First, we see them from a Midianite culture, given to an Egyptian-trained Hebrew named Moses, passed on to the Israelites as they entered Canaan, and then coming from a Tarsus-born, Jerusalem-trained Pharisee-turned-Christian leader dealing with Ephesian (Roman and Greek cultures) and Cretan cultures. They fit with any nation or people group, because people are people, God is God, and His Word is right for all. Talk with the Lord about anything on which He has focused your attention.

Lord, thank You for being the Leader and Savior in my life. Thank You for Your Word that is purer than silver from a furnace, "refined seven times" (Psalm 12:6). You and Your Word are always true, ever faithful, and filled with Your "Wisdom from Above" (James 3:13–18). Teach me what it means to worship and obey You, to trust You, listen and learn from You, and follow You and what You say day by day (Psalm 2:11–12; 32:8; Proverbs 3:5–7; Matthew 11:28–30). May I lead others to You day by day. In Jesus' name, I pray. Amen.

The Lord Is King and Judge

The Hebrew word *melek* (Strong's #4428), from the Aramaic *malaku* (to "counsel" or "advise"), is most often translated "king" and means "to reign." Linked to "consulting others" for counsel and advice, it is used over 2,500 times in the Old Testament, most referring to a human king over a city or kingdom. The Hebrew word *dayyan* (Strong's #1781) means "judge," referring to one who rules as umpire. The Hebrew word *shaphat* (Strong's #8199) means to "judge" or "pronounce sentence" for or against. The New Testament uses the Greek word *krites* (Strong's #2953, rooted in *krino* [#2919], to "distinguish"), translated "judge." It points to a just 'critic.' The Lord God, often spoken of as King and Judge in the Scriptures, needs no "counsel" or "advice."

The Lord Is King

Statement	Scripture
"The LORD sat as King at the flood; yes, the LORD sits as King forever."	Psalm 29:10
"Come, let us worship and bow down; let us kneel before the LORD our Maker."	Psalm 95:6
Speaking of Nimrod, Genesis 10:10 notes, *"the beginning of his kingdom was Babel,"* making him the first earthly king mentioned in Scripture. He also ruled over several other cities, including Nineveh.	Genesis 10:8–12
The prophecy found in Numbers 24 was to be fulfilled with a near fulfillment in the nation of Israel and a far fulfillment in the Messiah and His Kingdom, the King of Israel will be higher than all and His *"kingdom will be exalted."*	Numbers 24:3-9
The king Israel would have must be one that the Lord chooses.	Deuteronomy 17:14–20
In his blessing of the people of Israel, Moses spoke of the Lord as *"king in Jeshurun,"* another name for the nation of Israel.	Deuteronomy 33:2–5, note verses 2 and 5
The Angel of the LORD acted as a Commanding General as the *"Captain of the Hosts of the LORD"* leading Joshua at Jericho.	Joshua 5:13–15
Hannah praised the Lord for giving *"strength to His king,"* with a near fulfillment in Israel and a far fulfillment in the Coming Messiah-King Jesus.	1 Samuel 2:10
In the days of Samuel and the closing of the period of the judges, the people of Israel asked for *"a king to judge us."* The Lord told Samuel to give them their request, noting *"they have rejected Me from being King over them."*	1 Samuel 8:4–10; Acts 13:21
Referring to a former time before Saul as king, Samuel said to the Israelites, *"the LORD your God was your king."*	1 Samuel 12:12

The Queen of Sheba spoke to King Solomon, noting the Lord over all, even over Israel. She stated, "*Blessed be the LORD your God who delighted in you, setting you on His throne as king for the LORD your God...*"	2 Chronicles 8a
Referring to the Messiah King, the Father speaks of installing "*My King upon Zion.*"	Psalm 2:6
David speaks of the Lord as "*my King [melek] and my God.*"	Psalm 5:2
"*The LORD is King forever and ever.*"	Psalm 10:16
Crying out for deliverance, King David speaks of the Lord as Messiah King who can "*answer us in the day we call.*"	Psalm 20:9
Five times Psalm 24 speaks of "*the King of Glory,*" His might, salvation, and glory.	Psalm 24:7–10
The sons of Korah exclaim, "*You are my King, O God.*"	Psalm 44:4a
In a psalm to the Messiah King, the sons of Korah declare to the bride, "*the King will desire your beauty; because He is your Lord, bow down to Him.*"	Psalm 45:11
"*For the LORD Most High is to be feared, a great King over all the earth . . . Sing praises to our King, . . . For God is the King of all the earth. . . . God reigns over the nations, God sits on His holy throne.*"	Psalm 47:2, 6b, 7a, 8
"*Beautiful in elevation, the joy of the whole earth, is Mount Zion in the far north, the city of the great King.*"	Psalm 48:2; Matthew 5:35
Several verses speak of God as King or "*my King and my God.*"	Psalm 68:24; 84:3; 145:1; 149:2
Asaph penned, "*Yet God is my King from of old, who works deeds of deliverance in the midst of the earth.*"	Psalm 74:12
"*For the LORD is a great God, and a great King above all gods.*"	Psalm 95:3
"*Shout joyfully before the King, the LORD.*"	Psalm 98:6b
"*The LORD reigns, let the peoples tremble; He is enthroned above the cherubim, let the earth shake! ... Worship at His footstool; Holy is He.*"	Psalm 99:1, 5
Isaiah declared, "*My eyes have seen the King, the LORD of Hosts.*"	Isaiah 6:5; John 12:41
Isaiah prophesied about the coming Messiah who would reign—"*the government will rest on His shoulders.*" He is the "*Prince of Peace*" (Hebrew—*Sar Shalom*).	Isaiah 9:5–7
The Messiah—"*The LORD of Hosts will reign on Mount Zion and in Jerusalem.*"	Isaiah 24:23b

Speaking of the future Messiah King reigning, "Behold, a King will reign righteously."	Isaiah 32:1
"Your eyes will see the King in His Beauty..." "The LORD is our King..."	Isaiah 33:17a, 22c
"I am the LORD, your Holy One, the Creator of Israel, your King."	Isaiah 43:15
"Thus says the LORD, the King of Israel and his Redeemer, the LORD of Hosts; I am the first and I am the last, and there is no God besides Me."	Isaiah 44:6
Jeremiah assured Israel, "Is the LORD not in Zion? Is her King not within her?"	Jeremiah 8:19b
"Who would not fear you, O King of the nations?"	Jeremiah 10:7a
"But the LORD is the true God; He is the living God and the everlasting King."	Jeremiah 10:10a
"As I live," declares the Lord GOD, "surely with a mighty hand and with an outstretched arm and with wrath poured out, I shall be King over you."	Ezekiel 20:33
King Nebuchadnezzar spoke of "the Most High God" . . . "How great are His signs and how mighty are His wonders! His kingdom is an everlasting kingdom, and His dominion is from generation to generation."	Daniel 4:2-3, 34
King Nebuchadnezzar spoke of his dream and the angel's words, "the Most High is ruler over the realm of mankind." Daniel added, "It is Heaven that rules."	Daniel 4:17, 25, 26, 32; 5:21b
"Now I Nebuchadnezzar praise, exalt, and honor the King of heaven, for all His works are true and His ways just, and He is able to humble those who walk in pride."	Daniel 4:37
"I will make the lame a remnant, and the outcasts a strong nation, and the LORD will reign over them in Mount Zion from now on and forever."	Micah 4:7
A prophecy of the Coming Messiah who will rule: "But as for you, Bethlehem Ephrathah, too little to be among the clans of Judah, from you One will go forth for Me to be ruler in Israel. His goings forth are from long ago, from the days of eternity . . . . He will arise and shepherd His flock in the strength of the LORD, and in the majesty of the name of the LORD His God . . . . And this One will be our peace..."	Micah 5:2, 4a, 5a
"The King of Israel, the LORD, is in your midst..."	Zephaniah 3:15

"*Rejoice greatly, O daughter of Zion! Shout in triumph, O daughter of Jerusalem! Behold your King is coming to you; He is just and endowed with salvation, humble and mounted on a donkey, even on a colt, the foal of a donkey . . . . And He will speak peace to the nations; and His dominion will be from sea to sea, and from the River to the ends of the earth.*"	Zechariah 9:9, 10b Matthew 21:1–7 John 12:14–15
"*And the* LORD *will be king over all the earth; in that day the* LORD *will be the only one, and His name the only one . . . . Then it will come about that any who are left of all the nations that went up against Jerusalem will go up from year to year to worship the King, the* LORD *of Hosts, and to celebrate the Feast of Booths.*"	Zechariah 14:9, 16, 17
"*For I am a great King,*" says the LORD of Hosts, "*and My name is feared among the nations.*"	Malachi 1:14
"*Maji from the east*" sought and "*worshiped*" "*the Child*" Jesus as "*King of the Jews.*"	Matthew 2:1–2, 9–11
When Jesus revealed He knew Nathaniel, he replied, "*You are the King of Israel.*"	John 1:49
In Jesus' Triumphal Entry and at the Cross, people exclaimed, "*Hosanna, BLESSED IS HE WHO COMES IN THE NAME OF THE LORD, even the King of Israel.*" "*He is the King of Israel.*"	Matthew 27:42 Psalm 118:26 See also, Mark 15:32; Luke 19:38; 23:2; John 12:13.
Pilate questioned Jesus about being a king. Jesus said, "*You say correctly that I am a king. For this I have been born, and for this I have come into the world...*"	John 18:37
Pilate spoke to the Jews of Jesus as "*your King.*"	John 19:14, 15
Jesus was tried, condemned, and crucified as the "*King of the Jews.*"	Matthew 27:11, 29, 37; See also Mark 15:2, 9, 12, 18, 26; Luke 23:3, 37, 38; John 18:33, 39; 19:3, 12, 19, 21.
The dying thief, recognizing his sin and condemnation, repented of his sin and believed in Jesus as his sinless King and Savior, whose Kingdom would come—"*Lord, remember me when You come into Your Kingdom.*"	Luke 23:39–43
Certain Thessalonians derided Paul's message: "*there is another king, Jesus.*"	Acts 17:7c
Paul triumphantly declared about "*Jesus Christ,*" "*Now to the King eternal, immortal, invisible, the only God, be honor and glory forever and ever. Amen.*"	1 Timothy 1:16, 17

Paul spoke of "our Lord Jesus Christ" as "He who is the blessed and only Sovereign, the King of kings and Lord of lords." John saw Him this way in the Revelation.	1 Timothy 6:14, 15 Revelation 17:14; 19:16
Jesus, "the Son of Man," will return to earth as "King."	Matthew 25:31–34
"Great and marvelous are Your works, O Lord God the Almighty; righteous and true are Your ways, You King of the nations."	Revelation 15:3

The LORD Is Judge

Elihu spoke of the perfect "justice" of God "the Almighty." "For His eyes are upon the ways of a man, and He sees all his steps."	Job 34:10; see Job 24:23b; 31:4; Jeremiah 16:17
Hannah praised the Lord declaring, "The LORD will judge the ends of the earth."	1 Samuel 2:10
David spoke of the Lord as judge.	1 Samuel 24:15
"And He will judge the world in righteousness; He will execute judgment for the peoples with equity."	Psalm 9:8
"And the heavens declare His righteousness, For God Himself is judge."	Psalm 50:6
"But God is the Judge; He puts down one, and exalts another."	Psalm 75:7
"...The LORD... is coming to judge the earth; He will judge the world in righteousness, and the peoples in His faithfulness."	Psalm 96:13; 98:9
"The LORD is our judge..."	Isaiah 33:22a
Babylonian king Belshazzar, son of Nebuchadnezzar, faced an earthly judgment from God: "God has numbered your kingdom and put an end to it... you have been weighed on the scales and found deficient... your kingdom has been divided and given over to the Medes and Persians." He was slain that night (October 16, 539 BC).	Daniel 5:18, 21-28, 30
A judgment of condemnation rests on anyone not believing in Jesus for eternal life.	John 3:16-21
Jesus said that the Father "has given all judgment to the Son. . . . My judgment is just."	John 5:22-30
"And Jesus said, 'For judgment I came into this world, that those who do not see may see; and that those who see may become blind.'"	John 9:39
Speaking of Jesus of Nazareth, the Apostle Peter stated, "And He ordered us to preach to the people, and solemnly to testify that this is the One who has been appointed by God as Judge of the living and the dead."	Acts 10:38, 42

The Apostle Paul told the Athenians, "*Having overlooked the times of ignorance, God is now declaring to men that all everywhere should repent, because He has fixed a day in which He will judge the world in righteousness through a Man whom He has appointed, having furnished proof to all men by raising Him from the dead.*"	Acts 17:30-31
"*. . . we know . . . the judgment of God rightly falls on those who practice such things.*"	Romans 2:2, 3
Romans 2:5 speaks of "*the day of wrath and revelation of the righteous judgment of God, WHO WILL RENDER TO EVERY MAN ACCORDING TO HIS DEEDS.*"	Romans 2:5-6, 7-16 Psalm 62:12; Proverbs 24:12
"*Oh, the depths of the riches both of the wisdom and knowledge of God! How unsearchable are His judgments and unfathomable His ways!*"	Romans 11:33
All Christians will stand before the Lord at "*the Judgment Seat of God*" to acknowledge Jesus as Lord and give "*an account of himself to God.*"	Romans 14:10-12
Paul spoke of Christians receiving "*a reward*" or "*loss*" of a reward on "*the day*" when, through His "*fire,*" Christ will "*test the quality of each man's work,*" whether of "*gold, silver, precious stones, wood, hay, straw.*"	1 Corinthians 3:12-15
"*Therefore do not go on passing judgment before the time, but wait until the Lord comes who will both bring to light the things hidden in the darkness and disclose the motives of men's hearts; and then each man's praise will come to him from God.*"	1 Corinthians 4:5
"*For we must all appear before the judgment seat of Christ, that each one may be recompensed for his deeds in the body, according to what he has done, . . . good or bad.*"	2 Corinthians 5:10
Everyone, inclusive of all believers and unbelievers, "*shall give account to Him who is ready to judge the living and the dead.*"	1 Peter 4:5
Jesus, "*the Son of Man,*" will return to earth as "*King*" and judge the nations.	Matthew 25:31-46
John spoke of the Lord Jesus—"*In righteousness He judges and wages war.*"	Revelation 19:11
The Lord Jesus, on "*a Great White Throne,*" will judge every unbeliever, "*anyone*" whose "*name was not found written in the book of life.*" Each is "*judged from the things . . . written in the books, according to their deeds*" and "*thrown into the lake of fire.*"	Revelation 22:12, 13 Matthew 16:27

The Lord Jesus, *"the Alpha and the Omega,"* declares, *"Behold, I am coming quickly, and My reward is with Me, to render to every man according to what he has done."*	Revelation 22:12, 13
The Lord, the King and Judge, has written, *"'Blessed are those who wash their robes, that they may have the right to the tree of life, and may enter by the gates into the city...'I, Jesus, have sent My angel to testify to you of these things for the churches. I am the root and the offspring of David, the bright morning star.' Outside are the dogs and sorcerers and the immoral persons and the murderers and the idolaters, and everyone who loves and practices lying. And the Spirit and the bride say, 'Come.' And let the one who hears say, 'Come.' And let the one who is thirsty come; let the one who wishes take the water of life without cost."*	Revelation 22:14-17

Notes

LEADER'S GUIDE

TABLE OF CONTENTS

The best way to become a better discussion leader is to regularly evaluate your group discussion sessions. The most effective leaders are those who consistently look for ways to improve.

But before you start preparing for your first group session, you need to know the problem areas that will most likely weaken the effectiveness of your study group. Commit now to have the best Bible study group that you can possibly have. Ask the Lord to motivate you as a group leader and to steer you away from bad habits.

How to Guarantee a Poor Discussion Group:

1. Prepare inadequately.

2. Show improper attitude toward people in the group (lack of acceptance).

3. Fail to create an atmosphere of freedom and ease.

4. Allow the discussion to wander aimlessly.

5. Dominate the discussion yourself.

6. Let a small minority dominate the discussion.

7. Leave the discussion "in the air," so to speak, without presenting any concluding statements or some type of closure.

8. Ask too many "telling" or "trying" questions. (Don't ask individuals in your group pointed or threatening questions that might bring embarrassment to them or make them feel uncomfortable.)

9. End the discussion without adequate application points.

10. Do the same thing every time.

11. Become resentful and angry when people disagree with you. After all, you did prepare. You are the leader!

12. End the discussion with an argument.

13. Never spend any time with the members of your group other than the designated discussion meeting time.

Helpful Hints

One of the best ways to learn to be an effective Bible discussion leader is to sit under a good model. If you have had the chance to be in a group with an effective facilitator, think about the things that made him or her effective.

Though you can learn much and shape many convictions from those good models, you can also glean some valuable lessons on what not to do from those who didn't do such a good job. Bill Donahue has done a good job of categorizing the leader's role in facilitating dynamic discussion into four key actions. They are easy to remember as he links them to the acrostic ACTS:

*A leader ACTS to facilitate discussions by:

- Acknowledging everyone who speaks during a discussion.

- Clarifying what is being said and felt.

- Taking it to the group as a means of generating discussion.

- Summarizing what has been said.

*Taken from *Leading Life-Changing Small Groups* ©1996 by the Willow Creek Association. Used by permission of Zondervan Publishing House.

Make a point to give each group member ample opportunity to speak. Pay close attention to any nonverbal communication (i.e. facial expressions, body language, etc.) that group members may use, showing their desire to speak. The four actions in Bill Donahue's acrostic will guarantee to increase your effectiveness, which will translate into your group getting more out of the Bible study. After all, isn't that your biggest goal?

Dealing with Talkative Timothy

Throughout your experiences of leading small Bible study groups, you will learn that there will be several stereotypes who will follow you wherever you go. One of them is "Talkative Timothy." He will show up in virtually every small group you will ever lead. (Sometimes this stereotype group member shows up as "Talkative Tammy.") "Talkative Timothy" talks too much, dominates the discussion time, and gives less opportunity for others to share. What do you do with a group member who talks too much? Below you will find some helpful ideas on managing the "Talkative Timothys" in your group.

The best defense is a good offense. To deal with "Talkative Timothy" before he becomes a problem, one thing you can do is establish as a ground rule that no one can talk twice until everyone who wants to talk has spoken at least once. Another important ground rule is "no interrupting." Still another solution is to go systematically around the group, directing questions to people by name. When all else fails, you can resort to a very practical approach of sitting beside "Talkative Timothy." When you make it harder for him (or her) to make eye contact with you, you will create less chances for him to talk.

After taking one or more of these combative measures, you may find that "Timothy" is still a problem. You may need to meet with him (or her) privately. Assure him that you value his input, but remind him that you want to hear the comments of others as well. One way to diplomatically approach "Timothy" is to privately ask him to help you draw the less talkative members into the discussion. Approaching "Timothy" in this fashion may turn your dilemma into an asset. Most importantly, remember to love "Talkative Timothy."

Silent Sally

Another person who inevitably shows up is "Silent Sally." She doesn't readily speak up. Sometimes her silence is because she doesn't yet feel comfortable enough with the group to share her thoughts. Sometimes it is simply because she fears being rejected. Often her silence is because she is too polite to interrupt and thus is headed off at the pass each time she wants to speak by more aggressive (and less sensitive) members of the group.

It is not uncommon in a mixed group to find that "Silent Sally" is married to "Talkative Timothy." (Seriously!) Don't mistakenly interpret her silence as meaning that she has nothing to contribute. Often those who are slowest to speak will offer the most meaningful contributions to the group. You can help "Silent Sally" make those significant contributions. Below are some ideas.

Make sure, first of all, that you are creating an environment that makes people comfortable. In a tactful way, direct specific questions to the less talkative in the group. Be careful though, not to put them on the spot with the more difficult or controversial questions. Become their biggest fan—make sure you cheer them on when they do share. Give them a healthy dose of affirmation. Compliment them afterward for any insightful contributions they make. You may want to sit across from them in the group so that it is easier to notice any nonverbal cues they give you when they want to speak. You should also come to their defense if another group member responds to them in a negative, stifling way. As you pray for each group member, ask that the Lord would help the quiet ones in your group to feel more at ease during the discussion time. Most of all, love "Silent Sally," and accept her as she is—even when she is silent!

Tangent Tom

We have already looked at "Talkative Timothy" and "Silent Sally." Now let's look at another of those stereotypes who always show up. Let's call this person, "Tangent Tom." He is the kind of guy who loves to talk even when he has nothing to say. "Tangent Tom" loves to chase rabbits regardless of where they go. When he gets the floor, you never know where the discussion will lead. You need to understand that not all tangents are bad, for sometimes much can be gained from discussion that is a little "off the beaten path." But diversions must be balanced against the purpose of the group. What is fruitful for one member may be fruitless for everyone else. Below are some ideas to help you deal with "Tangent Tom."

EVALUATING TANGENTS
Ask yourself, "How will this tangent affect my group's chances of finishing the lesson?" Another way to measure the value of a tangent is by asking, "Is this something that will benefit all or most of the group?" You also need to determine whether there is a practical, spiritual benefit to this tangent. Paul advised Timothy to refuse foolish and ignorant speculations, knowing that they produce quarrels. (See 2 Timothy 2:23.)

ADDRESSING TANGENTS:

1) Keep pace of your time, and use the time factor as your ally when addressing "Tangent Tom." Tactfully respond, "That is an interesting subject, but since our lesson is on _____, we'd better get back to our lesson if we are going to finish."

2) If the tangent is beneficial to one but fruitless to the rest of the group, offer to address that subject after class.

3) If the tangent is something that will benefit the group, you may want to say, "I'd like to talk about that more. Let's come back to that topic at the end of today's discussion, if we have time."

4) Be sure you understand what "Tangent Tom" is trying to say. It may be that he has a good and valid point, but has trouble expressing it or needs help in being more direct. Be careful not to quench someone whose heart is right, even if his methods aren't perfect. (See Proverbs 18:23.)

5) One suggestion for diffusing a strife-producing tangent is to point an imaginary shotgun at a spot outside the group and act like you are firing a shot. Then say, "That rabbit is dead. Now, where were we?"

6) If it is a continual problem, you may need to address it with this person privately.

7) Most of all, be patient with "Tangent Tom." God will use him in the group in ways that will surprise you!

Know–It-All Ned

The Scriptures are full of characters who struggled with the problem of pride. Unfortunately, pride isn't a problem reserved for the history books. It shows up today just as it did in the days the Scriptures were written.

Pride is sometimes the root-problem of a know-it-all group member. "Know-It-All Ned" may have shown up in your group by this point. He may be an intellectual giant, or only a legend in his own mind. He can be very prideful and argumentative. "Ned" often wants his point chosen as the choice point, and he may be intolerant of any opposing views—sometimes to the point of making his displeasure known in very inappropriate ways. A discussion point tainted with the stench of pride is uninviting—no matter how well spoken!

No one else in the group will want anything to do with this kind of attitude. How do you manage the "Know-It-All Neds" who show up from time to time?

EVALUATION

To deal with "Know-It-All Ned," you need to understand him. Sometimes the same type of action can be rooted in very different causes. You must ask yourself, "Why does 'Ned' come across as a know-it-all?" It may be that "Ned" has a vast reservoir of knowledge but hasn't matured in how he communicates it. Or perhaps "Ned" really doesn't know it all, but he tries to come across that way to hide his insecurities and feelings of inadequacy.

Quite possibly, "Ned" is prideful and arrogant, and knows little of the Lord's ways in spite of the information and facts he has accumulated. Still another possibility is that "Ned" is a good man with a good heart who has a blind spot in the area of pride.

APPLICATION

"Know-It-All Ned" may be the most difficult person to deal with in your group, but God will use him in ways that will surprise you. Often it is the "Neds" of the church that teach each of us what it means to love the unlovely in Gods strength, not our own. In 1 Thessalonians 5:14, the apostle Paul states, "And we urge you, brethren, admonish the unruly, encourage the fainthearted, help the weak, be patient with all men." In dealing with the "Neds" you come across, start by assuming they are weak and need help until they give you reason to believe otherwise. Don't embarrass them by confronting them in public. Go to them in private if need be.

Speak the truth in love. You may need to remind them of 1 Corinthians 13, that if we have all knowledge, but have not love, we are just making noise. First Corinthians is also where we are told, *"knowledge makes arrogant, but love edifies"* (8:1). Obviously, there were some "Neds" in the church at Corinth. If you sense that "Ned" is not weak or faint-hearted, but in fact is unruly, you will need to admonish him. Make sure you do so in private, but make sure you do it all the same. Proverbs 27:56 tells us, *"Better is open rebuke than love that is concealed. Faithful are the wounds of a friend, but deceitful are the kisses of an enemy."* Remember the last statement in 1 Thessalonians 5:14, *"be patient with all men."*

Agenda Alice

The last person we would like to introduce to you who will probably show up sooner or later is one we like to call "Agenda Alice." All of us from time to time can be sidetracked by our own agenda. Often the very thing we are most passionate about can be the thing that distracts us from our highest passion: Christ. Agendas often are not unbiblical, but imbalanced. At their root is usually tunnel-vision mixed with a desire for control. The small group, since it allows everyone to contribute to the discussion, affords "Agenda Alice" a platform to promote what she thinks is most important. This doesn't mean that she is wrong to avoid driving at night because opossums are being killed, but she is wrong to expect everyone to have the exact same conviction and calling that she does in the gray areas of Scripture. If not managed properly, she will either sidetrack the group from its main study objective or create a hostile environment in the group if she fails to bring people to her way of thinking. "Agenda Alice" can often be recognized by introductory catch phrases such as "Yes, but . . ." and "Well, I think. . . ." She is often critical of the group process and may become vocally critical of you. Here are some ideas on dealing with this type of person:

1) Reaffirm the group covenant.

At the formation of your group you should have taken time to define some ground rules for the group. Once is not enough to discuss these matters of group etiquette. Periodically remind everyone of their mutual commitment to one another.

2) Remember that the best defense is a good offense.

Don't wait until it is a problem to address a mutual vision for how the group will function.

3) Refocus on the task at hand.

The clearer you explain the objective of each session, the easier it is to stick to that objective and the harder you make it for people to redirect attention toward their own agenda. Enlist the whole group in bringing the discussion back to the topic at hand. Ask questions like, "What do the rest of you think about this passage?"

4) Remind the group, "Remember, this week's lesson is about _____."

5) Reprove those who are disruptive.

Confront the person in private to see if you can reach an understanding. Suggest another arena for the issue to be addressed such as an optional meeting for those in the group who would like to discuss the issue.

Remember the words of St. Augustine: "In essentials unity, in non-essentials liberty, in all things charity."

Adding Spice and Creativity

One of the issues you will eventually have to combat in any group Bible study is the enemy of boredom. This enemy raises its ugly head from time to time, but it shouldn't. It is wrong to bore people with the Word of God! Often boredom results when leaders allow their processes to become too predictable. As small group leaders, we tend to do the same thing in the same way every single time. Yet God the Creator, who spoke everything into existence is infinitely creative! Think about it. He is the one who not only created animals in different shapes and sizes, but different colors as well. When He created food, He didn't make it all taste or feel the same. This God of creativity lives in us. We can trust Him to give us creative ideas that will keep our group times from becoming tired and mundane. Here are some ideas:

When you think of what you can change in your Bible study, think of the five senses: (sight, sound, smell, taste, and feel).

SIGHT:
One idea would be to have a theme night with decorations. Perhaps you know someone with dramatic instincts who could dress up in costume and deliver a message from the person you are studying that week.

Draw some cartoons on a marker board or handout.

SOUND:
Play some background music before your group begins. Sing a hymn together that relates to the lesson. If you know of a song that really hits the main point of the lesson, play it at the beginning or end.

SMELL:

This may be the hardest sense to involve in your Bible study, but if you think of a creative way to incorporate this sense into the lesson, you can rest assured it will be memorable for your group.

TASTE:

Some lessons will have issues that can be related to taste (e.g. unleavened bread for the Passover, etc.). What about making things less formal by having snacks while you study? Have refreshments around a theme such as "Chili Night" or "Favorite Fruits."

FEEL:

Any way you can incorporate the sense of feel into a lesson will certainly make the content more invigorating. If weather permits, add variety by moving your group outside. Whatever you do, be sure that you don't allow your Bible study to become boring!

Handling an Obviously Wrong Comment

From time to time, each of us can say stupid things. Some of us, however, are better at it than others. The apostle Peter had his share of embarrassing moments. One minute, he was on the pinnacle of success, saying, *"Thou art the Christ, the Son of the Living God"* (Matthew 16:16), and the next minute, he was putting his foot in his mouth, trying to talk Jesus out of going to the cross. Proverbs 10:19 states, *"When there are many words, transgression is unavoidable. . . ."* What do you do when someone in the group says something that is obviously wrong? First of all, remember that how you deal with a situation like this not only affects the present, but the future. Here are some ideas:

1) Let the whole group tackle it and play referee/peacemaker. Say something like, "That is an interesting thought, what do the rest of you think?"

2) Empathize. ("I've thought that before too, but the Bible says. . . .")

3) Clarify to see if what they said is what they meant. ("What I think you are saying is. . . .")

4) Ask the question again, focusing on what the Bible passage actually says.

5) Give credit for the part of the answer that is right and affirm that before dealing with what is wrong.

6) If it is a non-essential, disagree agreeably. ("I respect your opinion, but I see it differently.")

7) Let it go —some things aren't important enough to make a big deal about them.

8) Love and affirm the person, even if you reject the answer.

Transitioning to the Next Study

For those of you who have completed leading a Following God Group Bible Study, congratulations! You have successfully navigated the waters of small group discussion. You have utilized one of the most effective tools of ministry—one that was so much a priority with Jesus, He spent most of His time there with His small group of twelve. Hopefully yours has been a very positive and rewarding experience. At this stage you may be looking forward to a break. It is not too early however, to be thinking and planning for what you will do next. Hopefully you have seen God use this study and this process for growth in the lives of those who have participated with you. As God has worked in the group, members should be motivated to ask the question, "What next?" As they do, you need to be prepared to give an answer. Realize that you have built a certain amount of momentum with your present study that will make it easier to do another. You want to take advantage of that momentum. The following suggestions may be helpful as you transition your people toward further study of God's Word.

- Challenge your group members to share with others what they have learned, and to encourage them to participate next time.

- If what to study is a group choice rather than a church-wide or ministry-wide decision made by others, you will want to allow some time for input from the group members in deciding what to do next. The more they have ownership of the study, the more they will commit to it.

- It is important to have some kind of a break so that everyone doesn't become study weary. At our church, we always look for natural times to start and end a study. We take the summer off as well as Christmas, and we have found that having a break brings people back with renewed vigor. Even if you don't take a break from meeting, you might take a breather from homework—or even get together just for fellowship.

- If you are able to end this study knowing what you will study next, some of your group members may want to get a head start on the next study. Be prepared to put books in their hands early.

- Make sure you end your study with a vision for more. Take some time to remind your group of the importance of the Word of God. As D. L. Moody used to say, "The only way to keep a broken vessel full is to keep the faucet running."

Evaluation

Becoming a Better Discussion Leader

The questions listed below are tools to assist you in assessing your discussion group. From time to time in the Leader's Guide, you will be advised to read through this list of evaluation questions in order to help you decide what areas need improvement in your role as group leader. Each time you read through this list, something different may catch your attention, giving you tips on how to become the best group leader that you can possibly be.

Read through these questions with an open mind, asking the Lord to prick your heart with anything specific He would want you to apply.

1. Are the group discussion sessions beginning and ending on time?

2. Am I allowing the freedom of the Holy Spirit as I lead the group in the discussion?

3. Do I hold the group accountable for doing their homework?

4. Do we always begin our sessions with prayer?

5. Is the room arranged properly (seating in a circle or semicircle, proper ventilation, adequate teaching aids)?

6. Is each individual allowed equal opportunity in the discussion?

7. Do I successfully bridle the talkative ones?

8. Am I successfully encouraging the hesitant ones to participate in the discussion?

9. Do I redirect comments and questions to involve more people in the interaction, or do I always dominate the discussion?

10. Are the discussions flowing naturally, or do they take too many "side roads" (diversions)?

11. Do I show acceptance to those who convey ideas with which I do not agree?

12. Are my questions specific, brief and clear?

13. Do my questions provoke thought, or do they only require pat answers?

14. Does each group member feel free to contribute or question, or is there a threatening or unnecessarily tense atmosphere?

15. Am I allowing time for silence and thought without making everyone feel uneasy?

16. Am I allowing the group to correct any obviously wrong conclusions that are made by others, or by myself (either intentionally to capture the group's attention or unintentionally)?

17. Do I stifle thought and discussion by assigning a question to someone before the subject of that question has even been discussed? (It will often be productive to assign a question to a specific person, but if you call on one person before you throw out a question, everyone else takes a mental vacation!)

18. Do I summarize when brevity is of the essence?

19. Can I refrain from expressing an opinion or comment that someone else in the group could just as adequately express?

20. Do I occasionally vary in my methods of conducting the discussion?

21. Am I keeping the group properly motivated?

22. Am I occasionally rotating the leadership to help others develop leadership?

23. Am I leading the group to specifically apply the truths that are learned?

24. Do I follow through by asking the group how they have applied the truths that they have learned from previous lessons?

25. Am I praying for each group member?

26. Is there a growing openness and honesty among my group members?

27. Are the group study sessions enriching the lives of my group members?

28. Have I been adequately prepared?

29. How may I be better prepared for the next lesson's group discussion?

30. Do I reach the objective set for each discussion? If not, why not? What can I do to improve?

31. Am I allowing the discussion to bog down on one point at the expense of the rest of the lesson?

32. Are the members of the group individually reaching the conclusions that I want them to reach without my having to give them the conclusions?

33. Do I encourage the group members to share what they have learned?

34. Do I encourage them to share the applications they have discovered?

35. Do I whet their appetites for next week's lesson discussion?

Getting Started

The First Meeting of Your Bible Study Group

Main Objectives of the First Meeting: The first meeting is devoted to establishing your group and setting the course that you will follow through the study. Your primary goals for this session should be to . . .

- Establish a sense of group identity by starting to get to know one another.

- Define some ground rules to help make the group time as effective as possible.

- Get the study materials into the hands of your group members.

- Create a sense of excitement and motivation for the study.

- Give assignments for next week.

BEFORE THE SESSION

You will be most comfortable in leading this introductory session if you are prepared as much as possible for what to expect. This means becoming familiar with the place you will meet, and the content you will cover, as well as understanding any time constraints you will have.

Location—Be sure that you not only know how to find the place where you will be meeting, but also have time to examine the setup and make any adjustments to the physical arrangements. You never get a second chance to make a first impression.

Curriculum—You will want to get a copy of the study in advance of the introductory session, and it will be helpful if you do the homework for Lesson One ahead of time. This will make it easier for you to be able to explain the layout of the homework. It will also give you a contagious enthusiasm for what your group will be studying in the coming week.

You will want to have enough books on hand for the number of people you expect so that they can get started right away with the study. You may be able to make arrangements with your church or local Christian Bookstore to bring copies on consignment. We would encourage you not to buy books for your members. Years of small group experience have taught that people take a study far more seriously when they make an investment in it.

Time—The type of group you are leading will determine the time format for your study. If you are doing this study for a Sunday school class or church study course, the time constraints may already be prescribed for you. In any case, ideally you will want to allow forty-five minutes to an hour for discussion.

WHAT TO EXPECT

When you embark on the journey of leading a small group Bible study, you are stepping into the stream of the work of God. You are joining in the process of helping others move toward spiritual maturity. As a small group leader, you are positioned to be a real catalyst in the lives of your group members, helping them to grow in their relationships with God. But you must remember, first and foremost, that whenever you step up to leadership in the kingdom of God, you are stepping down to serve. Jesus made it clear that leadership in the kingdom is not like leadership in the world. In Matthew 20:25, Jesus said, *"You know that the rulers of the Gentiles lord it over them, and their great men exercise authority over them."* That is the world's way to lead. But in Matthew 20:26–27, He continues, *"It is not so among you, but whoever wishes to become great among you shall be your servant, and whoever wishes to be first among you shall be your slave."* Your job as a small group leader is not to teach the group everything you have learned, but rather, to help them learn.

If you truly are to minister to the members of your group, you must start with understanding where they are, and join that with a vision of where you want to take them. In this introductory session, your group members will be experiencing several different emotions. They will be wondering, "Who is in my group?" and deciding "Do I like my group?" They will have a sense of excitement and anticipation, but also a sense of awkwardness as they try to find their place in this group. You will want to make sure that from the very beginning your group is founded with a sense of caring and acceptance. This is crucial if your group members are to open up and share what they are learning.

DURING THE SESSION

GETTING TO KNOW ONE ANOTHER

Opening Prayer—Remember that if it took the inspiration of God for people to write Scripture, it will also take His illumination for us to understand it. Have one of your group members open your time together in prayer.

Introductions—Take time to allow the group members to introduce themselves. Along with having the group members share their names, one way to add some interest is to have them add some descriptive information such as where they live or work. Just for fun, you could have them name their favorite breakfast cereal, most (or least) favorite vegetable, favorite cartoon character, their favorite city or country other than their own, etc.

Icebreaker—Take five or ten minutes to get the people comfortable in talking with each other. Since in many cases your small group will just now be getting to know one another, it will be helpful if you take some time to break the ice with some fun, nonthreatening discussion. Below you will find a list of ideas for good icebreaker questions to get people talking.

____ What is the biggest risk you have ever taken?

____ If money were no object, where would you most like to take a vacation and why?

____ What is your favorite way to waste time?

____ If you weren't in the career you now have, what would have been your second choice for a career?

____ If you could have lived in any other time, in what era or century would you have chosen to live (besides the expected spiritual answer of the time of Jesus)?

____ If you became blind right now, what would you miss seeing the most?

____ Who is the most famous person you've known or met?

____ What do you miss most about being a kid?

____ What teacher had the biggest impact on you in school (good or bad)?

____ Of the things money can buy, what would you most like to have?

____ What is your biggest fear?

____ If you could give one miracle to someone else, what would it be (and to whom)?

____ Tell about your first job.

____ Who is the best or worst boss you ever had?

____ Who was your hero growing up and why?

DEFINING THE GROUP: 5–10 MINUTES
SETTING SOME GROUND RULES

There are several ways you can lay the tracks on which your group can run. One is simply to hand out a list of suggested commitments the members should make to the group. Another would be to hand out 3x5 cards and have the members themselves write down two or three commitments they would like to see everyone live out. You could then compile these into the five top ones to share at the following meeting. A third option is to list three (or more) commitments you are making to the group and then ask that they make three commitments back to you in return. Here are some ideas for the types of ground rules that make for a good small group:

Leader:

____ To always arrive prepared

____ To keep the group on track so you make the most of the group's time

____ To not dominate the discussion by simply teaching the lesson

____ To pray for the group members

____ To not belittle or embarrass anyone's answers

____ To bring each session to closure and end on time

Member:

____ To do my homework

_____ To arrive on time

_____ To participate in the discussion

_____ To not cut others off as they share

_____ To respect the different views of other members

_____ To not dominate the discussion

It is possible that your group may not need to formalize a group covenant, but you should not be afraid to expect a commitment from your group members. They will all benefit from defining the group up front.

INTRODUCTION TO THE STUDY:
15–20 MINUTES

As you introduce the study to the group members, your goal is to begin to create a sense of excitement about the Bible characters and applications that will be discussed. The most important question for you to answer in this session is "Why should I study _____?" You need to be prepared to guide them to finding that answer. Take time to give a brief overview of each lesson.

CLOSING: 5–10 MINUTES

Give homework for next week. In addition to simply reminding the group members to do their homework, if time allows, you might give them 5–10 minutes to get started on their homework for the first lesson.

Key components for closing out your time are a) to review anything of which you feel they should be reminded, and b) to close in prayer. If time allows, you may want to encourage several to pray.

PREPARATION OF THE DISCUSSION LEADER

I. Preparation of the Leader's Heart

A. Pray. It took the inspiration of the Holy Spirit to write Scripture, and it will require His illumination to correctly understand it.

B. Complete the Bible Study Yourself

1. Prayerfully seek a fresh word from God for yourself. Your teaching should be an overflow of what God taught you.

2. Even if you have completed this study in the past, consider using a new book. You need to be seeking God for what He would teach you this time before looking at what He taught you last time.

3. Guard against focusing on how to present truths to class. Keep the focus on God teaching you.

II. Keeping the Big Picture in Sight

One value of discussion: It allows students to share what God's Word says.

A. Looking back over the homework, find the one main unifying truth. There will be a key emphasis of each day, but all will support one main truth. Keep praying and looking until you find it (even if the author didn't make it clear).

B. Begin to write questions for each day's homework. Do this as you go through the study.

1. Consider key passage(s) for the day and ask questions of the text. For example, use the 5 Ws and an H (Who, What, When, Where, Why, and How): What was Jesus' main point? What is the context here? Do you see any cultural significance to this statement? How did this person relate to... (God? His neighbor? An unbeliever? The church? etc.)

2. Don't ask, "What do you think" questions unless it's "What do you think GOD is saying...?" It's easy to slip into sharing opinions if we don't carefully guide students to consider what God says. What I think doesn't matter if it differs from what God thinks.

3. Ask application questions as well. For example, "What steals our joy?" "How are we like these Bible characters?" "How can we learn from _____'s lessons so that we don't have to learn it the hard way?" "How can I restore/protect my _____ (joy, faith, peace...)?" Consider making a list where you write answers to "So what?" questions: So, what does this mean to me? How do I put this truth into practice?

4. Include definitions, grammar notes, historical/cultural notes, cross references, and so forth, from your own study. Go back over your notes/questions and add/delete/re-write after further prayer and thought. Go through your notes again, highlighting

(underlining, color coding, whatever works for you) what you believe is MOST important. This will help when time gets cut short. It will also jog your memory before moving to next day's homework,

III. Leading the Discussion

A. Begin with prayer

1. Consider varying the method - this will help to remind the group that we pray not as habit but as needy children seeking our loving Father Who teaches us by His Spirit.

2. If having a time of prayer requests, consider ways to make it time effective and to avoid gossip disguised as a prayer request. Time management is a way you can serve the group.

B. Start the Study with Review—Briefly review context of the study (or have a student come prepared to do it). This keeps the group together for those joining the study late or who've missed a week. This also serves as a reminder since it's been a week or so since your previous study session.

C. Go through the study questions day by day.

1. You may offer a "unifying theme" of study or ask if students can identify a theme.

2. Follow the Holy Spirit. Remember that you can't cover everything from every day. As you prepare, highlight any notes He leads you to consider as being most important.

3. Watch your time! When you are leading a group Bible study, you enter into a different dimension of the physical realm. Time moves at a completely different pace. What is 20 minutes in normal time flies by like 5 minutes when you are in the speaking zone.

4. Manage the questions raised by students and consider their value to the whole group within time constraints. Turn any questions raised back to the group.

5. Whether you make application day by day (probably best) or make application at the end, be sure to allow time for students to name ways to put knowledge into practice.

IV. Evaluation

1. After 1-2 days, evaluate how the lesson went.

2. Thank God—thank Him for using His Word in all participants' lives and ask Him to guard the good seed planted!

V. Begin Preparation for the Next Lesson

Lesson #1 - The Times of the Judges:
Coming Back to Following God

Memory Verse: Jeremiah 6:16

*"Thus says the LORD, 'Stand by the ways and see and ask for the ancient paths,
where the good way is, and walk in it; and you shall find rest for your souls,' But they said,
'We will not walk in it.'"*

BEFORE THE SESSION

- Your own preparation is key not only to your effectiveness in leading the group session, but also in your **confidence** in leading. It is hard to be confident if you know you are unprepared. These discussion questions and leader's notes are meant to be a helpful addition to your own study, but should never become a substitute.

- As you do your homework, study with a view to your own relationship with God. Resist the temptation to bypass this self-evaluation on your way to preparing to lead the group. Nothing will minister to your group more than the testimony of your own walk with God.

- Don't think of your ministry to the members of your group as something that only takes place during your group time. Pray for your group members by name during the week that they would receive spiritual enrichment from doing their daily homework. Encourage them as you have opportunity.

WHAT TO EXPECT

Knowing facts and figures about the history of Israel is useless if we do not apply these truths to our hearts, especially to our walk with the True God. Most people know very little of the times of the Judges or even the historical matters of the Old Testament. These events, people, and their faith or lack of faith give many illustrations for today's believer. They are like the 'box top' of a jigsaw puzzle that gives the 'Big Picture' and helps put more of the pieces together. This lesson begins by looking at the big picture from *Genesis* to *Judges*. It is important to help your group see the big picture without getting lost in the details. At the same time, it is essential to help focus the group on the personal applications of that time in history as well as seeing the applications from the people of those days.

Help your group see the importance of hearing what God is saying in the account of the "Judges." It mattered then and it matters now. Encourage them to share insights that God has shown them.

THE MAIN POINT

The main point to be seen in this introduction to the "Times of the Judges" is who is going to lead me and whom will I follow in life. The traps of idolatry, false worship, and the entanglements of "my opinion" did not go away after this period.

DURING THE SESSION

OPENING: 5–10 MINUTES

Opening Prayer – A good prayer with which to open your time is the prayer in Psalm 119:18, "*Open my eyes, that I may behold Wonderful things from Your law.*" Remember, if it took the illumination of God for the writing of Scripture, it will take the same for us to understand it.

Opening Illustration – Google "Leadership" and you will find 171,000,000 results— some helpful, some comical, and some very wrong. Many remain dissatisfied with the various suggestions and ideas, still looking for ways to be a better leader. What does it take to lead or to be a good leader? At least five key components come to mind.

1. **Following**—Someone or something worth following. Who is that? What is that?

2. **Fighting**—What is worth fighting for or against? What is worth my time and effort?

3. **Freedom**—What gives space, room to be creative and grow and be fruitful?

4. **Friends and Foes**—Who is with me, for me? Who is against me? Why? How? Where?

5. **The Forever Factor**—What matters forever? Is it last month's T-Ball winner, the Best Apple Pie at the County Fair, the latest "National" or "World" Champion in something?

It boils down to this: Whom or what **can I follow**? We know the answer is simple: someone or something that is good and real and true. Scripture is clear: God is good and real and true. He knows how to lead and how to guide others in leading.

DISCUSSION: 30 MINUTES

Study diligently in your preparation time. This will help you guide the discussion as well as answer many of the questions that arise in your group. Knowing the ways of God as The Leader in life can help your group in many areas of their Christian walk. Right Leadership is the need in every area of life. As you trek through the lesson, seek to keep the main point the main point and be sure to leave time for the application points in Day Five. There is nothing more important than emphasizing personal application.

Main Objective in Day One: In Day One, the main objective is to answer the question that has been surfacing since the beginning of time: "Who is Going to Lead?" God looks at the heart and wants each one to have His Wisdom that comes from a worshiping and obedient heart. In addition to any discussion questions you may have in mind, the list of questions below may also contain useful discussion-starter ideas.

___ Adam and the Woman thought they knew what was "good" or Best. What happened as a result?

___ What happens when we start comparing—comparing ourselves with others, comparing appearances, clothes, money or riches (or lack thereof), even comparing ministries? What did the people of Israel do when they started comparing their nation with other nations? Was this good or bad? How?

___ Why do you think the Lord let's people sometimes have what they 'want'?

___ What are some of the things people seek today? How does that affect people's lives? How does it (or could it) affect those around them? What is God's advice in these matters?

Main Objective in Day Two: In Day Two, the main objective is to see how Joshua led the people of Israel as he followed the Lord in the various challenges he faced. Check which discussion questions you will use from Day Two.

___ From your reading of the details of Joshua's life, what stands out about him?

___ How important is knowing the Word of God in making right decisions or going in the right direction?

___ What does it mean to listen to the Lord? How can we do that today? What do you learn from Joshua about this?

___ How can we influence others today? What should each of us be doing to help those who will lead in future days?

Main Objective in Day Three: In Day Three, our main objective is to see the successes and failures of the children of Israel and how these matters Impacted them. Below, are some suggested discussion starters for you to consider.

___ How important is prayer? Why does it matter that we follow the Lord and His guidance?

___ How does the *Book of Judges* show that we need the Lord and one another?

___ What characteristics of Caleb do you see in today's Scripture passages? Why are these important?

___ Do our 'successes' or 'failures' really matter? Why is it important to follow the Lord and what He says

Main Objective in Day Four: Day Four's main objective is to see how bad sin and self-will are and how good God and His Word are. Check any questions that are applicable for your Day Four-discussion time.

___ What do the words of the Angel of the LORD mean to you? Should the Israelites have listened to Him?

___ What should go with listening to the Lord and His Word? Is hearing alone enough? Why or why not?

___ Is the Cycle of Sin and Deliverance in Judges relevant for today? How or how not?

___ How important is it to know and follow the Lord and His Word? What 'fruit' does sin and stubbornness bring?

Day Five – Key Points in Application: The most important application point in "The Times of the Judges" is the crucial realities of knowing the Lord and His Word. This leads to right relationships and right actions—with Him and with others. Check which discussion questions you will use to help focus the applications from Day Five.

___ What about Jesus stands out to you in the passages explored in Day Five?

___ What one or two application points come to mind when looking at how Jesus lived?

___ Did you discover anything new about God's Word or its importance to you?

___ How important is knowing Jesus and obeying His Word?

CLOSING: 5–10 MINUTES

Summarize – Restate the key points highlighted in the class. You may want to reread "The Main Point" statement for this lesson.

Focus—Using the memory verse (Jeremiah 6:16), focus the group again on what it means to walk with God by faith. Remind the members of your group that life is meant to be lived walking with God not against Him.

Ask them to share their thoughts about the key applications from Day Five.

Preview – Take a few moments to preview next week's lesson on **"God's Reliability—Our Availability: Dealing with Sin and Evil God's Way."** Encourage your group members to do their homework in proper fashion by spacing it out over the week.

Pray – Close in prayer.

TOOLS FOR GOOD DISCUSSION

Some who are reading this have led small group Bible studies many times. Here is an important word of warning: experience alone does not make you a more effective discussion leader. In fact, experience can make you less effective. You see, the more experience you have the more comfortable you will be at the task. Unfortunately, for some that means becoming increasingly comfortable in doing a bad job. Taking satisfaction with mediocrity translates into taking the task less seriously. It is easy to wrongly assert that just because one is experienced, he or she can successfully "shoot from the hip" so to speak. If you really want your members to get the most out of this study, you need to be dissatisfied with simply doing an adequate job and make it your aim to do an excellent job. A key to excellence is regularly evaluating yourself to see that you are still doing all that you need to be doing. We have prepared a list of over thirty evaluation questions for you to review from time to time. This list of questions can be found on page 186 in this Leader's Guide. The examination questions will help jog your memory and, hopefully, will become an effective aid in improving the quality of your group discussion. Review the evaluation questions list, and jot down below two or three action points for you to begin implementing next week.

ACTION POINTS:

1.

2.

3.

Lesson #2—God's Reliability—Our Availability:
Dealing with Sin and Evil God's Way
Memory Verse: Judges 3:15

"But when the sons of Israel cried to the LORD,
the LORD raised up a deliver for them."

BEFORE THE SESSION

• Pray for your group as they study through this week's lesson.

• Remember that your goal is not to teach the lesson, but to facilitate discussion.

• As you walk through this lesson, keep in mind that the Lord does not change, that He longs to hear righteous, repentant prayer, and that He works in answer to prayer

• As you study, remember to highlight key statements and jot down those ideas and questions you want to discuss or ask as you go through this lesson with your small group.

WHAT TO EXPECT

God is God, ever reliable and faithful. God has not changed; the Scripture is very clear about that, but most people do not believe that. This was true in the days of the Judges; His reliability was very real in that day, just as for today. Sometimes (even often) in our day, people do not believe this; they think God and Scripture are outmoded concepts or old-fashioned beliefs, certainly not for the Twenty-first century. He also continues to call us to be available and will use the available life according to His wisdom and will. Expect your group members to come with hungry hearts, some with a few doubts. This is a great time to refocus on the reliability of God. Help each see that He can be trusted, and each needs to be available to Him. What He said and did thousands of years ago still matters today.

As mentioned in the last lesson, help your group grasp the significance of the period of the Judges, not just for the nation of Israel, but for each believer's life in any period of history. God encourages and empowers the available, teachable heart. Encourage them to share insights God has shown them.

THE MAIN POINT

The main point in this overview of Judges 3—5 is to see God's reliability and His readiness to use the available life, not the perfect life or the life with all the answers. He uses a variety of people, the one constant being readiness to worship and obey Him, the One True God. The snares of opposition and others' opinions are ever nearby. Follow God and His Word!

OPENING: 5–10 MINUTES

Opening Prayer – Ask someone in your group to open the session in prayer.

Opening Illustration – For years the slogan, "The Quality Goes in Before the Name Goes On" was used by the Zenith Company about their radios and TVs. In a similar, but much greater way, our Heavenly Father has always been marked by quality, perfect in every way. He is good and righteous and wants His people to be the same, revealing that in actions and words. When people in Israel acted evil, He dealt with it, chastening them in His covenant faithfulness. When they cried out to Him, He responded. The members of your group need to understand the character and power of God. Jesus revealed that and by His Spirit is continuing to make the Father more clear and real in daily life. In this week's lesson, God's reliability and His willingness to work through the available life are clearly illustrated. Help your group grasp these truths and their application points.

DISCUSSION: 30 MINUTES

Make your preparation time a priority this week. Diligent preparation can help you as you guide the discussion. It can also aid you in answering many of the questions that arise in your group. Knowing God's reliability, His character and power, can encourage you and your group in many areas of their walk. Knowing God is reliable and ready to use the available heart is a truth for every heart. As you walk through this Scripture adventure, seek to keep the main point the main point and be sure to leave time for the application points in Day Five. Knowing how these truths apply to any and every heart can encourage and help each believer grow.

Main Objective in Day One: In Day One, the main objective is to see God's reliability and His creativity in how he uses people. How does He want to creatively use any one life this week? Think through your discussion questions as well as the list of questions given below as you look for useful discussion-starter ideas.

___ Define *"evil"* using Judges 3:7. What matters to God?

___ What do God's chastening actions reveal about Him? Is chastening good for a person? How so or not so?

___ Is prayer really effective? What did you discover in the lives of the Israelites in Othniel's day?

___ What significance did the Spirit of the LORD have in Othniel's life? What came as a result?

Main Objective in Day Two: In Day Two, the main objective is to see how God sometimes simply uses who and what is available to reveal Himself and fulfill His will. Check which discussion questions you will use from Day Two.

___ Does *"evil"* ever get better or "OK"? What does God's response to Israel's "evil" tell you about God and about "evil"?

___ How important is prayer? In a difficult day, God answered prayer by raising up Ehud, an imperfect leader—what does this tell you about some of God's ways?

___ Apparently, where *"evil"* rules, battles must come. What do Ehud's victories tell us?

___ How important is 'peace' to a person? To a nation? What would 80 years of being *"undisturbed"* mean?

Main Objective in Day Three: In Day Three, our main objective is to see the successes and failures of the children of Israel and how these matters impacted them. Below, are some suggested discussion starters for you to consider.

___ How important is prayer? Why does it matter that we follow the Lord and His guidance?

___ How does the *Book of Judges* show that we need the Lord and one another?

___ What characteristics of Caleb do you see in today's Scripture passages? Why are these important?

___ Do our 'successes' or 'failures' really matter? Why is it important to follow the Lord and what He says?

Main Objective in Day Four: Day Four's main objective is to better understand how God evaluates the actions of people, especially in their responses to the Lord, His Word, or the needs of those close by. God wants each doing His will His way. Check any questions that are applicable for your Day Four discussion time.

___ What does it mean that the Lord knows every heart and that we are accountable to Him?

___ Knowing that God knows everything, how can we better know what God wants us to do?

___ How can we bolster our belief in God and His Word and thus better do His will?

___ What does it mean to know and apply God's "wisdom from above" in various situations?

Day Five—Key Points in Application: The most important application points in "God's Reliability—Our Availability" are are the certainties of knowing some of what Jesus faced in His life on earth and how He knows how to lead us day by day in whatever tests each of us faces. Check which discussion questions you will use to help focus the applications from Day Five.

___ What about Jesus stands out to you in the passages explored in Day Five?

___ What one or two application points come to mind when looking at how Jesus lived?

___ How does Paul's testimony help in seeing how Jesus and His Word give guidance?

___ How does the testimony of other believers help you in your trials and tests?

CLOSING: 5–10 MINUTES

Summarize—Review the main objectives for each day.

Focus—Using the memory verse (Judges 3:15a), focus the group again on heart-filled righteous prayer and how vital this is in one's walk with God. Remind the members of your group that prayer is always the right direction to take.

Ask them to share their thoughts about the key applications from Day Five.

Preview—Take a few moments to preview next week's lesson on **"Willing Hearts—Victorious God: God Directs Willing Hearts."** Encourage your group members to dig into Scripture each day, spacing the Scripture Adventure out over the week.

Pray—Close in prayer.

TOOLS FOR GOOD DISCUSSION

While wayward discussions can be a waste of time and actually hurtful to spiritual growth, healthy discussion can help each member of your group grow. There are four actions that can help you in your small group discussion times—just remember the acrostic **"A.C.T.S."** and review the four actions given on page 179. This is part of the information in the "Helpful Hints" section of **How to Lead a Small Group Bible Study,** beginning on page 178.

Lesson #3—Willing Hearts—Victorious God:
God Directs Willing Hearts

Memory Verse: Judges 6:14

"And the LORD looked at him and said, 'Go in this your strength and deliver Israel from the hand of Midian. Have I not sent you?"

BEFORE THE SESSION

- Pray each day for the members of your group. Pray that they spend time in the Word, grasp the message God wants to bring to their lives, and that they surrender to what God is saying.

- Remember, your goal is to facilitate discussion, help lead people to clear applications, and encourage each person in the group.

- As you walk through this lesson, recall that the Lord is willing to use willing hearts, even like Gideon. Always, the key is who God is, not who any person is (or thinks he or she is).

- Highlight key statements. Jot down ideas and questions you want to discuss or ask as you go through this lesson with your small group

WHAT TO EXPECT

The Cycle of Sin and Deliverance is clear in the *Book of Judges*. The events and lessons surrounding Gideon is a clear example. Knowing about this does not mean truly understanding how subtle sin can be. Help the group grasp something of the dilemma Gideon and others faced and how anyone today can face a similar dilemma because of one's own sin or disobedience or the sin and disobedience of someone else. God is very concerned to guide His children, but He will not force the issue. He wants willing hearts, and obviously, not perfect people. Help focus the group on personal application, how God used Gideon, and how He is willing to work in the lives of each of His children.

It is important to grasp the significance of this time in Israel's history as well as the issues evident in Gideon's life and in the lives of those around him. Every believer faces similar tests and trials. God does not change, nor do people. Help each one see how these truths apply in daily life and encourage them to share the insights and applications God has given.

THE MAIN POINT

The main point in this overview of Judges 6-8 is to see how God works with willing hearts. People are fickle, often defeated, but God is reliable and victorious. He uses all kinds of people, even Gideon-like people. God seeks obedience and desires we love Him.

OPENING: 5–10 MINUTES

Opening Prayer—It is good to pray. Have one of the group members open the time with prayer.

Opening Illustration—Those Willing— Among leadership discussions, there is a phrase sometimes used: "The Coalition of the Willing." It refers to those willing to listen, learn, and sometimes lead. In any team, organization, business, or church only the willing make things move forward. It is true in most of life. The same is true in a small group Bible study—people have to be willing to learn, adjust, grow, and apply what God says. God worked this way with Gideon and many more in his day. He does the same today. The members of your group need to know how crucial it is for each one to be a "willing" vessel in God's hands with a "willing" heart toward Him and others. Jesus showed this in His ministry with the Twelve and many more, even in His trial before Pilate. In this week's lesson, the willingness of Gideon and others is on display as are God's paths to victory. Help your group see and apply these truths

DISCUSSION: 30 MINUTES

Prioritize your preparation, study, and prayer times this week. These times can certainly aid your thought processes, your leadership in the discussion, and your ability to answer many questions that could arise. Remembering that God is our victorious God can encourage those going through difficult seasons as well as those seemingly living in the calm areas of life. As you walk through this Scripture Adventure, focus on what it means to have a "willing" heart and seek to keep the main point the main point. Always be thinking of ways to make the application points clear, especially in Day Five.

Main Objective in Day One: In Day One, the main objective is to see that people continually sin and face the consequences, especially God's children. He lovingly chastens. God does not 'wink' at sin or rebellion, He deals with it. Think through the list of questions given below as you look for useful discussion-starter ideas.

___ What kinds of things do we face simply living on a "fallen" earth?

___ How are some of the things we face like loving "fences" to keep us from worse choices? As we considered last week, what do God's chastening actions reveal about Him? How could chastening be good for a person?

___ How does God respond to the genuine prayers of His people? What actions did God take in Gideon's day?

___ What is significant in the way God first responded? How does this apply to us today?

Main Objective in Day Two: In Day Two, the main objective is to see how God responds to His people in pain and in prayer. Review these questions and check which ones you will use from Day Two.

___ What is significant about the Angel of the LORD coming to where Gideon was?

___ What does God see in Gideon that Gideon apparently does not see? What do Gideon's questions reveal about him?

___ How did the Angel encourage Gideon? How did He address Gideon's fears, doubts, worries, and pains?

___ How important is the Lord's presence? What could this thought have meant to Gideon? How did Gideon respond to the Angel of the LORD?

Main Objective in Day Three: In Day Three, our main objective is to see how God uses tests, new assignments, and fresh insights to accomplish all He wants to do... with each of us, with the situation, with His will. Consider these questions as you ponder the ways of God with Gideon and Gideon's responses.

___ What does obedience to the Lord and His Word tell about a person? What do God's commands tell us about Him?

___ What do Gideon's 'fleece' questions reveal about him? What do God's responses reveal about Him?

___ What is significant about God giving Gideon further encouragement just before the actions of the 300?

Main Objective in Day Four: Day Four's main objective is to see how God uses many different people in accomplishing His will. Look over these questions and check any that are applicable for your discussion time.

___ What part did God call Gideon to play in dealing with the Midianites and their companions? What part did the 300 play?

___ Not everyone is called to do the same thing, while some do not want to do the will of God, whatever it is. What do the events surrounding Gideon reveal about following God and how others do or do not follow?

___ Even though the *"land was undisturbed"* for many years, Gideon and the people failed to follow the Lord. What does this say about us and the circumstances in which we find ourselves?

Day Five—Key Points in Application: Application points matter very much for Christian growth. In **"Willing Hearts—Victorious God,"** we find several matters that should be taken very seriously, specifically, "Sin," "the Lord," "His Word," "Friends and Enemies," and the "Part" each of us should take. In light of these "serious" matters, check which discussion questions you could use to help focus applications.

___ Why should we treat "sin" seriously? Why does it matter? How does this relate to taking the Lord seriously?

___ How can we take the Word of God seriously in daily life?

___ Someone wisely quipped, 'The world wouldn't have so many problems if it weren't for people.' How important are our friends? What are some applications Scripture gives about enemies?

___ How important is it for each to play some part in God's working? What practical pointers do you find in Day Five?

CLOSING: 5–10 MINUTES

Summarize—Restate the key points the group shared. Review the objectives for each of the days found in these leader notes.

Focus—Using the memory verse (Judges 6:14), focus the group again on the importance of having a "willing" heart and of following the Lord's will, His Word, and acting in His strength to obey.

Ask them to share their thoughts about the key applications from Day Five.

Preview—Take a few moments to preview next week's lesson on "**Deception—Rebellion—Stumbling.**" Encourage your group members to focus intently on the Scriptures like one searching for buried treasure. Work each day, giving time over the week for this Scripture Adventure.

Pray—Close in prayer.

TOOLS FOR GOOD DISCUSSION

Often a "**Talkative Timothy**" will show up in a Study Group. He (or she) tends to talk too much and dominate the discussion, which gives less time for others to give their input or share their insights. What should you do with a group member who talks too much? In the "Helpful Hints" section of **How to Lead a Small Group Bible Study** (page 179), you'll find some practical ideas on managing the "Talkative Timothy" situation.

Lesson #4—Deception—Rebellion—Stumbling:
The Failure of Not Following God

Memory Verse: Judges 8:34

"...The sons of Israel did not remember the LORD their God, who had delivered them from the hands of all their enemies on every side."

BEFORE THE SESSION

- Be sure to do your own study far enough in advance so as not to be rushed. You want to allow God time to speak to you personally.

- Don't feel that you have to use all of the discussion questions listed below. You may have come up with others on your own, or you may find that time will not allow you to use them all. These questions are to serve you, not for you to serve.

- You are the gatekeeper of the discussion. Do not be afraid to "reel the group back in" if they get too far away from the subject of the lesson.

- Remember to keep a highlight pen ready as you study to mark any points you want to be sure to discuss.

- Pray each day for the members of your group—that they spend time in the Word, grasp the message God wants to bring to their lives, and that they surrender to what God is saying.

WHAT TO EXPECT

Not everyone wants to know God or His will. Some want to follow their own selfish pursuits. We see that in some of the people in this week's lesson. This lesson presents several caution points for anyone, especially for a follower of Christ. We must always be aware of our wayward tendencies; as the old hymn lamented, "prone to wander, Lord, I feel it." At the same time, we can make an extra effort to draw near to the Lord, to call on Him in prayer, to read and meditate on His Word more consistently. As you walk through this lesson, it is essential to help focus the group on personal application, ever aware that Scripture was not written simply to convey data, but *"for our instruction"* and well-being (Romans 15:4).

Help your group understand the subtle ways we can encounter deception or be tempted with rebellion against the Lord and His Word. This is for any believer in any location. Each one needs to attend to the cautions and receive encouragement. Encourage your group members to share insights that God has shown them.

THE MAIN POINT

The main point in this overview of Judges 9-12 is to see the subtle ways deception can creep in to anyone's life. It is also crucial to guard against rebellion. God is the God of

Truth and wants us to walk in truth. We can learn from the stumbling of others; we do not have to repeat the same missteps.

DURING THE SESSION

OPENING: 5–10 MINUTES

Opening Prayer—Have one of the group members open the time with prayer.

Opening Illustration—From time to time, we come upon "Caution" signs on the highway or even in a neighborhood street. Those signs are meant to protect us or our vehicle from danger or damage. The same is true about God's "Caution" signs, whether through the details of a deceptive life or the downward spiral of a series of missteps. In Scripture, God does not paint perfect pictures of perfect people; He gives accurate information about motives, choices, and consequences along with His cautions and calls to follow Him. Your group members need to grasp this about Him and how He does what He does in His faithful love. Jesus often showed this or spoke of this. Today, He continues to do so by His Spirit's working. In this week's lesson, carefully look at this matter of deception, rebellion, and stumbling—the "Caution" signs are in place for our good and for immediate application.

DISCUSSION: 30 MINUTES

Good preparation time is vital to help you in guiding the discussion as well as in answering various questions from the members of your group. The matters of deception, rebellion, and stumbling are not foreign to any of us and knowing how to recognize and deal with these can help you and your group in their daily walk. Knowing God is the God of Truth gives us a sense of security in His Word and helps us in following Him. He never deceives anyone. As you walk through this Scripture adventure, make sure you keep the main point the main point. Leave time for the application points in Day Five. Knowing what matters is always helpful.

Main Objective in Day One: In Day One, the main objective is to see how easily deception can sneak in, how gullible or self-deceived we can be, and sometimes how we too can be deceptive. God deals with deception and rebellion in His ways and timing. Look over the questions listed here along with others you may have as you consider what might be the most useful discussion starters.

___ How important is gratitude? How can one fail to be grateful—where does ingratitude come from? How can we increase gratitude in our daily lives?

___ What connections do you see between people being deceived about the various "Baal" idols and being deceived about Abimelech?

___ Jotham directed his parable/exhortation to the people of Shechem and to Abimelech. How did this reveal God's mercy and His justice?

___ Sowing and reaping are integral to life on earth. How is this seen in the details of Judges 9?

Main Objective in Day Two: In Day Two, the main objective is to see how needy the people of Israel were and how God provided leaders who helped in many ways. In spite of God's loving direction, people often walked away from Him into idolatry. Check which discussion questions you will use from Day Two.

___ What do the lives and deeds of Tola and Jair say about God's faithfulness to His people?

___ What does the false worship of many Israelites say about the lure of false gods?

___ What do you see about the relationship between Israelites in Gilead and the Lord? What does the interaction with the Lord and how He dealt with them tell about the Lord?

___ How important is it to "*put away the foreign gods*" and focus on the true God?

Main Objective in Day Three: In Day Three, our main objective is to see how the Israelites in Gilead dealt with foreign oppressors, not knowing which way to turn. Listed below are some suggested discussion starters for you to consider.

___ How important is prayer when under God's chastening hand or when facing new oppressive circumstances?

___ How important are relationships with others?

___ What part did details about the Lord have in the interaction between the Gileadites and Jephthah?

___ Can you think of any needless ways we try to adjust our situation or our relationship with the Lord?

Main Objective in Day Four: Day Four's main objective is to see how conflicts continue between various people and how various ones work out these issues. Many issues go unanswered. Look over the questions here and choose those that are applicable for your Day Four-discussion time.

___ What can we do to help resolve conflicts? What if someone refuses to accept what is said or done?

___ What can one person do to help someone or some group deal effectively with conflicts?

___ No one can help everyone. Who did the judges of Israel help?

___ Helping those around us with who we are and with what we have is a good starting point. How did the judges of Israel show this?

Day Five—Key Points in Application: The most important application points in "Deception—Rebellion—Stumbling" are the issues each of us faces where we are, with the people near us—where God has placed us. Check which discussion questions you will use to help focus the applications from Day Five.

___ How important is it to recognize that "your place matters"? How should one respond to this truth?

___ What can we learn from others about the time in which each of us is living? What are some ways to make the most of our time?

___ As someone once said, "People are the Problem," but they can be part of the answer. What should each of us do about the people we deal with each day?

___ What are some ways in which the Lord is the most important matter in life? How should we live in light of this?

CLOSING: 5–10 MINUTES

Summarize—Restate the key points that were highlighted in the discussion. You may want to briefly review the objectives for each of the days found at the beginning of these leader notes.

Focus—Using this lesson's memory verse (Judges 8:34), focus the group on gratitude toward God (and toward people). What are some practical ways we can show our gratitude to God (and others)?

Ask the members of your group to reveal their thoughts about the key applications from Day Five.

Preview—Take a few moments to preview next week's lesson on **"Behind the Scenes: When We Cannot See All God Is Doing."** Encourage your group members to be diligent in searching the Scripture each day, and to anticipate God speaking to each of them throughout the week.

Pray—Close in prayer.

TOOLS FOR GOOD DISCUSSION

As mentioned earlier, there are certain people who show up in every discussion group. Last week we looked at "Talkative Timothy." Another person who is likely to show up is **"Silent Sally."** She doesn't readily speak up. Sometimes, her silence is because she doesn't yet feel comfortable enough with the group to share her thoughts. Other times, it is simply because she fears being rejected. Often, her silence is because she is too polite to interrupt and thus is headed off at the pass each time she wants to speak by more aggressive (and less sensitive) members of the group. In the "Helpful Hints" section of **How to Lead a Small Group Bible Study** (p. 180), you'll find some practical ideas on managing the "Silent Sallys" in your group.

Lesson #5—Behind the Scenes:
When We Do Not See All God Is Doing

Memory Verse: Hebrews 11:1–2

"Now faith is the assurance of things hoped for, the conviction of things not seen. For by it the men of old gained approval."

BEFORE THE SESSION

- Resist the temptation to do all your homework in one sitting or to put it off until the last minute. You will not be as prepared if you study this way.

- Make sure to mark down any discussion questions that come to mind as you study. Don't feel that you have to use all of the suggested discussion questions included in this leader's guide. Feel free to pick and choose based on your group and the time frame with which you are working.

- Make some personal applications of **"Behind the Scenes"** in your time this week. Your testimony and example can be a powerful encouragement to your group members.

- Remember your need to trust God with your study. The Holy Spirit is always the best teacher, so stay sensitive to Him!

WHAT TO EXPECT

From time to time, everyone wonders what's going on. We don't always know, nor can we always see or perceive what's next. In this lesson, expect some of your group to have questions about what's going on—in their lives, in the church, in the town, or any number of other places. The overarching big truth in this lesson is the work of God Himself—He is 'behind the scenes' in many ways. He knows the hearts of each person and He is not restricted in who He uses or how He uses circumstances and He always works in line with His holy, loving character. Some may question that, but this adventure in Scripture can help people realize that God always sees the bigger picture and, most of the time, is at work in numerous ways we cannot see (and ways we could not understand if we could see). Help your group members realize afresh how important it is to trust Him and His Word. Help them see that knowing the Scripture is a life-long process. Each of us needs the experience of ever-growing and understanding of deeper levels of God's work and ways.

THE MAIN POINT

The main message from "Behind the Scenes" is that God is at work in ways we cannot see and many we could not understand if we could see. He calls us to trust Him, His Word, His will, and His ways.

DURING THE SESSION

OPENING: 5–10 MINUTES

Opening Prayer—Remember to have one of your group members open your time together in prayer.

Opening Illustration—John 11:1-44 records the earnest plea from Mary and Martha sent to Jesus about their brother Lazarus being sick. They included the statement *"he whom You love,"* aware of His great love for him and for them. Here is a mystery: Jesus did not immediately travel to Bethany; He waited two days. In that time, Lazarus died and was buried. Then, Jesus, knowing Lazarus had died, left the place *"beyond the Jordan"* and traveled to Bethany near Jerusalem. There, Jesus called Lazarus from his tomb, raising him from the dead. While Mary and Martha expressed their concerns and questions, it became obvious that, while Mary and Martha wanted Jesus to heal Lazarus, Jesus had in mind raising him from the dead. This resurrection led to many more believing in Jesus as the promised Messiah.

In every era of history, God is doing more than can be seen; He has more in mind so that His purposes and plans are carried out in greater ways. That was true in Samson's day and it is true today. There are times when we want 'healing' while God is working to bring about a 'resurrection' of some sort. It is a mystery, but it is one of the ways of God as He works "Behind the Scenes."

DISCUSSION: 30 MINUTES

Remember that your job is not to teach this lesson, but to facilitate discussion. Do your best to guide the group to the right answers, but don't be guilty of making a point someone else in the group could just as easily make.

Main Objective in Day One: The main point in Day One is to see the faithfulness of God with His people, even when they had disobeyed in many ways. Choose a discussion question or two from the list below.

___ The Angel of the LORD came to Manoah's wife with words of hope. How does this reveal the faithfulness of God?

___ Manoah showed concern about raising this son. What does that tell us about Manoah and his wife?

___ Manoah prayed and the Angel of God came to Manoah's wife once again. What does this tell us about God and prayer?

___ In the encounter between the Angel of the LORD and Manoah and his wife, what stands out to you?

Main Objective in Day Two: In Day Two, we are introduced to Samson, some of his character, his desires, and his ways. Below, check any discussion questions you might use from Day Two.

___ While Samson proved questionable in many ways, how did God use him in dealing with the idolatrous Philistines?

___ How do Samson's actions reveal the seriousness of sin and idolatry?

___ Someone once told me, "Man's setbacks are God's setups." How might that apply to Samson's situations?

___ Samson's thirst seems to have overpowered him. He prayed. God answered. What insights and applications do you see?

Main Objective in Day Three: Day Three introduces us to new situations: Samson still wandering into Philistine ways, even getting involved with the Philistine woman named Delilah. Review the questions below and see if any are suitable to your group discussion on Day Three.

___ Samson continued to test the boundaries of life among the Philistines. What did the Philistines think of Samson?

___ Greed can arise anywhere, anytime. What can we do to deal with temptations to greed?

___ Often people think money can buy anything. Not so. It cannot buy the will of God, nor His purposes and plans. What other things can money do or not do?

___ The Lord was the source of Samson's strength. How do we find His strength today for each of us?

Main Objective in Day Four: In Day Four, we see some more of Samson's foolish choices and the consequences of those choices in fuller view. Check which discussion questions you will use from Day Four.

___ Delilah kept on hounding Samson until he gave in. What lessons can we learn from this about our own battles with thought darts, faulty thinking, and temptations?

___ How important is it to stay sensitive to the Lord? What can we do to maintain a sensitive conscience and heart (see Acts 24:16)?

___ Being taunted by unbelievers is never enjoyable. Samson had to deal with this. What is significant about Samson's calling on the Lord in this situation?

___ Apparently, Samson continued in 'battle mode,' seeking to deal with the Philistine menace in whatever way he could. What applications do you see for your life?

Day Five—Key Points in Application: The important thing to see in Day Five is the difference between a God-pleasing, God-willed life and a God-resistant, self-willed life. Decide on some discussion-starter topics for the application section of Day Five. The following questions are suggested questions you may want to use for your discussion:

___ Paul prayed for the Colossian believers to be filled with the knowledge of God's will. Jesus told us to pray *"Your will be done."* What does this say about daily seeking God and His will.

___ Where there's a vacuum, all kinds of things can be 'sucked in.' What does this say about not seeking, knowing, or doing God's will each and every day?

___ What are some things that can 'fill the vacuum' today? What should each of us do when we see empty places in our lives/hearts?

___ What is the fruit of "sensualism," "materialism," or "me-ism"? What fruit does God want in our lives?

CLOSING: 5–10 MINUTES

Summarize—Go over the key points of the lesson.

Remind your group members that we can trust God, even when we do not see what He is doing. Charles Spurgeon said it well, "God is too good to be unkind and He is too wise to be mistaken. And when we cannot trace His hand, we must trust His heart." [www.goodreads.com, accessed April 28, 2020]

Ask the group members what they thought were the key applications from Day Five.

Preview—Take a few moments to preview next week's lesson **"Going Astray: Following the Wrong Way**." Encourage them to be sure to complete their homework..

Pray—Close in prayer.

TOOLS FOR GOOD DISCUSSION

Hopefully your group is functioning smoothly at this point, but perhaps you recognize the need for improvement. In either case, you will benefit from taking the time to evaluate yourself and your group. Without evaluation, you will judge your group on subjective emotions. You may think everything is fine and miss some opportunities to improve your effectiveness. You may be discouraged by problems you are confronting when you ought to be encouraged that you are doing the right things and making progress. A healthy Bible-study group is not one without problems but is one that recognizes its problems and deals with them the right way. At this point in the course (only three more lessons), it is important to examine yourself and see if there are any corrections needed. Again, review the evaluation questions list found on pages 186 and 187 of the Leader's Guide, and jot down two or three action points for you to begin implementing next week. Perhaps you have made steady improvements since the first time you answered the evaluation questions at the beginning of the course. If so, your improvements should challenge you to be an even better group leader for the final lessons in the study.

ACTION POINTS:

1.

2.

3.

Lesson #6—Going Astray:
Following the Wrong Way

Memory Verse: Proverbs 14:12 (and 16:25)

"There is a way which seems right to a man, but its end is the way of death."

BEFORE THE SESSION

- George MacDonald said, "The best preparation for the future is the present well seen to, and the last duty done" [www.brainyquote.com, accessed April 28, 2020]. One of the main reasons a Bible study flounders is because the leader comes in unprepared and tries to "shoot from the hip."

- Make sure to jot down any discussion questions that come to mind as you study.

- Keep in mind the importance of personal daily application of these lessons for **your** life. As your group members ponder those who have gone astray, they will be warned, challenged, and encouraged to follow the Lord and His Word.

- Don't forget to pray for the members of your group and for your time studying together. You don't want to be satisfied with what you can do—you want to see God do what only He can do!

WHAT TO EXPECT

In studying this lesson on "**Going Astray**," be observant of ways in which anyone could ignore God or His Word. We need to avoid the traps and hidden potholes on the roadways of life. Depending only on ourselves, our friends' opinions, or simply "what others think" instead of going to the Lord and His Word, can be a recipe for disaster. At the same time, we need to watch out for presumptuousness, thinking we have all the answers, even in knowing much of the Bible or in being a believer for many years. Ever watchful, ever listening and learning from the Lord is always crucial. Be sensitive to any discussion questions that may surface in this lesson and guard your group from applying it only to others rather than to themselves..

Main Point: The main point to be seen in this lesson is the ever-present danger of following a presumed "right way," though it may not be in line with God's character or Word.

DURING THE SESSION

OPENING: 5–10 MINUTES

Opening Prayer—Remember to have one of your group members open your time together in prayer.

Opening Illustration—The mapping service gave very detailed directions, where to turn, how far to travel before the next turn, but the final place was not the right place. There was only a field—no building, no address, no people, just open country. That can happen with GPS services or mapping services, but God and His Word never lead astray. The same is true in life. If one follows the current fad or popular direction or opinion, it can lead astray in the wrong path and even lead to harm or destruction. Help your group members walk through this lesson on "Going Astray," understanding the essential of following the Father and His Word. Pray for yourself and each member to grow, make progress, and experience the difference between going "astray" in *a* way and following *The* Way.

DISCUSSION: 30–40 MINUTES

Remember to pace your discussion so that you will be able to bring closure to the lesson at the designated time. You are the one who must balance lively discussion with timely redirection to ensure that you don't end up finishing only part of the lesson.

Main Objective in Day One: In Day One, the main objective is to see the horrendous choices one can make when not following God or His Word. Check which discussion questions you will use from Day One.

___ Just because one says "this belongs to the Lord" does not mean that is true. What errors do you see in the actions and words of Micah and his mother?

___ Scripture often speaks of remembering or recalling something. Why is it important to "remember"?

___ Why do we sometimes (or often) think we are "right" about something? How can the Word of God help balance our opinions?

___ What kinds of "opinions," "justifications," or "excuses" do we make today for what we do or do not do?

Main Objective in Day Two: In Day Two, we see how an entire tribe chose to follow their own opinions instead of the counsel of the Lord and His Word. Choose a discussion question or two from the Day Two list below.

___ How easy is it for human reasoning (without God or His Word) and/or feelings to lead us astray? In what ways could people do this today?

___ We may never know what could have been for the Tribe of Dan. It is often natural to want less battles or easier days, but could our "tough" issues be better for us in the long run?

___ Sometimes our ideas appear "successful." Does that make them right? What should be our 'litmus test'?

___ How or where should trust in God—His ways, His timing—enter the decisions of daily life?

Main Objective in Day Three: Day Three introduces us to the wayward choices of many in the Tribe of Benjamin (likely in the fourteenth century BC). Decide on some discussion-starter questions for your session in "Thinking Wrong and Calling It Right." Below are some possible discussion questions to consider.

___ With no king, no leader in Israel, people took leadership into their own hands. How did the Levite of Ephraim do that, according to Judges 19:1?

___ The Levite, the concubine, and her father interacted for several days. What's wrong with this picture?

___ Judges 19 and 20 take wrongs seriously, using several different Hebrew words. What does this say to you about any wrongs in your life?

___ What should any person do about any sin revealed by the Word of God or by the Holy Spirit?

Main Objective in Day Four: In Day Four, we see the extreme discord and division brought by wrongdoing. Check which discussion questions you will use from Day Four.

___ What were the men of Israel willing to fight about?

___ Two Words: "Wrong." "Right."—The same two words for coming to faith in Christ— "Wrong." "Right." Admit and turn from wrong to do what is right (the Bible word is "repent"). Come to Jesus Christ for forgiveness, cleansing (being made "righteous"), and eternal life. Is this true of you? If not, it can be.

___ God wants what is right in every life—it is a matter of life and death. The seriousness and the sadness of Judges 20-21 reveal this. How should we view any sin in our lives?

___ After much weeping, all sought peace. Romans 12:18 exhorts believers, *"if possible, so far as it depends on you, be at peace with all men."* How can peace come to each person and each relationship?

Day Five—Key Points in Application: The most important application point in Day Five is the essential of true worship. Below, check any discussion questions that are best suited to your group for application.

___ What does it mean to value the Lord and His Word?

___ What are some ways to show the "fear of the Lord" today?

___ What does it mean to "give wholeheartedly"?

___ What does prompt obedience to the Lord or His Word look like?

CLOSING: 5–10 MINUTES

Summarize—Restate the key points.

Remind those in your group that "Going Astray" is a matter of the heart, not merely outward actions. It also means going in the right way, His way, with a right heart.

Preview—Take a few moments to preview next week's lesson on **"The Life of Eli: Finishing Wrong."**

Pray—Close in prayer.

TOOLS FOR GOOD DISCUSSION

As discussed earlier, there are certain people who show up in every discussion group that you will ever lead. We have already looked at "Talkative Timothy" and "Silent Sally." This week, let's talk about another person who tends to show up. Let's call this person **"Tangent Tom."** He is the kind of guy who loves to talk even when he has nothing to say. Tangent Tom loves to "chase rabbits" regardless of where they go. When he gets the floor, you never know where the discussion will lead. You need to understand that not all tangents are bad. Sometimes, much can be gained from discussion "a little off the beaten path." But these diversions must be balanced against the purpose of the group. In the "Helpful Hints" section of **How to Lead a Small Group** (pp. 180–182), you will find some practical ideas on managing the **"Tangent Toms"** or the **"Agenda Alices"** in your group. You will also get some helpful information on evaluating tangents as they arise.

Lesson #7—The Life of Eli:
Finishing Wrong

Memory Verse: 1 Samuel 2:2

"There is no one holy like the LORD, indeed, there is no one besides You, nor is there any rock like our God."

BEFORE THE SESSION

- Try to get your lesson plans and homework done early this week. This gives time for you to reflect on what you have learned and process it mentally. Don't succumb to the temptation to procrastinate.

- Make sure you keep a highlight pen handy to highlight any things you intend to discuss, including any questions that you think your group may have trouble comprehending. Jot down any good discussion questions that come to your mind as you study.

- For additional study, you may want to look at Following God: Life Principles for Worship from the Tabernacle, especially Lesson Two, "Where We Meet God."

- Review the Chart at the end of this lesson—**"The Glory Cloud of the LORD and the Fire of God"**—and consider a few ways to use it in your discussion.

- Don't think of your ministry to the members of your group as something that only takes place during your group time. Pray for your group members by name during the week that they would receive spiritual enrichment from doing their daily homework. Encourage them as you have opportunity!

WHAT TO EXPECT

The life of Eli occurred during some of the most momentous years in Israel's history. At the same time, vast changes were on the horizon. Eli judged Israel during his last forty years, but he and his sons did not follow the Lord as they should have. Many in Israel continued in doing *"what was right in his own eyes,"* but some were seeking the Lord and His Word. Hannah was one of those individuals. Barren for many years, she grieved over her situation, but she prayed in earnest, pleading for a son. God answered in the birth of Samuel. His birth and life were at a hinge point in Israel's history with Eli and his sons at one of the dark points. We do not have to learn from our own blunders and wayward choices; we can learn from others like Eli and his sons. Expect that everyone in your group will have some aspect of their life to which these factors apply. Be prepared to share what these truths mean to you. This can help you guide your group members toward personal evaluation and personal application to their walk with God.

Main Point: The main point to be seen in "The Life of Eli" is the folly of failing to follow the Lord and His Word. The consequences affected many, but the Lord did not stop His work.

DURING THE SESSION

OPENING: 5–10 MINUTES

Opening Prayer—It would be a good idea to have a different group member each week open your time together in prayer.

Opening Illustration—"In Bounds"—No matter how fast one runs, how accurately one throws or catches a football, or how amazing the flight of a golf ball; if at any time one is "out of bounds" it doesn't count, it's null and void, no gain, no points, certainly no win. The same is true in following God and His Word. If one fails to stay "in bounds" where God says the boundary lines are, then it is useless, even sinful. One of the words for "sin" is "transgression" which means to be out of line or to step out of bounds or over a boundary line. God, in His infinitely holy character, knows what is right and wrong and, in His great grace and love, He tells us and shows us this several times, in many ways throughout His Word. Eli and his sons ignored God and His Word several times over the years, and it cost them and others. "In bounds," God has many blessings and wonderful works. Look closely and listen carefully as you walk through "The Life of Eli."

DISCUSSION: 30–40 MINUTES

A key objective in how you manage your discussion time is to keep the big picture in view. Your job is not like a schoolteacher's job, grading papers and tests and the like, but more like a tutor's job, making sure your group understands the subject. Keep the main point of the lesson in view, and make sure they take that main point home to the heart.

Main Objective in Day One: In Day One, the main objective is to see the importance of what's on the "inside" versus outward appearances alone. Start thinking now about what discussion starters you will use in your session on Lesson Seven, "Knowing 'About' Something Is Not All—Eli's Ministry." Review the question list below. Perhaps there is a question or two that might be helpful to your group time.

___ Words reveal one's heart and thinking. What do Eli's words to Hannah reveal about Eli?

___ How did Hannah express her inner turmoil?

___ What difference does prayer make? What difference can God make in a life? In a situation?

___ What difference can someone's words make in another's life?

Main Objective in Day Two: In Day Two, we see **part** of the lives and "ministries" of Hophni and Phinehas. Check which discussion questions you will use from Day Two.

___ What difference can one's attitude make? What about one's words spoken, or choices made?

___ What were some of the apparent elements in the relationship between Eli and his two sons Hophni and Phinehas?

___ How can one show his or her estimation or evaluation of another? How can one show his or her estimation of the Lord?

___ How important is it to honor God and obey His Word? What are some ways we can do this today?

Main Objective in Day Three: Day Three introduces us to the reality of "God Means What He Says." Take a look at the discussion questions given below to see if any are applicable to your group session.

___ What did Samuel do right as a boy? What does this reveal about his heart?

___ What do you discover about Eli in this series of events?

___ What connections might Samuel have seen between what he saw day by day and what God revealed to him?

___ How important is it to pay attention to what God says? How can we do that today?

Main Objective in Day Four: Day Four explores "When Judgment Comes" and how that affected the Israelites and the Philistines. Choose some discussion starters for your group session.

___ Do we have to deal with any "Philistine" issues today? What kinds of battles do we face?

___ Are we ever guilty of being presumptuous or superstitious in our battles in life? If so, how?

___ In this instance, much, if not everything, centered around the Ark of the Covenant. What did this "Ark" mean to the Israelites? To the Philistines?

___ What is so important about the "Glory of the LORD"? What does the "Glory of the LORD" mean today?

Day Five—Key Points in Application: The most important application points in Day Five revolve around how the Philistines and the Israelites dealt with the "Ark," thus revealing their understanding of and attitude toward God, and how He dealt with them. Below, check any discussion questions that you might consider using for your application time.

___ What are some ways people might try to "use" God today?

___ How do people try to "capture" or "imprison" God? What correct action should a person employ?

___ What does it mean to "trivialize" God?

___ How are people guilty of "ignoring" God? What are some ways we can honor and value Him?

CLOSING: 5–10 MINUTES

Summarize—You may want to reread "The Main Point" statement at the beginning of the leader's notes on **"The Life of Eli"** to help you summarize the lesson.

Review—Using the memory verse (1 Samuel 2:2), note the heartbeat evident in Samuel's mother Hannah and the lack in Eli or his sons. Encourage your group members to meditate on and use this verse in their prayer times.

Preview—Take a few moments to preview next week's lesson on **"The Life and Times of Samuel."** Encourage your group to finish strong in completing their homework, especially for the final lesson, Lesson 8.

Pray—Close in prayer.

TOOLS FOR GOOD DISCUSSION

One of the issues you will eventually have to combat in any group Bible study is the enemy of **boredom**. This enemy raises its ugly head from time to time, but it shouldn't. It is wrong to bore people with the Word of God! Often boredom results when leaders allow their processes to become too predictable. As small group leaders, we tend to do the same thing in the same way every single time. Yet God the Creator, who spoke everything into existence is infinitely creative! Think about it. He is the one who not only created animals in different shapes and sizes, but different colors as well. When He created food, He didn't make it all taste or feel the same. This God of creativity lives in us. We can trust Him to give us creative ideas that will keep our group times from becoming tired and mundane. In the "Helpful Hints" section of **How to Lead a Small Group** (pp. 183–184), you'll find some practical ideas on adding spice and creativity to your study time.

Lesson #8—The Life and Times of Samuel:
Faithful to the Lord

Memory Verse: 1 Samuel 12:23–24

"Moreover, as for me, far be it from me that I should sin against the LORD by ceasing to pray for you; but I will instruct you in the good and right way. Only fear the LORD and serve Him in truth with all your heart; for consider what great things He has done for you."

BEFORE THE SESSION

- Your own preparation is key not only to your effectiveness in leading the group session, but also in your confidence in leading. It is hard to be confident if you know you are unprepared. These discussion questions and leader's notes are meant to be a helpful addition to your own study but should never become a substitute.

- As you do your homework, study with a view to your own relationship with God. Resist the temptation to bypass this self-evaluation on your way to preparing to lead the group. Nothing will minister to your group more than the testimony of your own walk with God.

- It is always good to pray. Pray for your meeting time and for your group members by name during the week. Encourage them as you have opportunity (even with a simple text message).

- For a clearer grasp of the inner workings of Samuel and others, review the Chart at the end of this lesson, **"The LORD is King and Judge."** This can be a great source of conviction, comfort, and encouragement for you and the members of your group.

WHAT TO EXPECT

Spiritual decline is not something new. Israel saw many times of decline and revival. The same is true for each believer and each church today. Needs never stop. As we begin to look at "The Life and Times of Samuel," we will see both times of decline and revival, how Samuel and others responded, and how the truths evident in that period could be applied today. Samuel had no "secret sauce" or special "recipe" for life; he followed the Lord and His Word. The same is true for us today. While times and cultures change like the weather, God, His Word, and people do not change. In the midst of His ministry, Jesus faced challenges, but He continued faithful to His Father and His Word. As Samuel did this, he found God faithful as well. This lesson finds very ready application to everyday life. While everyone has needs, not everyone looks to the Lord and His Word about those needs, nor how to proceed. All of us are on a journey. Expect some members of your group to find a new sense of hope as they walk through the life of Samuel. Others will face their need for correction or course adjustments. Be ready to share your own insights. Those can be an encouragement to others. Pray for and expect your group to grow as they walk through the Word with the Lord.

Main Point: The main point in "The Life and Times of Samuel" is seeing the faithfulness God as well as of Samuel and a few others in contrast to Eli, Hophni, Phinehas, and several others.

DURING THE SESSION

OPENING: 5–10 MINUTES

Opening Prayer—A good prayer with which to open your time is the prayer expressed in Psalm 119:18, "*Open my eyes, that I may behold wonderful things from Your law.*" Remember, if it took the illumination of God for men to write Scripture, it will take the same for us to understand it.

Opening Illustration—Faithfulness—Decades ago, the Timex Corporation used a famous sales slogan that pointed to the 'faithfulness' of their watches. That company often said of the Timex watch, "It takes a licking and keeps on ticking." That statement helped sell many watches. People want a reliable product whether it's a watch or a phone or a car. God and His Word are reliable; Scripture says, "*God is faithful*" and He wants the same from His people—faithful to Him and His Word (1 Corinthians 1:9; 4:2; Matthew 25:21). Hannah, Samuel, and several others proved faithful to the Lord and His Word. Help your group members grasp the importance of this in their lives.

DISCUSSION: 30–40 MINUTES

Remember to pace your discussion so that you don't run out of time to get to the application questions in Day Five. This time for application is perhaps the most important part of your Bible study. It will be helpful if you are familiar enough with the lesson to be able to prioritize the days for which you want to place more emphasis, so that you are prepared to reflect this added emphasis in the time you devote to that particular day's reading.

Main Objective in Day One: In Day One, the main objective is to see the details of Samuel's family, his birth, and first years of spiritual formation in contrast with the ways of Eli and his family. Choose a discussion question or two from the list below.

___ How should we handle difficult or grievous situations in life?

___ Hannah revealed a humble attitude in prayer. What does this say about how each of us should pray?

___ How can knowing the character of the Lord affect our relationships with others? Our prayers?

___ What are some correct ways we can "listen" to the Lord, His Word, or Word-filled people? What could result?

Main Objective in Day Two: We explore in Day Two Samuel's years at the Tabernacle and his life as a judge and prophet. Check which discussion questions you will use from Day Two.

___ What is the heart attitude of the statement, "*Speak, LORD, Your servant is listening*"?

___ Name some of the marks of Samuel in his early years (and later years)? What should mark each of us?

___ What is the difference between having "heart" in one's relationship with God or with others and simple knowledge or activity?

___ How important is integrity in one's life, one's work, or one's interactions with others? How can we build more integrity and better "trust-bridges" with one another?

Main Objective in Day Three: Day Three introduces us to what Samuel faced in his later years and shows us some of his interactions with Saul. In addition to any discussion questions you may have in mind for your group session, the following questions below may also be useful:

___ People have differing ideas. Why is it so important to go to the Lord about any ideas (even our own)?

___ What does it mean that God sometimes gives us what we want though He knows it is not best?

___ Part of Saul's "job" was to deal with the Philistine menace. How does God work today to deal with whatever "menace" there is that keeps us from fully seeing, knowing, or obeying Him?

___ Samuel did what God told him to do. How important is it to obey God, even though others resist Him or His Word?

Main Objective in Day Four: In Day Four, we see the work of Samuel continuing and how he dealt with Saul then David. Place a checkmark next to the discussion question you would like to use for your group session. You may want to place a ranking number beside a question to note your order of preference.

___ Samuel lived a life of integrity. How might that have affected the people as he spoke to them?

___ What were some of the key issues in the life of Saul that Samuel dealt with?

___ What is God's main concern for people? How does God respond to obedience? To disobedience?

___ How important is God's Word or God's promises in the lives of Samuel, Saul, or David?

Day Five—Key Points in Application: The most important application points from Day Five are following the Lord as the Best Leader and growing in character by His grace to be made a right person and leader. Check which discussion questions you will use from Day Five.

___ What are some ways that the Lord is the Best Leader?

___ What are some of the essential marks of a leader anywhere (in the heart, in the home, in the church, in business or at work, in school, in the community, in the nation)?

___ Though many cultures, economies, and nations have come and gone, in what ways are people still the same?

___ What are some essentials everyone wants in his or her life? What kind of leader do (most) people want?

CLOSING: 5–10 MINUTES

Summarize—Restate the key points. You may want to reread "The Main Point" statement for "The Life and Times of Samuel" as well as the main objectives for each of the days found in these leader notes.

Focus—Using the memory verse (1 Samuel 12:23–24), direct the group's focus to the heartbeat of Samuel toward the Lord and toward the people of God. Remind them of ways this can apply to each of us today.

Ask the group to express their thoughts about the key applications from Day Five.

Pray—Close your time in prayer thanking the Lord for the journey He has led you on over the past eight weeks.

TOOLS FOR GOOD DISCUSSION

Congratulations! You have successfully navigated the waters of small group discussion. You have finished all eight lessons in *Following God: Judges: Who Will Lead Us?*, but there is so much more to learn, so many more paths to take on our journey with the Lord, so much more to discover about what it means to follow Him. Now What? It would be wise for you and your group to not stop with this study. In the "Helpful Hints" section of **How to Lead a Small Group Bible Study** (p. 185), there is information on how you can transition to the next study. Share those insights with your group. Encourage your group to continue in some sort of consistent Bible study. Time in the Word is much like time at the dinner table. If we are to stay healthy, we will never get far from physical food, and if we are to stay nourished on "sound" or "healthy" doctrine, then we must stay close to the Lord's "dinner table" found in His Word. Job said it well, "*I have not departed from the command of His lips; I have treasured the words of His mouth more than my necessary food*" (Job 23:12).

When you purchase a Bible or book from **AMG Publishers, Living Ink Books,** or **God and Country Press,** you are helping to impact the world for Christ.

How? AMG Publishers and its imprints are ministries of **AMG International,** a Gospel-first global ministry that meets the deepest needs – spiritual and physical – while inspiring hope, restoring lives and transforming communities. Profits from the sale of AMG Publishers' books are poured into AMG International's worldwide ministry efforts.

For over 75 years, AMG International has leveraged the insights of local leaders and churches, who know their communities best to identify the right strategies to meet the deepest needs. AMG's methods include child and youth development, media evangelism, pastor training, church planting, medical care and disaster relief.

To learn more about AMG International and how you can partner with the ministry through your prayers and financial support, please visit **www.amginternational.org**.

AMG | MEETING THE
INTERNATIONAL | **DEEPEST NEEDS**